Also by Dorothy Wade
and Justine Picardie

HEROIN: CHASING THE DRAGON

MUSIC

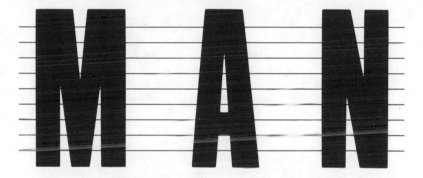

*Ahmet Ertegun, Atlantic Records,
and the Triumph of Rock'n'Roll*

MAN

Dorothy Wade and Justine Picardie

W · W · NORTON & COMPANY · New York · London

Library of Congress Cataloging-in-Publication Data
Wade, Dorothy.
Music man: Ahmet Ertegun, Atlantic Records, and the triumph
of rock 'n' roll. / by Dorothy Wade and Justine Picardie.
p. cm.
Includes index.
1. Ertegun, Ahmet M. 2. Sound recording executives and producers—
United States—Biography. I. Picardie, Justine. II. Title.
ML429.E72P5, 1990
784.5'0092'4—dc19
[B]   89-30820

ISBN 0-393-02635-3

W. W. Norton & Company, Inc., 500 Fifth Avenue, New York, N. Y. 10110
W. W. Norton & Company Ltd., 37 Great Russell Street, London WC1B 3NU
1 2 3 4 5 6 7 8 9 0

Dedicated with love to Neill and James,
Gerard, and Rebecca.

CONTENTS

Authors' Note   11

Acknowledgments   13

PROLOGUE *The Greatest Rock-and-Roll*
                Mogul in the World   17

1 *Young Turks*   28

2 *A Really Lovely Guy*   44

3 *Hoodlums and Hustlers*   52

4 *Booze, Bribes, and Broads*   76

5 *Ill Feelings, Bad Grace*   97

6 *Black Soul, White Rock*   122

7   *Selling Out*   144

8   *Mayhem in Miami,*
        Murder in Memphis   170

9   *In Pursuit of the*
        Rolling Stones   197

10 *In with the New*   217

11 *Madness and Money*   232

12 *The Guys with Funny Names*   252

13 *Long Live the King*   277

Index   291

AUTHORS' NOTE

RESEARCH FOR THIS BOOK BEGAN IN 1986. Music is a fickle business, and since then the circumstances of some people mentioned in the text will have inevitably changed. To those who are now more elevated or more successful than we describe them, our apologies—and congratulations.

ACKNOWLEDGMENTS

FIRST AND FOREMOST, our thanks are due to Ahmet Ertegun. He and his wife, Mica, invited us to countless social occasions, and to their homes in New York and Turkey where Ahmet submitted, with great patience, to hours and hours of interviews. Our thanks and respect are also due to Nesuhi Ertegun, who died in 1989. His intelligence, generosity, and courtesy were boundless.

Morris Levy also gave up many hours of his time to extensive and frank interviews in his New York office and at his farm, Sunnyview—for which we are grateful.

Yves Beauvais of Atlantic Records mined the picture archives. Seymour Stein, Jerry Wexler, Tom Silverman, Tom Dowd, and Hy Weiss proved to be constant and able guides through the labyrinth of the music business of yesterday and today. Countless others offered more time and advice than they need have done: Miriam Bienstock, Jerry Leiber, Herb Abramson, Al Bell, Doc Pomus, and Noreen Woods are names which stand out—but there were many more. To all of them, thank you.

Some fellow journalists helped us. Michael Graham and Sara Walden are warmly thanked for their contributions to the chapter on Alan Freed and the payola scandal. Thanks are also due to Tracey Nicholas and Charlie Gillett for invaluable help in the early stages of our research.

Last, we are especially grateful to Paul Eddy and Robert Ducas, who made the whole project possible.

MUSIC MAN

PROLOGUE:
THE GREATEST ROCK-AND-ROLL
MOGUL IN THE WORLD

One balmy June evening in New York City, Ahmet Ertegun, the founder and chairman of Atlantic Records, and his wife, Mica, are hosting a party. It is "to raise money for a school run by a poet," says Ertegun, somewhat vaguely. At six o'clock an assortment of grand people begins to arrive at the couple's Upper East Side house: Kathleen Tynan, Kenneth Tynan's widow, who looks terrifyingly elegant; the Watergate journalist Carl Bernstein, who does not; a refined European art historian; some brittle Manhattan society ladies in high heels and cocktail dresses; and Nancy Reagan's ubiquitous "walker," Jerry Zipkin, who bears a disconcerting resemblance to Mr. Toad of Toad Hall. The guests are plied with drink and small talk and allowed to enjoy their cool and airy surroundings enhanced by vast windows looking out onto a garden. Two imposing bronze palm trees stand on a gallery overlooking the ground-floor dining room and on the walls hang paintings by Matisse, Magritte, and Hockney. "And this is a small Picasso," says Ertegun in passing.

Amidst the splendid art collection there are fading photographs of Ertegun's Turkish and Romanian relatives and, next to a picture of his mother and an oil painting of his grandfather, there is photographic evidence of more recent memories: Ahmet Ertegun with Mick Jagger; another of Ertegun with Phil Collins, who sells far more records for Atlantic than Mick Jagger ever did. Perhaps the contrasts in

Ertegun's life are at their most apparent in the library, where books about jazz and the blues, about American film stars and singers, about Turkish art and architecture, compete for shelf space with the leather-bound works of Proust and Tennyson, and French editions of poetry by Gautier and Verlaine.

The party, it transpires, is to be held elsewhere and once the guests are assembled they are ushered outside to await the charabanc that has been hired to transport them. No bus is in sight, so the party straggles along the street in desultory fashion to Park Avenue where Ertegun spots a yellow school bus. He steps into the middle of the rush-hour traffic to flag it down. The traffic stops, the bus stops, and the guests climb aboard for a journey of fewer than fifty blocks but nonetheless to a distant world—East 129th Street in Harlem.

When the bus arrives a party is in full swing in the street. A jazz band plays in the middle of the road. Old men are dancing. Girls are skipping on the sidewalk. Everyone else is on the street drinking beer and Ahmet Ertegun is in his element. Pausing only to say hello to a fellow fund-raiser, the suave fashion designer Oscar de la Renta, he heads off down the street to talk to the band. With shouts of recognition, the black musicians shake his hand and slap him on the back. Then they launch into a funky blues number, and Ertegun starts dancing, much to everyone's delight, with Mercedes Kellogg, a glamorous lady with glittering teeth and a penchant for fine cigarillos.

At eight o'clock, the party moves into the basement of All Saints' Church a little way down the street. The large, barn-like hall has been transformed with streamers and balloons, and tables overloaded with mounds of barbecued ribs, southern fried chicken, corn bread, and sweet potato pie, all served up in large portions by motherly women who encourage everyone to come back for more.

Like the street, the hall is filled with a bizarre mixture of party-goers: New York high society people mingle with sharply dressed black men, fat Harlem ladies with babies and toddlers in their arms, and the local schoolchildren—who are the reason for this party—squeeze their way between the adults, with scrubbed faces and starched clothes, the girls in frilly dresses, the boys in meticulously ironed shirts and suits.

The party is a wild success. The Harlem Blues and Jazz Band plays, and everyone dances (Ertegun well; Carl Bernstein badly). After a while, Ertegun disappears backstage to talk to the musicians, and Mama Lu Parks and her Savoy Lindyhoppers take the floor. It is an awe-inspiring sight: Mama Lu, solidly built and middle-aged, who has toured with the likes of Cab Calloway and Count Basie (at a time when Ahmet Ertegun's Atlantic Records was a very insignificant company), can still dance as lithely as her young troupe. Lindyhopping is the most athletic form of dancing imaginable— demanding jumps and leaps and splits and cartwheels to unrelentingly energetic swing-time music. The little Harlem children, standing at the front watching, clap their hands with delight and wiggle to the music that their grandparents danced to.

The strange cultural contrasts of the evening become even more apparent when Yo Yo Ma, a brilliant young cellist of international renown, takes the stage of All Saints' Church in Harlem and plays a Bach recital. As in Paris, London, and Berlin, he receives a standing ovation. Then follows a speech, from Ned O'Gorman, the poet who started the school—the Children's Storefront—twenty years ago. He thanks Ertegun, who has put the considerable weight (and fortune) of Atlantic Records behind the venture, and then introduces the schoolchildren, who sing a song. They receive thunderous applause and their mothers and fathers beam with parental pride.

And finally, to bring the evening to a close, Roberta Flack takes the stage, resplendent in a sequined gown. With her soaring voice and gospel roots she is an Atlantic star in the old tradition: a one-time schoolteacher, plucked from the obscurity of the nightclub circuit which Ertegun habitually attends. Afterward, Ertegun takes his friends backstage to meet her, introducing them one by one. And this, he says, is Miss So-and-So, "the distinguished archeologist . . ."

Roberta Flack did well for Atlantic, earning four gold records in less than three years, and well enough for herself to be able to neglect her singing career to work for improved educational programs for disadvantaged children.

But there are other Atlantic artists of the old school, exemplars of modern popular music, who were not among the major beneficiaries of its rewards. Take, for example, the case of "Big" Joe Turner. Between 1951 and 1956 he gave the fledgling Atlantic Records a string of hit records, each one of which now stands as a rock-and-roll classic: among them, "Sweet Sixteen"; "Shake, Rattle and Roll"; and, the biggest of them all, "Corrina, Corrina." When his run of successes ended, Big Joe continued working for the next quarter-century—touring Europe, recording with the likes of Dizzy Gillespie and Pee Wee Crayton, starring in a movie with Count Basie, and appearing in nightclubs long after age and arthritis should have dictated his retirement. Even so he died flat broke, leaving a tangle of debts, and an impoverished widow with no money for the funeral. That may have been because Big Joe was not good with money, but it is also true that he—along with most of his contemporaries, many of whom were black—was not awarded the lucrative recording contracts that are commonplace today. They were, if they were lucky, paid meager royalties, and often the sum of those royalties was exceeded by the bill for "studio time" which the artists were required to pay.

When Joe Turner died in 1987, at the age of seventy-six, it was Ahmet Ertegun who paid for the funeral, and paid off the mortgage on Turner's widow's house, and he did so quietly, in such a way that his gesture was not instantly reported in the columns of *Rolling Stone.* Since then—in an industry not noted for its charity—Atlantic Records has "recalculated" the royalties due on foreign sales and reissues of old records, and has so far paid out hundreds of thousands of dollars to meet its newly discovered obligations. Atlantic has also contributed $2 million to establish a foundation that makes tax-free grants to the down-on-their-luck pioneers of rhythm and blues.

It could be argued that Ahmet Ertegun can easily afford such generosity and, anyway, that he is merely paying a debt long overdue. Similarly, it can be said that when Ertegun buses his white jet-set friends into Harlem for a street party, he receives plaudits and publicity at no great cost to himself—and when the evening is over he returns to his own world in the safety and comfort of a black limousine.

But the truth is, Ahmet Ertegun has been going to Harlem since he was not much more than a boy because Harlem was where he could find the music for which he has a passionate love. He sponsored racially mixed gatherings when the Jim Crow laws made such assemblies illegal, and—in an industry not noted for its compassion, either—he has cared for his artists as much as, and sometimes more than, the music they made. His record is not flawless. There have been periods when Ertegun has been obsessed with the business side of his business, when he has become remote to his friends and would not take their calls. But, almost always, Ahmet Ertegun has paid his dues.

Along the way he has acquired unique distinction in his industry—as a profile in the *New Yorker* magazine described it, a stature "in his line of work that Irving Thalberg and Louis B. Mayer had in theirs." In the same sense that they represented Hollywood at its most powerful, he is the Music Man, and when he gives up the reins of Atlantic Records, or they are taken from him, popular music will have lost a patriarch. Tom Dowd, a producer of more hit records than anyone can count, puts it this way: "When Ahmet goes, an image will disappear. Nobody could replace him. When he goes the charisma, the love, will change, and people will say 'It's not like it was.' When it comes down to dollars and cents, Atlantic will still be a profit-making organization. Atlantic won't suffer—but music will suffer when Ahmet leaves."

.   .   .

The man whom the *New Yorker* called the "Greatest Rock-and-Roll Mogul in the World" spends each August in a remarkably beautiful house overlooking the Mediterranean at Bodrum, in his native Turkey. The house is built out of marble taken from the tomb of King Mausolus, and to enjoy what is left of what was one of the Seven Wonders of the ancient world there is an endless procession of guests kept amused by Ertegun's endless collection of jokes and anecdotes. Princess Margaret (with whom Ertegun likes to sing the old songs) flits through while a leading Democratic congressman arrives for a "taste of paradise." Rudolf Nureyev, Mick Jagger, the Turkish ambassador, the earl of Warwick—all of them come to visit Ahmet Ertegun in Turkey. Long, lazy days are spent on his stately wooden yacht, *Miss Leyla,* in the shade of white awnings, reclining on soft cushions. At noon the boat is anchored and Turkish *mezze* are served by two barefoot sailors in crisp uniforms while Ertegun proffers the local aperitif, *raki.* Later, Ertegun plays with his brother's children (who call him "Uncle Omelette"), swimming around the boat with them on his back and telling them stories. Before they go to bed at night he will, if they are lucky, sing them songs—the blues and the jazz that he listened to when he was a child and that were the foundation of his considerable fortune.

When the gentle pace of days on the boat begins to pall, Ertegun organizes an expedition to the local bazaar, where he bargains for lengths of striped cotton, and buys himself voluminous undershorts: "The first ones that I've bought for thirty cents each," he says with glee.

The same expert haggling is in evidence at the Galeri Anatolia carpet shop in the center of Bodrum. Ertegun is welcomed as an honored guest, and a little boy is dispatched to acquire glasses of mint tea. Settling down on a pile of rugs, looking like a cross between the hookah-smoking caterpillar in *Alice in Wonderland* and an enigmatic sultan, Ertegun begins the long negotiations. Dozens of kilims are laid out for his perusal, and a great deal of rapid Turkish is spoken, accompanied by emphatic gesticulations. After an hour or so,

Ertegun departs, leaving the shop owner to mull over his prices. Ertegun will return the next day, and the day after that, until a satisfactory deal has been struck.

According to those who know him, watching Ahmet Ertegun buy undershorts or carpets reveals a great deal about the man and his phenomenal career. In the words of one of his closer associates: "Ahmet takes nothing seriously on the surface but cares deeply underneath, especially when his pocketbook is in question. Ahmet is a trader." ·

Back in New York there are Turkish diplomats and trade delegations to entertain, and a dinner to host for Henry and Nancy Kissinger at Le Cirque, where Manhattan society gapes (discreetly) at the Erteguns' sought-after center table. Politics is discussed in a civilized way until Ertegun, like a naughty schoolboy disturbing the solemnity of the proceedings, launches into a tale of the trip he made to China with Kissinger in November 1985. Ertegun—having been warned by Kissinger not to tell jokes, he naturally could not resist— regaled his hosts with the story of a Chinese rabbi who went to New York to attend a service at the Temple Emmanu-El. Afterward he was asked if he had enjoyed the experience. "Oh, it was wonderful," said the rabbi. "I loved the service, and the synagogue is the most beautiful I have ever seen. The only thing is, I didn't see any people who looked Jewish." Ertegun's Chinese hosts did not get the joke, thus forcing an embarrassed Kissinger into one of his more laborious explanations.

It is typical of Ertegun to poke fun at his friends but Kissinger does not seem to mind. Ahmet Ertegun is perhaps the only man in the world who could lure Henry Kissinger, in full evening attire, to a gigantic rock concert—held at Madison Square Garden to celebrate Atlantic Records' fortieth anniversary—and with the pungent sweetness of marijuana in the air, and the ear-shattering sounds of Led Zeppelin in the background, introduce the former secretary of state to "my friend" Wilson Pickett, presently on probation for taking a loaded shotgun into a bar.

"Henry Kissinger, my man," said Pickett, hugging him.

"Mr. Pickett, a pleasure," said Kissinger, meaning it.

"I think I would be a rather good president," says Ahmet Ertegun after a long evening of polished tact and small talk. He laughs as he says it, but there is no doubt that his personal skills far exceed those required for successful commerce— and Ertegun has gently declined overtures from Turkey urging his entry into ambassadorial service. He has survived and prospered in a very tough business for far longer than anybody else, while avoiding almost all of its taints. He has done more than most to attack racial bigotry in the United States, by bringing black music to white people, and he began doing that long before civil rights was a fashionable cause. He has won the friendship and respect of presidents, painters, and pop stars, and he crosses effortlessly the boundaries between their separate worlds. He is sufficiently shrewd to have outlasted all his partners, and to have sold his company more than once. He can be tough, even ruthless, but rarely is he cruel.

In the London offices of Atlantic Records Ertegun greets the earl of Worcester, who is known to his friends as Bunter. The earl, it seems, has pulled all the strings he can to meet Ertegun in the hope that Atlantic Records will sign his aristocratic rock group, the Business.

The Business has already recorded one single, with Lady Theresa Manners on lead vocals, but even after widespread publicity (including a double-page spread in the society magazine the *Tatler*), the record sank without trace. Undaunted, Bunter has taken over the vocals from Lady Theresa, and the band has produced a tape recording of two songs it has written for Ertegun to hear.

Chain-smoking and painfully nervous as the tape is played, Bunter does not look like an earl. His singing voice is unre-

markable, and the songs are memorable only for their awful-
ness. One is entitled "Freddie." Freddie went back to the
jungle—or, perhaps, came *from* the jungle—so at first the
song sounds as if it might be a mournful dirge about an aged
African retainer. But as the tape continues it becomes clear
that Freddie is a dead parrot.

Ertegun is very kind. He listens carefully and nods his head
in time to the music. When the tape ends he compliments
the earl on his voice, and then does something rather tactful:
He offers the earl some advice on the kind of songwriting the
Business might progress to—and, in that way, the question of
whether the group will be signed by Atlantic Records simply
does not arise. Ertegun tells the earl to "get in touch" when
he has written more songs. Never mind that this British aristocrat has as much chance of joining the pop aristocracy as a
child from the Liverpool slums has of going to Eton. "I'm
always kind to artists," says Ertegun.

Mica Ertegun, Ahmet's second wife, is an elegant Romanian
aristocrat who in harder times worked on a chicken farm in
Canada for eight years. She is on record as saying "It's hard to
know what makes a marriage work"—by which she may
mean her marriage to Ahmet. That is partly because the Erteguns see very little of each other. Mica is now an interior
designer, much in demand in Manhattan, and the pressures
of her business require that she retire to and rise from her
bed at reasonable hours. Ahmet does not.

It is two-thirty in the morning in New York and Ertegun
has spent much of the evening deprecating his own skills as a
record producer. ("People like Ray Charles and Aretha
Franklin can produce themselves," he says. He does admit,
however, that somebody has to organize the studio, book the
musicians, and soothe monumental egos. And, if nothing else,
he adds, laughing all the while, "the producer can roll the
joints.") Now he wants to go out and with a party of friends
sets off for a jazz bar in Greenwich Village where, sup-

posedly, Gil Evans is playing. Of course, Gil Evans has long since finished and gone home, but there are still some black musicians hanging around waiting for a party to happen. Though the bar has officially closed, drinks are served and everyone lines up to shake Ertegun's hand. A young Rastafarian begins to play the piano and sing, while Ertegun sits listening, smiling, clapping, and quietly humming the harmonies. "I can always hear them in my head," he says. "I just can't sing them the way I want to."

Even drunk in Greenwich Village at four o'clock in the morning Ertegun remains the diplomat, reserving judgment until the "artist" is not present to be hurt by it: "It was a somewhat eccentric performance—middle-of-the-road songs, with cocktail piano playing and some gospel wails." Like the earl of Worcester, the young Rastafarian is not destined for musical stardom—but it is not Ahmet Ertegun who will disabuse him.

The record company that Ahmet Ertegun started, on money borrowed from his dentist, gave Ray Charles his first record to sell one million copies, and it "discovered" and nurtured, among others, Ruth Brown, Joe Turner, and Aretha Franklin. If Ray Charles was one of the originators of soul music, Aretha Franklin reshaped it, and if Ruth Brown was, briefly, "Miss Rhythm"—the leading black female singer in the world, who inspired and influenced a generation of future stars—Big Joe Turner was, without challenge, the Boss of the Blues. Examining the roster of Atlantic's early artists is like reading the roll call of the founding fathers of rock and roll, and that, by itself, would earn Ahmet Ertegun a place in the Rock-and-Roll Hall of Fame (an institution he founded). But his contribution to modern music goes far beyond that.

At precisely the right moment Ertegun turned his attention from black rhythm and blues to the white music that imitated it, and made shooting stars of, among others, Bobby Darin, Sonny and Cher, Buffalo Springfield, and Crosby,

Stills, and Nash. With equally impeccable timing he brought to the United States the British rock groups Yes and Cream (and thus Eric Clapton), and Led Zeppelin—which, in the course of a U.S. tour in 1973, broke the supposedly unbreakable box office records set by the Beatles. And if Ahmet Ertegun did not discover the Rolling Stones, he did pursue them through a legendary, exhausting courtship, much of it conducted in a drug-induced haze, that ultimately won the group to Atlantic Records at a time when they were the most sought after rock stars in the world.

It is, perhaps as much as anything else, Ertegun's prodigious energy, and his ability and willingness to woo what others call (unkindly) the "rockoids," to soothe their egos and become their friends, that has made Atlantic Records a monumental company. For a good deal of his career, Ahmet Ertegun has not made records so much as made them possible. He is all things to all men: a caring, cultured, urbane, debonair connoisseur of jazz and the blues who can, nevertheless, endure the thunderous volume of music from the edge of mayhem and announce, "That sounds like a hit record to me."

And more often than not, and more often than most, he has been right.

Chapter 1
YOUNG TURKS

On October 29, 1923—some three months after Ahmet Ertegun was born—President Mustafa Kemal declared Turkey a republic. He diminished the power of Islam, rid the Turkish language of all Arabic words, and began the long process of dragging his country into the twentieth century. As part of his modernization campaign Kemal (or Ataturk as he later renamed himself) pressed Ahmet's father into diplomatic service. Munir Ertegun was a bookish man who would have preferred teaching or writing or philosophy, but he had been recruited to the Turkish revolution when Ataturk was still a rebel, and he was dedicated to it. In 1925, when Ahmet was two years old, Munir Ertegun took his family abroad to help negotiate Turkey's entry into the modern world, and to translate Ataturk's speeches. He served as the Turkish ambassador to Switzerland, France, and then England. Thus it was that at the age of ten, Ahmet Ertegun was able to go to the London Palladium to listen to the orchestras of Cab Calloway and Edward Kennedy "Duke" Ellington. He had never before seen black men; never heard a jazz band perform live. It was an experience that transformed his life— and, arguably, the course of popular music.

When, in 1934, Munir Ertegun was next transferred to Washington, he was depressed, Ahmet elated: This, after all, was the land of gangsters, cowboys and Indians—and jazz. In Washington Munir Ertegun withdrew entirely into his work, and Ahmet's mother concentrated on "having a good time." She was an exceptionally modern woman by the Turkish standards of her time, inclined to a life of dancing, playing cards, and gambling—and Ertegun, his brother, and his sister were expected to entertain themselves. She did, however, take time to pass on to her children a great love of music and she filled the embassy with recordings of the popular songs of the day. She also bought Ahmet a small device that allowed him to cut discs of his own, and he would make records of himself singing.

Another influence on young Ahmet was Cleo Payne, the Turkish embassy's black janitor. He taught Ertegun to box and took him to fights. He introduced him to beer joints, and he gave him an appetite for soul food. Ertegun became fascinated with black America and, above all, with its music. By age fourteen he had lived in the splendid embassies of four capitals, he was fluent in three languages, he attended one of the best schools in the Washington area, he was surrounded by comfort, and he was served by chauffeured limousines— and all the boy wanted to do was go to Harlem.

He got the chance when the commander of the Turkish air force arrived in Washington to buy airplanes. He and Ertegun became friends, and when the commander went to New York to visit the Turkish consul he took Ahmet along. Once there, Ertegun won permission to go to the cinema alone. He bought a ticket, waited until the coast was clear, and then hailed a cab: "Take me to Harlem," he said. It did not matter where in Harlem; all of it was, for him, the promised land. The cab deposited him at the Plantation Club where, at eight o'clock at night, Ertegun was the only customer. At four o'clock the following morning, with the place now packed, Ertegun was still there, enjoying the music of "Hot Lips" Page—and the company of a chorus girl whom Hot Lips had sent to Ertegun's table. Persuaded that her schoolboy escort was a suave young student from Harvard, she took him to an after-hours club, and Ertegun did not get back to the Turkish consulate in midtown until 8 A.M. By that time the police had been called, and the consulate had launched a full-scale search for the ambassador's son. He was returned to Washington under the strict personal supervision of the consul.

Harlem was now out of bounds for the time being, but nothing could cure Ertegun's obsession with black music. The owners of Washington's black record stores became used to the bizarre sight of a sleek chauffeur-driven limousine pulling up outside their modest premises. Ahmet and his older brother, Nesuhi, would emerge from the car to begin insatiable searches through the stock, looking for long-forgotten recordings of jazz and blues that nobody else wanted and that were available for ten or twenty cents apiece. The brothers would pile boxes of them into the back of the limousine, and return to the embassy to listen to their latest finds. According to another avid jazz collector from that era, "They knew every record and who played on it, like other kids knew about football and baseball teams."

Their zeal was such that when an article appeared in *Esquire* magazine in 1938 about what was then a very small band of jazz-record collectors, the sons of the Turkish ambassador were included. Ertegun's headmaster telephoned the embassy to warn the ambassador he should not allow his son to be mentioned in the press because it would give the boy "a big head." The headmaster also warned that young Ertegun had "Communist leanings" (a suspicion which Ertegun attributes to his liking for the works of D. H. Lawrence).

Certainly the Ertegun brothers held radical views, and they were confident enough to act on them. Washington was then as segregated a city as the Jim Crow laws could make it, and Nesuhi—recently returned from Paris where he had studied at the Sorbonne—was outraged by what he found: "We had a lot of black friends in Washington, and we could never go to a restaurant together, never go to a movie, or to the theater with them. It was impossible to go out. I couldn't even take Duke Ellington, who is one of the geniuses of our century, to a restaurant. Or Count Basie. That's how it was—

and we could not accept it." And Ahmet still remembers the embarrassment of inviting Benny Carter, a black jazz musician, out to dinner. The only place they were allowed to sit at the same table was the restaurant at the Union rail station.

But the laws that applied to the nation's capital did not apply to the sovereign territory of the Turkish embassy—and so members of the bands of Duke Ellington and Benny Goodman, and the legendary Lester Young himself, would be invited to that sanctuary for Sunday lunch. The impromptu jazz sessions that followed would invariably last for the rest of the day.

In time the Ertegun brothers were able to find another refuge—the Jewish community center in Washington—where they arranged and promoted jazz concerts featuring racially mixed performers for racially mixed audiences. It was only a small step on the road to desegregation but it set in concrete the careers of Ahmet and Nesuhi Ertegun.

In 1944 Munir Ertegun died and his wife and daughter returned to Turkey. The Ertegun brothers did not. Nesuhi (five years older than Ahmet) moved to Los Angeles where he edited a well-respected music magazine, ran a jazz and blues record shop, and recorded albums for connoisseurs like himself. He also found time to teach a course at the University of California—the first of its kind, on the roots of American music. Ahmet remained in Washington, ostensibly to do postgraduate work at Georgetown University, but in reality to hang out at Waxie Maxie's record store in the black section of Washington where he gained an invaluable education in the newly burgeoning record business from a variety of hustlers.

Business was booming because World War Two had created a shortage of shellac—the varnish contained in 78 r.p.m. records—and therefore a shortage of product. With the war over, and shellac once more available, there was a rush to fill the vacuum and a whole host of new record companies sprang up, run by entrepreneurs with almost no musical knowledge. "I met these guys, and I realized that none of them knew anything about the music," says Ertegun. "One of them had been . . . a jukebox operator who thought, 'Well, we're having trouble getting records so we might as well make some ourselves.' I met all these people and they had no idea of songs, they had no idea of musicians." On the slender basis of "if they can make it, I can make it," the second son of the recently deceased Turkish ambassador to Washington, a student of philosophy, economics, and literature, with no money and no business experience whatsoever, determined to enter the record industry.

Ertegun needed both capital and a partner—preferably one who knew *something* about making, distributing, and promoting records—and he found both from the unlikely source of the world of dentistry. Dr. Vahdi Sabit, who had taken care of the Ertegun family's teeth in Washington, was persuaded by Ertegun to invest $10,000 in the as-yet-un-named record company. For a partner Ertegun recruited Herb Abramson, a dapper man from New York City who had trained as a dentist during the war but whose hobby and passion was jazz.

Abramson's hobby had become his career when he met a certain Al Green, a paint manufacturer from Chicago. Green knew nothing about music but he had somehow acquired a shellac-manufacturing plant and, on that foundation, had launched National Records. To find artists for his new label Green recruited a pretty young classical piano teacher he met at a record-manufacturers convention, where she gave a talk on music appreciation for children. Unfortunately her own musical appreciation did not extend to jazz. Casting around for a replacement, Green persuaded Abramson— without much difficulty—to abandon dentistry and become the talent scout and producer for National Records.

By all accounts Abramson soon distinguished himself among the new music men of New York City. According to Jerry Leiber (who, with his partner Mike Stoller, would become one of the most successful songwriters of the 1950s),

Abramson was the most fashionable and handsome man-about-town: "He really looked exquisite—not just good, exquisite. And he was the one who was really the most professional and experienced of the group. He produced great records." He also acquired for National Records artists of the caliber of Big Joe Turner and Billy Eckstein.

But National Records did not grow quickly enough for Abramson's liking and by 1947 he had grown restless. There was, he believed, a vast reservoir of black talent in America, and a growing market for black music. When the young Turk Ertegun approached him, offering a partnership, Abramson agreed to invest his experience and, incidentally, $2,500 of his savings.

So, in October 1947, Atlantic Records was launched on an unsuspecting world. (The name was settled on at the last moment after Ertegun and Abramson discovered their original six or seven choices of name had already been registered with the Musicians Union.) Their first office was a room in the Ritz Hotel in Manhattan but it proved to be too expensive. Atlantic moved to the much more modest Hotel Jefferson where for $65 a month they rented enough space for their desks and somewhere for Ertegun to sleep. For a while Ertegun was obliged to share his cramped sleeping quarters with a cousin, a bohemian poet, and the city later condemned the Hotel Jefferson as being unsafe. The ambassador's son had never been happier.

Having returned to live in Turkey, Ertegun's mother told her friends that Ahmet had remained in the United States in order to study "Afro-American music." She was not too far wrong.

The early days of Atlantic were consumed by a constant search for artists to record. "I spent almost every night in Harlem," says Ertegun. And when he was not in New York's jazz clubs "hanging out with the musicians," Ertegun was on a train with Abramson, scouring the country's nightclubs and theaters for talent. When they found suitable candidates they would persuade them to go to their New York office, where the furniture was pushed to one side and Atlantic's offices became Atlantic's recording studios. There was nothing remotely sophisticated about it. Tom Dowd, a classically trained musician and physicist who had been recruited as Atlantic's recording engineer (and who would become essential to Atlantic's success over the next thirty years), recalls: "You put one microphone up and told the band to play louder or softer. The band would drive up to New York, go into the studio for three hours, get four sides down—and that was it, 'goodbye,' in and out in a day."

There was also a constant quest for new material to record, and it was no easier to find—which is how the compositions of "A. Nugetre" came to be written. Ertegun, who could not write music, would compose tunes in his head and then sing them in his rasping voice in the twenty-five-cent recording booths of Times Square. The resulting disc was given to an arranger to transcribe, or simply played to the musicians who would re-record it. "I wrote those songs not out of talent, but out of necessity," says Ertegun, who spelled his name backwards for the author's credit so as not to embarrass his family. (In fact, there was no need for embarrassment: A. Nugetre wrote twelve songs that became hit records, including "Chains of Love" for Big Joe Turner.)

In the main the records that Atlantic produced were not typical "blues" but a cross between what Ertegun calls "city and southern." This came about because the session players available in New York were, on the whole, sophisticated jazz musicians from the big bands put together by Count Basie and Duke Ellington who regarded traditional southern blues as "ignorant," and something they really did not like to play. But the "ignorant" sound was exactly what Ertegun wanted, because that was what was selling, and he would cajole the musicians into diluting their suave sophistication with at least some basic, raw blues.

Meanwhile, Abramson worked at his ambition to make Atlantic "an eclectic record company of varied style" by recording a full-length version of "Romeo and Juliet," a book of poetry narrated by a young actor, and 256 stories for children.

But it was Atlantic's jazz and rhythm-and-blues recordings that were the label's main output. Despite their strenuous efforts, Ertegun and Abramson produced no hits at all in the first two years and Atlantic barely survived. Then in 1949 a distributor in New Orleans called Atlantic to inquire if the company knew of any wholesaler that could supply 5,000 copies of a record by Stick McGhee called "Drinking Wine, Spo-Dee-O-Dee." The answer was no. But since Stick McGhee's label was now extinct, Ertegun offered to make an exact copy of the record to sell to the distributor.

The only problem was, he could not think of anybody in New York who could sing authentic country blues—until he remembered a musician named Brownie McGhee whom he had met on one of his endless trips to Harlem. "I called him up, and he said he could to it, but as it happened his brother Stick was staying with him, so he might as well remake his own record," said Ertegun. Ertegun and Abramson recorded Stick McGhee that night, and "Drinking Wine, Spo-Dee-O-Dee" went on to sell 400,000 copies, reaching number three in *Billboard* magazine's rhythm-and-blues chart. (Almost forty years on, Ertegun has an understandable fondness for "Drinking Wine. . . ." In Turkey, as Uncle Omelette, he sings it for his niece and nephew as a bedtime treat.)

That lucky break marked the beginning of Atlantic's rise. In 1949 the company recorded 187 songs—three times the output of previous years—and, in Ertegun's words, "we began to make a little noise." The noise was sufficient to attract the attention of two executives from CBS Records, then the giant of the industry, who approached Ertegun and Abramson with the offer of a deal: CBS would manufacture and distribute Atlantic's records, and pay a royalty of 3 percent for each copy sold.

"What about the artist's royalty?" said Ertegun.

"You mean you're giving these artists royalties?" said the men from CBS as they looked at each other in amazement. (Their reaction was not surprising for it was then common practice to pay recording artists, at best, a one-time fee for their work: For his original version of "Drinking Wine . . ." Stick McGhee had received the princely sum of ten dollars.)

"We certainly are," replied Ertegun.

"You're going to ruin the business for all of us."

In addition to his savings and his experience, Herb Abramson had made one other significant contribution to Atlantic Records: his wife. Miriam Abramson was, and is, a formidable woman. She was also a collector of jazz records—which was how she had met Herb. She had no previous business experience—she worked as a proofreader for a New York advertising agency—but that did not deter her from taking on the business affairs of Atlantic. As far as she was concerned, all it took was common sense. "You see, one of the advantages of the record business at that time was that it was so small," she says. "You could see every aspect of it. Anybody could. You may not have done the actual work, but you could perceive what was being done in recording, in selling, in distribution. Everything that was done, you could really see."

Miriam was not always easy to deal with, as she herself admits: "Everybody said I was fair, but very tough. It was my business to get records out, which meant, in many cases, fighting with factories . . . I was the one who had to talk to the factories all the time, which I did. I yelled." As Tom Dowd says: "Tokyo Rose was the kindest name some people had for her. At some other companies, they would take it in turns to answer the phone if they knew that she was calling."

Her attitude was exactly what Atlantic needed to survive in its dealings with not always scrupulous record distributors and manufacturers. But problems arose when she turned her wrath on someone within the company—when, as Dowd puts it, "she would walk around like Popeye the sailor look-

ing for a fight." Doc Pomus, who was one of Atlantic's first—
and best—regular songwriters, puts it more strongly: "Miriam could be an extraordinarily vitriolic woman. I was writing for Joe Turner—at that time, we would come in and play
our songs live, and get advances. Once, in a room full of people, she said to me, 'Are you coming in to beg for money
again?' She would go around screaming at people all day."

Tough—but fair. According to Francine Wakschal, who
was hired as Atlantic's bookkeeper and first salaried employee in 1949, Miriam insisted that the company's books
were always to be kept in order: "That was the one thing that
we were always sticklers for—paying artists, paying bills, paying the musicians . . . We had schedules, we had a procedure.
We ran a disciplined company, with strict regulations."

It could not have been easy to maintain tight fiscal control
at Atlantic because Ertegun has never been one to allow a
lack of ready cash to prevent what he calls "having a good
time." On his relentless tours of New York's nightclubs he
insisted on being seen wearing the best suits and with the
prettiest girls on his arm—and Miriam was somewhat taken
aback to discover that his impeccable suits from Brooks
Brothers were simply put on the Ertegun account, in the
expectation that one day he would be able to pay the bill. "I
used to see these bills coming in to him which he hadn't paid,
and I'd say, 'Why don't you pay your bills?' And he'd say, 'If I
do, they'll think I'm closing the account.' I'd never heard that
kind of attitude before." ("The older I get, the more I realize
how Turkish I am," says Ertegun. "I display the prime char-
acteristics of Turkish vices: indolence and excess.")

There were other excuses. In 1948 Herb Abramson and
Ertegun went to the Crystal Caverns club in Washington to
listen to the singing of a twenty-year-old girl from Virginia
who had got her first booking after winning an amateur talent show. Ruth Brown had a magical voice and Ertegun immediately invited her to New York to record for Atlantic. She
never made it: En route to New York, just outside Philadelphia, the car in which she was traveling was involved in a

head-on collision and Brown ended up a patient in Chester Hospital, Pennsylvania, unable to walk for several months. She did not yet have a contract with Atlantic, but the company paid her bills and supported her—which as Miriam says, with her customary frankness, was "absolutely ridiculous. Nobody sensible would do that. But we did it."

She signed the contract on her twenty-first birthday, while she was still recovering in hospital, and where Ertegun visited her. "We thought that we would be very good for each other," she says. "We thought that maybe we could grow together." Indeed they did. Her first release, "So Long," reached number six in the rhythm-and-blues chart, and Ruth Brown went on to record more than eighty songs for Atlantic, becoming the company's most prolific and best-selling artist of that period.

The thriving Atlantic Record Company moved out of its shabby suite at the Hotel Jefferson and took offices at 301 West 54th Street in Manhattan. Francine Wakschal, the bookkeeper, remembers it as "quite a building"—a "walk-up" surrounded by drunks, where it was prudent for her to be escorted to work by the shipping clerk. "But it was fun," she says, because Atlantic was not run like a company: "Ahmet, and Herb, and Miriam—they were like my family." And Doc Pomus's best memories of the music business come from those days with Ertegun and Abramson. Atlantic had to endure seedy surroundings but it was determined to be what Miriam calls "the Tiffany" of record companies. According to Pomus: "Other record companies or music publishers were all the same to me: Their cultural and intellectual level was somewhere between the palm tree and the potted plant."

What mattered most was that Ertegun and Abramson were not executives so much as "absolute fans" who respected their artists, and were even a little in awe of them. Ruth Brown would go to see Ertegun, "the head honcho," and "prop my feet on his table, and we'd talk one-to-one. You never worried about not being able to sit down and talk to him."

For a black artist like Ben E. King, who was born in South Carolina where segregation was still a way of life, the Atlantic approach was nothing short of revolutionary: "This was a whole different bunch of people to those I had been meeting in the South—people that would not only accept you as a talent, but accept you as a person and leave room for you to make suggestions. I am from an era and a place where people would say, 'Hey, you don't talk until you're talked to.' And then I was brought to New York City where people asked *me* for advice! I said, 'Wow, where is this guy Ahmet coming from?' "

Not everybody appreciated where Ahmet Ertegun was coming from.

In 1953 he learned that Clyde McPhatter had been fired as the lead singer of a group called the Dominoes, and Ertegun tracked him down to a rented room in Harlem in order to sign him to Atlantic. To Ertegun, McPhatter's voice was "thrilling." It had "an angelic quality," and he sang with "an incredible amount of gospel soul." McPhatter duly signed with Atlantic and became lead singer for the Drifters (so called because most of its members had drifted from group to group), which recorded "Money Honey"—the biggest rhythm-and-blues hit of the year.

But there were those who regarded the Drifters' songs as lascivious smut. The group's next record for Atlantic, "Such a Night," was banned by the WXYZ radio station in Detroit after a vociferous campaign launched by angry mothers fearful of its corrupting influence on their children. Their next release, "Honey Love," was similarly banned in Memphis and southern outrage was such that, according to Tom Dowd, "you could have got arrested just for selling it or owning it."

But success breeds success and Atlantic was now attracting

not only its own discoveries but relatively established artists of the quality of Ray Charles, whom the company signed in 1952. He was not an easy man to work with—a genius, yet, as Miriam puts it, "no saint." Atlantic had moved offices again, to above Patsy's Restaurant on West 56th Street, where the desks would be pushed aside to make way for the microphones, and Charles would arrive for recording sessions which Miriam found hair-raising: "He had a drug problem, and we had a tiny loo. Really, it was just like a cupboard and it had a loo in it. And during the session he would go in and you could hear him hitting his head against the wall. It was quite weird . . ."

Nevertheless, with his pounding gospel piano and exuberant voice, the blind singer from Georgia gave Atlantic Records yet more hits. The company was not yet secure, and Ertegun constantly worried about "a good release for *next* month"—but there was now every prospect that the bills from Brooks Brothers would be paid.

One test of Atlantic's strength was that it survived the sudden departure of one of the founding partners. In 1953 Herb Abramson was drafted into the army and sent to Germany (where he served as a dentist). To replace him for the two years he would be away, Ertegun enlisted the help of Jerry Wexler, who was working as a reporter at *Billboard* magazine where he had coined the phrase "rhythm and blues" to replace the derogatory description of black music as "race records."

Wexler was another zealous collector of jazz records who regarded the people at Atlantic Records as "pals": "We used to go to each other's houses and play our Louis Armstrong 78s, that sort of thing. And then we'd go to Fire Island together for summer vacations." The son of Jewish immigrants to New York, his father, Harry, was a Talmudic scholar who became a window cleaner, helped out by Jerry when he was not at school or working at his evening job as a liquor store delivery boy. Wexler's background—"he came out of strife, out of oppression," in Tom Dowd's words—gave him an insight into black music. As Dowd emphasizes, his was not the cool appreciation of a distant connoisseur: "By living in New York and being gregarious—and so conscious of oppression— he had a natural empathy for the blues and jazz musicians. He loved dancing. He'd always be in Harlem dancing, picking it up firsthand, and just having a good time." Wexler, who had originally trained as a journalist, nursed a fierce desire to write the great American novel, but "I need to get into a kind of white heat to write—and if I don't, I hate what I write. I'm a perfectionist. It has to be as good as Faulkner, or not at all." Shelving his literary ambitions, he channeled his considerable energies into making hit records for Atlantic, throwing himself into the business entirely.

There was something magical about the Ertegun-Wexler partnership. They sat with their desks side by side and, as Wexler says, "everything was done together. If somebody came up to speak to one of us, the other was there. This wasn't because we needed to keep an eye on each other, but because we were in it together." Wexler had never produced a record before; he simply jumped in at the deep end, going into the studio with Ertegun, picking things up as he went along—as, indeed, did Ertegun. "The truth is, there was no state of the art in record-making at that time," says Wexler. What they did not know, they invented.

Of course, Ertegun and Wexler did have the benefit of Tom Dowd as their engineer, who—"for the sake of decency," says Wexler—was promoted to producer. The three of them worked as a team: "We always found an accommodation," says Wexler. "Very rarely would there be an impasse or confrontation—and this partnership worked very well in the studio and in the office, because the affirmative prevailed. There was no right of veto. If somebody *really* wanted to do something, he would carry the day."

It is also true that Ertegun and Wexler were both far too unsure of themselves for either to insist that the other was wrong: "Each of us had a certain quotient of narcissism, but the whole thing was much too frightening to let narcissism prevail. If we had been as secure as we are now, then maybe it wouldn't have gone so smoothly. But we were just reaching out and feeling our way, and trying to find out where we were going. We didn't know what we were doing . . . Really we were frightened to death that the next minute would snuff this thing out. So nobody would want to stand fast and insist that his opinions were sacrosanct, because we didn't really know." (Now, Wexler adds, "our opinions are insistent, and have been cast in bronze and marble and are unchangeable.")

For Wexler the biggest ordeal was going into the studio: "It was frightening for years. It took me a long time to get over being scared, because I was sure that the musicians would find me out. I don't know if this could have worked if we weren't the bosses, and we paid their checks. If we'd been employees, we probably would have been fired for incompetence or vagueness."

But they obviously did something right. With increasing speed and frequency the major companies began issuing "covers" of Atlantic's hits: sanitized versions of the black music performed by more acceptable, clean-cut white artists.

The original Atlantic versions would often outsell the covers, though that was never reflected in the charts. To the chagrin of Atlantic, the sales of R&B (meaning black) records and the sales of pop (meaning white) records were measured separately and kept distinct. Tom Dowd remembers receiving a royalty statement for a song he had "scribbled" for the B side of a Clyde McPhatter record showing it had sold 450,000 copies. At the time, the number one pop single in the country had sold under 200,000 copies—yet Clyde McPhatter was not even listed in the Top 100.

But what did it matter? In its first two years the Ertegun-Wexler partnership produced thirty R&B hits, including Big

Joe Turner's version of "Shake, Rattle and Roll" (with Ertegun and Wexler singing the backup vocals). Atlantic was flying.

The question was: What would happen when Herb Abramson came back from the army to reclaim his partnership?

Chapter 2
A REALLY LOVELY GUY

Nowadays Herb Abramson lives in a little green house in Culver City, within a stone's throw of a busy Los Angeles freeway, and beside the Naugles takeout restaurant. The front door leads directly into a small room where there is a sagging divan that he sleeps on, and some old car seats that provide makeshift chairs. There is a dusty backroom, which has been turned into a tiny studio stacked with old tapes, records, books, and—for reasons he does not explain—stage makeup stacked next to a mirror. Crammed into remaining corners is Abramson's elaborate filing system, housed in crates and cardboard boxes from the neighboring restaurant. Packed full of fading memorabilia and yellowed newspaper cuttings, it is all he has left of his founding partnership in Atlantic Records.

Renowned for his charm and good looks in the 1950s, Abramson is now overweight, dressed in shabby ill-fitting clothes. But although his hair is long and unkempt, he has a neatly trimmed beard and an air of dignity. At the start of a conversation, he stammers and finds it difficult to speak, almost as though it has been a long time since he talked to other people. Once started, however, a stream of memories comes flowing out.

In January 1953, he remembers, when he was drafted by the army, Atlantic had reached a turning point: "Nineteen fifty-three was the time when black music began to go pop.

The important disc jockeys were playing black music all over the country, and the kids of America, when they heard 'Shake, Rattle and Roll' and things like that, they took to it—and rock and roll spread over the whole world." Atlantic could not have been healthier when Wexler arrived to fill Abramson's place: "When he came in Atlantic had a very nice roster of artists such as Ruth Brown, and Joe Turner, and Clyde McPhatter, and Ray Charles . . .

"I would like to make the point that it is easy to do something once you have been shown. Columbus said he could stand an egg on end and they said, 'Oh no, that's impossible.' He said, 'Do you want to know how it's done?' and he cracked the bottom of the egg and the egg stood up. In the same way, when you come into a company like Atlantic which had artists that meant something, and when the scene was such that the records one put out got to be hot, it was possible to get even bigger sellers . . . I was off the scene, and Ahmet and Jerry were on the scene and the Atlantic hits started to be covered by other hit artists. They were in the right place at the right time."

Then he adds: "Having gone away as the top executive—and being the president of the company even when I was away—when I came back I expected to carry on as usual. But I was surprised to see that there was not too much desire to work with me. They had a hot team going, and they wanted to keep it."

What is striking is his valiant attempt to be fair toward his old colleagues. Every note of betrayal that creeps into his voice is soon followed by an almost guilty effort to keep his bitterness at bay: "I admit they had a hot swinging thing going, and it wasn't necessary to break it. If they wanted to work together, fine." But then he adds he was the one who taught Ertegun everything he knew about record production and, "When I left for the army, Ahmet said to me, 'I don't know what we are going to do—after all, you used to supervise most of the sessions.' I said, 'Ahmet, you make three or four recording sessions entirely on your own, and even if each one bombs, by that time you will have learned enough to be confident in yourself.' "

Unfortunately for Abramson, by the time he returned to Atlantic in 1955, Ertegun had grown entirely confident—as had Jerry Wexler. And the balance of power shifted even farther away from Abramson with the arrival at Atlantic of Ertegun's older brother, Nesuhi, who was brought into the company as a partner shortly after Abramson's return.

Nesuhi had been living in Los Angeles for ten years, and contact between the two brothers was irregular. "We'd talk on the phone once in a while, every few months," said Nesuhi, who treated his younger brother like a wayward child, scolding him for talking too much or being flippant. (Ahmet, in retaliation, teased Nesuhi about his number of marriages—four. As Jerry Wexler observes, the two brothers always had a relationship based on "exasperation and exacerbation." At times, he says, he was closer to them than they were to each other—"except when it came to the bone, the Turkish nitty-gritty.") It was during one of the brothers' infrequent telephone conversations that Nesuhi told Ahmet, almost in passing, that he had been offered a partnership in Imperial Records, based in Los Angeles, and intended to join the company as a jazz record producer. "Ahmet went crazy: 'You can't do that. You can't join our biggest competitor. We need you in New York.' " Ahmet and Wexler went to California to talk Nesuhi out of joining Imperial, and into joining them. Nesuhi was not keen on moving to New York, but "they dragged me into agreeing."

Nesuhi Ertegun and Herbert Abramson did not much like each other. Abramson says, with some disdain, that until he joined Atlantic Nesuhi had produced only "moldy fig" records—an epithet that jazz critics apply to traditional jazz: "That was a very fine little hobby, but he wasn't in the mainstream of the record business." Nesuhi, for his part, thought that Abramson was not in touch with jazz musicians: "I remember at a session for National Records, Herb said to Billy Eckstein, 'Have you vocalized this morning?' Of course Billy didn't know what on earth Herb was talking about."

Even so, Abramson agreed that Nesuhi should become a partner in Atlantic Records. In his little green house in Culver City he recalls what happened: "So, foolish me, I said to Ahmet, 'Give Nesuhi some of your stock, that doesn't cost me anything.' Then boom, what do I know, there is another hostile partner. Ahmet and Nesuhi used to talk in Turkish in my presence to say things that I wasn't supposed to know."

Far away from the Naugles restaurant and the exhaust fumes of the Los Angeles freeways, Miriam Abramson—or rather Mrs. Freddie Bienstock, as she has been since 1957—lives in a comfortable apartment on Park Avenue, Manhattan. A smiling black maid shows visitors into the spacious living room where Persian rugs are scattered on wood floors and a neat pile of logs lies by the fire. The room is a traditional one, decorated in navy, cream, and red, but there are a few modern touches, such as the Picasso woodcuts hanging on the wall. Miriam, who wears a stylish outfit and bouffant hair, is still recognizable as the vigorous, formidable businesswoman of the 1950s. "When Herb came back from the army in 1955, we were doing pretty well—everybody had cars . . . This whole shift in balance was something that he couldn't adjust to. He couldn't come back as number one, and he certainly couldn't come back as number three. He had an ego, because he started the company and he had experience. So it was rather an awkward situation. I think that neither Jerry nor Ahmet felt comfortable working with him." And, she adds briskly, Herb did not get on well with Wexler.

There was one other ingredient in this potent mix—one that made an already difficult situation explosive. Abramson returned from the army in Germany with a girlfriend. She was pregnant and, he announced, he wanted to marry her.

Miriam and Herb, who had a three-year-old child, continued to work together at Atlantic while divorce proceedings were going on. "It was very awkward, it really was," she

says quietly, choosing her words with care. "We were working in the same office, but we weren't working under the
same circumstances."

"He came back with a Brünnhilde!" says Wexler, with an
air of amused exasperation, as if that might explain everything. But he does admit: "Of course it must have been difficult for him, because Ahmet and I had formed this team,
and we were clicking away like mad. Nothing but euphoria
and mad success. Things kept going up and up."

Abramson felt excluded from the new power structure at
Atlantic in every way, down to the last detail of office layout.
When he left the company in 1953 his desk was next to Ertegun's. When he returned in 1955, it was Wexler who sat
next to Ertegun and there was no room for a third desk. "We
had an interesting setup," Abramson says. "Ahmet and Jerry
had an office at one side, and I had an office at the extreme
other side, and in the middle there was a conference room."

After a few tense months, it was decided by the partners
that Abramson should have a separate company, too. He was
placed in charge of a new Atlantic subsidiary, named Atco.
According to Ed Ward, writing in *Rolling Stone*'s history of
rock and roll, *Rock of Ages*, the reorganization of the company was "to welcome home Herb Abramson from his two
year stint in the Army Dental Corps . . . Atco was an ideal
niche for the returning soldier who had missed out on Atlantic's rise to glory, and Wexler and Ertegun turned it over to
him to run." Unfortunately, the returning soldier did not see
it that way. He recognized the logic of starting a subsidiary
that would allow Atlantic to use an additional set of distributors, thus providing added muscle to promote the company's
artists—but being shunted off to Atco only increased his
sense of isolation.

And though Tom Dowd thought the creation of Atco was a
good way of defusing the tension within the company ("Jerry
was flying, Ahmet was flying—and Herb stepped onto a
wheel going at seven hundred miles an hour"), and though
Abramson was given his own budget and "a couple of artists

that would be better suited to him—a new breed, another culture," the consequences were disastrous.

One of the "new breed" artists that Abramson acquired was Walden Robert Cassotto, a twenty-one-year-old college dropout from the Bronx, better known as Bobby Darin. He was an avid fan of Atlantic's black musicians, particularly Ray Charles, and wanted to sing just like Charles. "He started off really being a would-be R&B artist," says Ertegun. His early releases on Atco met with little success but, in the course of recording them, he did make a considerable impression on Ertegun: "Bobby used to come to the office all the time . . . He didn't have a penny, so I'd give him money to come in on the subway. He used to wait to see Herb, or whatever, and he used to sit in a room next to my office which had a piano in it. And he used to sit and mess around at the piano while he was waiting. I was taken by how bluesy his piano playing and his singing were. And we became friends, just because I used to go into the room and he'd say, 'Do you remember this?'—and he'd do Ray Charles's songs and other songs. I thought he was a fantastic artist, and just needed to be recorded properly."

Abramson thought otherwise and announced he was dropping Darin from Atco. Ertegun, however, decided that he would have one go at producing Darin. In less than two hours, he recorded three sides—including "Splish Splash," a song Darin had composed in twelve minutes. The record sold 100,000 copies in the first month of its release in 1957, and went on to sell one million. That success transformed Darin into a teen idol and gave Atlantic its first breakthrough into the white pop market. "It was the beginning of a whole new era," says Tom Dowd. For Abramson it was the end of the road: "Herb just looked and said, 'I'm not where these guys are,' and he left."

Thirty years later, in his dusty little house in Culver City, Abramson tries to be philosophical about his fate: "In entertainment entities there is cutthroat politics, but it is the way of the world." He does not feel that Ertegun betrayed him; rather that he was the loser in a merciless game of cards. "You read about the factionalism and the politics that goes on in the movie business, where they play musical chairs, each striving for themselves—well, it was a similar situation at Atlantic. I sometimes look at it like a poker game, in that originally there are quite a few participants, but some of them are dealt out and some of them end up with all the chips. That is the way the cookie crumbles."

Jerry Wexler insists there was no reason for Abramson to have left—certainly no financial reason: "There was plenty of money. Let's suppose one of us had a fallow period. Well, that's fine—everything continued. You drew your salary and it would all come around full circle at some other point. And if it never came around, well that's fine too. You paid your dues and you were a part of it, and everybody gets treated alike . . . It was like having a mound of money on the table, and saying, 'I think I need two and a half inches of money.' "

Ertegun confines himself to one brief comment on the subject, unadorned by anecdote or humor: "Herb insisted on being bought out. He didn't have to go." And, in a way, Abramson agrees with this simple analysis: "I had a big ego and after a while I couldn't take it, so I said, 'Buy me out.' It was the stupidest thing I ever said, but that was it."

Some of Abramson's stock was assigned to Nesuhi Ertegun. The rest went to Miriam (who, having married Freddie Bienstock, helped him build up the vast Chappell music publishing company) as a substitute for alimony for her, and child support for their son. And that, as far as Miriam is concerned, was the end of it. She does not know where Abramson lives nowadays, nor, she says, does she care. "I haven't seen him since we were divorced, and neither has my son."

Abramson went on to set up his own independent label, recording R&B artists such as Louisiana Red, but without a great deal of success. His departure from Atlantic was not greatly mourned by the partners and colleagues he left behind. The songwriter Doc Pomus says that by the time

Abramson left, "he was an absolutely professional flake" whose behavior grew more erratic by the day. "He fancied himself as a songwriter, and always called me up in the middle of the night to help him write a song. He grew weirder as time went on." But then he adds: "Even so, he really was a lovely guy."

Jerry Leiber, another Atlantic songwriter of that era, has a more compassionate view. He believes "Miriam's lunch money and what she spends on her hair would allow Abramson to live a relatively decent life in southern California. It's really pathetic . . . They should save him. But there's not enough heart there to save a mouse.

"I think he was intimidated or overwhelmed . . . He was a very gentle soul, and very unassuming. He was not at all aggressive, he struck you as someone who could not defend himself in life . . . It's terribly sad what happened to him—like the worst sackcloth and ashes fantasy. It's Dickensian: to hit the bottom of the well, after being almost at the very top."

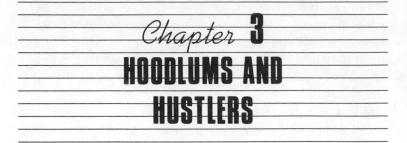

Chapter 3
HOODLUMS AND HUSTLERS

Ahmet Ertegun's favorite nightclub in New York was Birdland, the largest and liveliest of Broadway's jazz clubs. Perhaps part of the attraction for Ertegun was that Birdland managed to straddle several layers of urban culture, providing a microcosm of American life and in some way uniting the various strands of Ertegun's experience. A strange social mix would fraternize into the small hours: society people who saw it as *the* place to go; black musicians staying at the Alvin Hotel across the road; members of the emerging black middle class; young kids who could not afford to sit at the tables and stood at the bar to listen to the jazz; rough-and-ready entrepreneurs who were looking for musicians to record; and sinister underworld characters who wielded some undefinable but palpable form of power over New York's club land.

A party from Atlantic Records—usually consisting of Ertegun, his brother Nesuhi, Miriam Abramson, and Jerry Wexler—would be treated as honored guests at Birdland. As they descended a grand staircase into the basement club, they would be met by the maître d'—a black midget, in full dinner dress, named Peewee Marquette who would show them to one of the best tables. (If Nesuhi arrived without Ahmet, Peewee would inevitably greet him, "Hi, Ahmet, how's your brother?" Peewee knew full well that Nesuhi was not Ahmet, but he could not learn to pronounce Nesuhi's name.) The Dizzie Gillespie Band might be playing, or Charlie Parker, whose nickname, "Bird," had inspired the club's name. The owner of Birdland, a tall, well-built young man named Morris Levy, would send drinks over to Atlantic's table or join Ertegun's party to discuss the fortunes of the still fledgling record business—a business in which Levy was taking an increasing interest. While he played host, his brother, Zaccariah—a former cabdriver and a thinner, more lugubrious version of Morris—took care of the nuts and bolts of business.

"I liked the Erteguns' company," says Morris Levy. "They were very talented people and we used to have laughs together." Ertegun and his brother would sometimes stay late into the night at Birdland for after-hours drinking sessions with musicians such as Levy's close friends Count Basie and Dinah Washington, and Levy would regale them with the latest insights he had gained from wire-tapping the pay phone in the ladies' cloakroom at another club he owned, the Roundtable. "We would break up laughing at the things broads would tell their husbands when they were cheating, or they were out with some guy," says Levy. "It was a hell of a lesson in learning about women."

Besides the fun, there was an important business reason for Ertegun's frequent visits to Birdland. One of the club's attractions was "Symphony Sid"—a small, thin, undistinguished-looking man who was never without a beautiful woman at his side. Symphony Sid was a disc jockey from Boston who had been "discovered" by Levy and brought to Birdland from where he broadcast a live radio program. Since airplay was crucial to any record's success, it was important to persuade the likes of Symphony Sid to play Atlantic's jazz records on his program. And, since Atlantic was still too small to hire any promotion men, Ertegun had to do the job himself.

It was not easy. The little disc jockey had been immortalized in song by Lester Young, the legendary saxophonist who wrote "Jumping with Symphony Sid," but those who sang it would make up their own irreverent words for the tune—of which "Symphony Sid was a jive motherfucker" were the most polite. He was an obsessive and stubborn man who played only music that met his own quirky but rigorous standards. He might broadcast one record twenty times a night; another he would refuse to play at all. Miriam Abramson found him unbearable: "He had a beautiful speaking voice and was a complete idiot." She recalls that he would deliberately exasperate Ertegun. It was a time when many jazz musicians, influenced by the nascent black power movement, took Muslim names. "One time Sid said, 'What's your name again?' Ahmet said, 'Here's my card.' And Sid said, 'What's that? Ahmet Ertegun? Suddenly everybody is a Mohammedan.' "

Ertegun could, of course, have asked Morris Levy to use his influence with the intractable Sid—but, on the whole, he preferred not to. Birdland may have been "the jazz center of the world," as Levy called it, and Levy undoubtedly a growing power in the music business as he opened up more nightclubs (in addition to the Roundtable, Levy owned the Down Beat and the fashionably elegant Embers—leading *Variety* to call him "The Octopus of Broadway"), but Ertegun believed there were reasons to keep a judicious distance from Morris Levy, and particularly from some of his friends.

Morris Levy's early childhood, so very different from Ertegun's, is reminiscent of a New York version of *Oliver Twist.* He was born in Harlem in 1927, the son of the owner of a small grocery store. When he was four months old both his father and his older brother died of pneumonia. A surviving brother was placed in an orphanage while Morris remained at home with his mother. "The shock of my father and brother dying gave her every sickness known to man," he says. "First her jaw froze, then she had diabetes and heart trouble. She was never a well woman. I was very close to her." In spite of his filial affections, Levy can only have compounded her anxieties by running away from home at the age of thirteen.

"School bored me and I wanted to get out and work. I had always made money. I was shining shoes at nine years old." By thirteen Morris had virtually stopped going to school and he was hauled in by the truant officer and "sentenced" to live in a children's home until the age of twenty-one. That night he ran away to Florida, and conspired to cover up his traces. "I got my school records destroyed. I had someone apply for a transfer to another school, and the old school gave them my records to take to the new school—and they made them disappear. So *I* disappeared as a student in the U.S."

He was already five feet, eleven inches tall, with the looks of a young Marlon Brando, and had no trouble persuading a Florida nightclub owner he was old enough to be taken on as the darkroom boy, developing the souvenir photographs of guests. After more nightclub jobs, and a spell in the U.S. Navy, Levy returned to New York where he worked as a chauffeur, driving New York gamblers to crap games in New Jersey clubs. (He would while away the waiting time in the clubs' kitchens, learning from the Italian chefs the best way to serve eggplant with ricotta, and to reheat spaghetti.) By the time he was twenty he had earned enough, and learned enough, to open Birdland.

It was during this period of his life that Levy made the contacts that were to bolster him for the rest of his career—and which made more cautious businessmen, such as Ahmet Ertegun, keep their distance.

Levy has never made any secret of his connections with the New York Mafia: "When I was fourteen or fifteen I worked for people that were in the Mob because they were the people that owned the clubs. They liked me because I was smart, I was hard-working, and I was a tough kid," says Levy in his very low gruff voice. Many have speculated that it was the Mob who put Levy in business, and that he is beholden to gangsters to this day. True or not, the notion Levy was "connected," together with his own impatient manner and his impressively broad appearance, earned him a certain fearful respect—and a reputation as a tough guy which he assiduously cultivated. "Morris talked like the Godfather," says a radio station manager who knew him during that period. "He'd walk around his clubs with his gun showing . . . Oh yes, he carries a gun. I went into his office one day for a meeting and his jacket fell open and there was a gun. It scared the hell out of me. It was in his belt, like a detective's. He was a colorful character."

Levy's fearful reputation only grew when his brother Zaccariah was murdered at Birdland in what many people said was a gangland killing. "His brother was stabbed to death in the middle of a performance," says a regular visitor to the club. "I think Stan Kenton's band was playing at the time . . . Whoever did it thought they were getting Morris." Levy says that Zaccariah had thrown a prostitute out of the club the night before, and her pimp turned up and stabbed him to death. Nevertheless, the suspicion that Morris Levy was the real target of a Mob vendetta strengthened the air of menace which surrounded him (and still does today)—and was greatly to his advantage when he decided to extend his business into the profitable world of music publishing.

Levy's introduction to publishing came almost by chance when he discovered that some of the interests muscling in on club owners were entirely legitimate. "These guys came into the club one night and said to me, 'You have to pay us if you want to play music in the club.' I thought it was a shakedown and I had them thrown out.

"I went to my lawyer and told him about it. He said, 'You know, Morris, that's the law. By an act of Congress you have to pay if you want to play music in a club." He explained to Levy about the 1909 Copyright Act and the role of the American Society of Composers, Authors, and Publishers (ASCAP), and Broadcast Music Incorporated (BMI), which collect royalties on behalf of songwriters and their publishers from every establishment where music is performed in public.

Levy paid his dues, but he also registered with ASCAP and

BMI immediately—as the "publisher" of songs first performed in his club. "I thought it was a hell of a thing that by
an act of Congress I could now collect royalties from every
bar in the area." From such beginnings Levy went on to
create a considerable publishing empire that now holds the
worldwide rights to works as diverse as "The Yellow Rose of
Texas" and "Celebration" by Kool and the Gang (which became a kind of alternative national anthem when the U.S.
hostages were returned from Iran). "I love my publishing,"
says Levy. "It's very intimate, very straight, and it never talks
back to you. Publishing was always my first love . . . I only
fooled with records to get more publishing."

Levy began "fooling with records" in 1956 when he
founded Roulette Records—the first of a bewildering number of labels Levy has owned, some of which have only ever
released a handful of records. His attitude to what might be
called artist relations was robust, and very different from that
of Atlantic. "Artists are pains in the asses," he says. "Artists, a
lot of them, are just imbeciles and they are ignorant. They
say, 'Look what big thieves . . . Roulette were, that they paid
four cents a record and they took advantage of the artists.'
Bullshit. There is no need to apologize. I don't apologize for
it. If anyone was abused it was the record companies. They
were damn fools to take all that shit from the artist."

Despite that attitude—or perhaps because of it—Levy's record companies scored some solid successes. For example, in
1956 the Gee label (which Levy took over from its founder,
George Goldner) produced four Top Twenty hits from just
one album by Frankie Lymon and the Teenagers, including
"Why Do Fools Fall in Love?"—one of the more durable
songs from that era. (Frankie Lymon himself was less durable: A career that began when he was thirteen was over at
eighteen. At twenty-five he died of a heroin overdose.)

And the truth is, with or without Mob connections, Morris
Levy was much more typical of the new music moguls than
either Ahmet Ertegun or Jerry Wexler (who may well be the
only record industry executive of his time to have read the

works of William Faulkner). The world in which Atlantic had to survive was populated largely by hoodlums and hustlers.

"In those days no one gave a shit whether you had a college degree, or what kind of tie you wore, and whether or not you had Gucci shoes on," says Bob Krasnow in what is his characteristically blunt way. "This was a tough business and you had to be tough. You had to be funny too, because everybody was tough. So, you could lighten up the slap on the hand when they didn't pay you on time—because nobody paid you on time. You had to be a juggler, you had to be a magician, you had to be an artist, you had to be a painter, a con man, a high-wire walker—everything to everybody." What mattered was how sharp you were, and whether you could hustle your way through the business faster than anyone else, says Krasnow. "You had to do everything: You gotta make the record, you gotta sell the record, you had to promote the record . . ."

Krasnow is one of the survivors of the 1950s who went on to become head of Elektra Records—now one of Atlantic's sister companies, and the label of such artists as Simply Red, Tracy Chapman, and Anita Baker. Today he sits in a stylish office with matte-black furniture, twenty floors up in the towering New York headquarters of Warner Communications, surrounded by his eclectic art collection. (It was, he says, his ethnic credentials more than anything else that got him the job: "I could work for a big company like Warner Brothers because I had all of the ethnic qualities—I was white, I was Jewish, they could invite me over to their house for dinner, and I could talk to black people.")

In 1958 he worked for King Records of Cincinnati, which was to country music what Atlantic was to rhythm and blues. He was, he says, among the "gunslingers. I was like a guy on the frontier.

"You see, in those days nobody really understood what the record business was. There was no business. It was like digging the first ditch—you know, the Israelis trying to irrigate the desert. Who knew they would build cities?"

There were, of course, well-established record companies, such as CBS and RCA/Victor, but they largely recorded classical music, or Rosemary Clooney and Bing Crosby and the rest of the white balladeers. Then suddenly the "majors" found their entrenched position under siege from the myriad of new "independents" recording music derived from country and delta blues. As Krasnow says: "Hey, [we were] a small group of people who were like Green Berets. It was the opposite of England beating up on the Falklands, you know. It was like the Falklands beating up on England. It was reverse warfare."

Even by the late 1950s many people had never even heard of the so-called record industry: "My mother used to always call me and say, 'Bob, what are you doing for a living? What is it exactly you are doing for a living? My girlfriends are sitting here, and we're playing canasta, and they keep saying, "What does your son Bob do?" and I can't remember. What is it?' And I'd say, 'Mom, I'm in the record business.' She'd say, 'There is no record business—I've looked it up everywhere. No one knows what the record business is. What is it?' And I'd say, 'Mom, you know all those records I brought home for you to listen to?' She says, 'I'm not playing those records for anybody. Did you hear those records?' My mother just couldn't understand what the hell we were doing."

What Krasnow was actually doing was learning the tricks of the trade from the owner of King Records, Sydney Nathan—"this fat old Jewish guy who could barely speak the English language. Well, he spoke in the English language, but he spoke it like a member of the Gambino family."

Syd Nathan was perhaps the quintessential record man of the pioneering days. He was, in the words of one his junior employees, "a short, round, rough, gruff man with a nose like Porky Pig and two Coca-Cola bottles for eyeglasses." King Records, though an independent, was exceptional in that it was a complete record-producing operation—like the majors—with its own pressing plant and branch distribution network. It began as something much smaller when Nathan, who owned a shop selling radios in Cincinnati, collected a long-overdue debt from a jukebox operator who, short of cash, paid up with a mountain of old 78 r.p.m. records in lieu. Nathan sold the records in his radio store, and when they were gone—and shellac became available again after the war—he decided, like so many others, to make his own product. He became legendary for his parsimony (he supposedly fired Bob Krasnow every other week because of his expenses) and his worldly-wise maxims.

Nathan once congratulated one of King's most successful country artists, "Cowboy" Copus, for refusing to pay $50 for the rights to a song he discovered on one of his scouting forays down to Nashville. "You did the right thing, Copus; ain't no song in the world worth fifty bucks," said Nathan. (That might have been a shortsighted view: The song was "The Tennessee Waltz.") But Nathan had an uncanny eye for talent. For as well as recording innovative artists such as James Brown and Hank Ballard (who inspired the Twist), he gave many of today's prominent figures in the record industry their first jobs. He also gave them their first lessons in "playing the game."

"You want to be in the record business?" he said to Dickie Kline, who went on to become head of promotion for Atlantic Records. "The first thing you learn is everyone is a liar, and the only thing that matters is the song. Buy the song, own the song, but remember, no matter what anyone tells you, they are liars until they have convinced you that they are telling the truth."

None of the protégés that Nathan bequeathed to the record industry has been more successful than Seymour Stein, who—like Bob Krasnow—is now ensconced in Warner Communications' headquarters, as head of Sire Records (another of Atlantic's sister companies), and who is very much the rising star of Warner's record empire.

Seymour Stein was always determined to enter the music

business. Tom Noonan, the charts editor at *Billboard,* remembers the gauche and awkward boy who came to him with a rather strange request in the 1950s. "Seymour came to me as a thirteen-year-old Brooklyn student, with this unbelievably thick Brooklyn accent—he used to whine when he talked—and said he had a hobby." Stein's hobby was the charts and he won permission from *Billboard* to go to its offices every day after school to write out by hand every chart back to the year he was born. The task took two years to complete, in the course of which Stein demonstrated not only his dogged determination but also his financial meanness: "Then and now," says Noonan, "Seymour is very, very cheap—he won't spend a lovely afternoon. He is incredible with money, and in those days he was ridiculous."

Stein is also one of today's most talented record industry executives, and the most eccentric. His reputation depends, in equal parts, on signing Madonna while lying in a hospital bed after heart surgery; wild, not to say unfettered, behavior at parties; and his obsessive collecting of old china, prints, furniture, and almost anything else that he can get his hands on.

Just as his vast, two-storied New York apartment overlooking Central Park West has become a storehouse for a jumble of *objets d'art,* his mind is a repository for old songs and extraordinary anecdotes from the days when the music moguls were a special breed.

Sitting in a private room of Chez Vong, an expensive Chinese restaurant in New York City, Seymour Stein holds court. He entertains his guests with croaky renditions of girl-group songs from the 1960s, and tales of hoary old record men from the 1940s. Between his versions of Elvis Presley's "Wooden Heart" (in German) and "Golden Teardrops" by the Flamingos, he employs the few phrases of Chinese he knows to order a sumptuous meal. Although he claims to be on a diet of papaya and no alcohol, he attacks the food hungrily—and the wine. As the evening progresses, and the wine takes effect, the stories, in particular those about Syd Nathan, grow more and more outrageous.

He recounts his first meeting with Nathan at the tender age of sixteen: "I went out to Cincinnati and got there at about three in the morning. Sydney's stepdaughter came into my room. She was about fourteen and she says to me, 'You're the kid that's going to live with us for the summer. You want to go for a swim? We go skinny-dipping here.' So, we go swimming [in Nathan's pool] and all of a sudden this huge hulk says, 'Get out of the pool.' It's her stepbrother Nat. 'He's crazy,' she says, 'don't pay any attention to him.' So he starts screaming, 'Get out of the pool,' and all of a sudden Sydney comes out, wearing nothing more than one of those undershirts—but he is so old that his balls were hanging all the way down. 'Having a swim, kids?' [Stein here adopts a gruff Syd Nathan voice.]

"Sydney couldn't see. He had these Coca-Cola glasses [and he had] cataracts. So he says to me, 'Seymour, have you met my son?' His son had the unfortunate name of Nathaniel Nathan Nathan—can you imagine?—they called him Nat Nat Nat. He [the son] turns around and says, 'Do you think I'm crazy? Do you think you could fool me? I'm Al Capone. And I know that's Bugsy Malone in the pool.' Syd says, "You're so smart, I wanna tell you a secret'—and he punches the kid in the face. And the kid runs off . . . And then he [Nathan] waddles off. So he never knew that I was skinny-dipping with his daughter—not that he would have cared."

Stein says that Nathan was "a genius"-a unique character. But he trusted nobody (which was why King pressed and distributed its own records, and even printed the jackets) and he could not delegate. When he died, the company died with him. Stein had long since left King Records ("I couldn't stand Cincinnati") and had engaged in a long series of fights with Nathan, but he went to the funeral as a pallbearer. So, too, did James Brown ("Soul Brother Number One") though he had sued Nathan for unpaid royalties. And, Stein says, both of them cried.

Stein quickly changes the subject to divulge another Syd Nathan story that "must be told." It concerns a period when King Records—and just about every other record company in America—was attempting to imitate Atlantic's success with rhythm and blues. Nathan hired a former music publisher from New York, down on his luck, and sent him out on the road to find and buy R&B songs that King Records might record.

The man—"Don't use his name," says Stein (we will call him John)—was a country fan not attuned to black music, and he failed miserably. Under increasing pressure from Nathan, he disappeared for a month and there was no trace of him until a letter and a tape arrived in the mail. In the letter John said that, having scoured the Midwest and the South for songs, he had found eighty—of which the ten best were on the tape. If none of those had hope, said John, he would leave King Records because "I'm not cut out for R&B."

Nathan was "overwhelmed," says Stein. He had been "nasty" to John but "he hadn't meant anything by it—he really liked him." In King's basement studios Nathan recorded his own tape in reply, first telling John, "I love you and I can't believe you're ready to quit." Then, with the tape still running, he assembled his staff in the studio so they could give their verdicts on John's ten songs. Nathan said that because some of the men in the room were "yes-men" he would reserve his own judgment until last.

"So he puts on the first song and it was dreadful," says Stein. "I was so self-conscious I hid under the piano because I didn't want him to call on me and ask for a comment. So he said [Stein readopts his gruff Syd Nathan voice]: 'All right, boys, what do you think? I won't say a word.' And nobody opened their mouth because everybody liked [John] very much . . . Finally Syd loses his patience and he says, 'All right, Sonny Thompson,' and he points over to Sonny Thompson—

and he's such a nice guy—and Syd says, 'Sonny, you're the oldest one in the room. I'm not going to say a word. I'm going to say nothing at all. Sonny, tell us, what do you think of this load of crap?' "

The guests at Stein's table roar with laughter. When it has subsided he adds: "The very sad part of this is, about fourteen days later, the day the guy got this tape, he dropped dead of a heart attack. So it's not that funny."

According to Stein, King Records was a relatively honest company—"they actually employed bookkeepers!" As for the rest of the independents, there was Atlantic—"as honest as any major company was in those days, and that's where it ended. Underneath that there was a big drop." Indeed there was.

Everybody in the business knows Morty Craft: He occupies a very special place in the folklore of the music industry. The rumbustious parties he hosted in the "hospitality suites" at the record industry's conventions were sufficient to make his name legendary. "Morty Craft—what a character, what a character," says Bob Krasnow with more than a hint of nostalgia in his voice. "Oh, man, I've had some wild nights with him . . . wow"—and nobody else can leave the garrulous Krasnow at a loss for words.

Craft started his career in the 1940s as an arranger. "I did some very lush things with big orchestras," he explains. "It was Morty Craft and His Swinging Strings." He then worked for the "artists and recording" (A&R) departments at a number of independent New York labels throughout the 1950s when "you couldn't walk up and down Broadway without bumping into fifty groups who wanted to sing for you." At the pinnacle of his career, as head of A&R for MGM Records, his star artists were Connie Francis and Conway Twittie. Industry legend says that Connie Francis's father took her away from MGM after he caught Craft chasing his daughter around the studio; he nearly killed Morty.

Today Craft is reduced to hustling for business for his little-known Twintower Records label, which is most notable for the rumor that it was financed by ex-president Ferdinand Marcos of the Philippines. He conducts his affairs from the Sunlight Restaurant—a warm, down-to-earth diner on Broadway which is both social mecca and improvised office for the slightly faded music moguls of yesteryear who can no longer afford high Manhattan rents.

Craft mourns the good old days: "That was an era when there was really romance, and there was more music, pure music. In those days a handshake was better than a contract is today. There was a little more honesty, and less ego-tripping, and more creativity . . . These days, you're talking business, not romance. It's all changed . . . Mitch Miller [the head of A&R for CBS Records in the 1950s and early 1960s] and I were very into romance. Between the two of us, there could have been nine marriages—it used to be a very romantic era. We wined and dined and traveled a lot. These things were uplifting as far as I was concerned."

As he tells it, the fine art of "payola" (bribing a radio disc jockey to play records) was also more gentle in the old days, and not practiced extravagantly: "You might buy somebody a five-dollar meal. I can't see anything corrupt about a five-dollar meal. But if you buy them a hundred-dollar meal and give them cocaine—that's corrupt." He admits that the disc jockeys might have been sent a call girl, but only one costing $25. "It's quite another thing if you send a call girl that costs five hundred . . ." (Craft's indignation may be misplaced: Perhaps the difference in prices is not so much moral as inflationary.)

Hy Weiss, a more gritty and down-to-earth stalwart from the early days of the record business, does not share Craft's romantic illusions. After thirty years' experience in every nook and cranny of the industry—from operating jukeboxes, to distribution companies, to pressing plants, to running his own label—Weiss is very blunt about most of what happened. He was not interested in wining and dining disc jockeys:

"Why waste time going out with someone you don't like, and sit down and feast with them when you can't stand them. Just give them the money and let them play the fucking record." That seems to have been the industry norm. Dickie Kline of Atlantic Records, who spent those days on the road driving to radio stations from the Midwest to the deep South, remembers the standard line from the disc jockeys who took bribes: "Don't take me, *send* me."

The music industry never made Hy Weiss rich and he lives in quiet retirement in the most dilapidated of the spacious middle-class homes in Woodbury Estate on Long Island. That is partly, he claims, because he never took bribes himself: "I was a giver, I was never a taker." But lack of material success did not stop him becoming a vivid strand in the industry's highly colorful mythology.

The son of Romanian Jewish immigrants who brought their young family to the Bronx in the 1920s (where they lived just a few blocks from the young Morris Levy), Weiss epitomized the swashbuckling life of the hustlers on Broadway. There is hardly a deal in the history of the modern music business that he will not take credit for "putting together"; no action that he will not claim "a piece of." Whenever seasoned entrepreneurs gather in the Sunlight Restaurant to swap anecdotes from the early days, Weiss's name will crop up again and again in one tall tale after another.

His initiation into the music business came when he graduated from working as a bouncer in a bar and grill to a job with a record distribution company called Runyon Sales. Distributors in those days were sales and promotion men who contracted with record companies to get their releases into the stores and onto the jukeboxes. They were essential to the success of the independent companies, which had no other way of getting their records out. As a result of this dependence, distributors often held the record companies to ransom, refusing to pay for the last consignment until they knew the next was on the way. The record manufacturers, however, would not press the next consignment until they had

been paid for the last. Caught in this Catch-22, many an undercapitalized record company was driven to the wall, and
distributors were generally regarded as the villains of the
industry. Bob Krasnow, whose own dealings with distributors
forced him to sell Blue Thumb, an independent label he
started, says: "They weren't what I would call criminals, but
let's put it this way—I wouldn't like either of you two girls to
ever marry an independent distributor."

Weiss is uncharacteristically reticent about the details of
Runyon Sales—for example, who owned it? "I don't want to
get into that one. Just leave that one out. Don't even *talk*
about Runyon Sales." He claims to have been good at his job,
which was to place the records Runyon Sales distributed onto
jukeboxes, but, again, he is not very forthcoming as to how he
achieved his success: "I knew all these jukebox guys intimately. They liked me for some other reason—I can't go into
that, but they liked me. So I could do whatever I wanted with
them. I had a good rapport with them on another level, not as
a record guy." He does reveal how he got his records into the
large department store chains—by paying the stores' buyers
half of his own commission. "That effected a relationship
where I didn't have to go out of the house to work. All I
would do was call these folks and say, 'I'm sending you this
and I'm sending you that,' and I'd have control of the whole
market." His technique for selling to the five-and-dime stores
was to persuade the owners to put his records at the front of
the store, where they were more likely to be stolen, in the
hope of winning reorders.

After leaving Runyon Sales, Weiss made a couple of unsuccessful attempts to become a distributor in his own right, one
of which ended when the building where he had his office
caught fire. (Rumor in the industry has it that Weiss set the
fire himself to destroy a rival distributor's office; he denies it.)
He then took his buccaneering sales techniques to a New
York company called Cosnat which distributed four independent labels: Jubilee (owned by Cosnat's owner), Chess,
Checker, and—most lucratively—Atlantic. Weiss, who re-

garded himself as the best salesman in the business "then, now, later, and after and before," developed an understandable fondness for Atlantic since it provided the bulk of his income. As he puts it: "They made it possible for me to put bread and potatoes on the table."

In those rough, tough days Weiss was never afraid to throw his weight around. He was "tough like a young bull," says one of his contemporaries. "He was strong and he would fight all the time." He was also one of the few people who ever stood up to Morris Levy.

As Levy became a growing force in the music business, and as his reputation preceded him, he was almost always accompanied by two bodyguards—even at industry conventions—who became notorious for their rough tactics. Anybody who wanted to collect what Levy owed them had first to deal with the bodyguards. Doc Pomus, the Atlantic songwriter (who wrote such classic hits as "Save the Last Dance for Me"), once sent his partner to Levy's office to collect songwriting royalties: "When he got there, he was threatened by a guy with a gun. He ran out of Levy's offices—without the royalties." Similarly, an emissary for Ronnie Hawkins (best known as the man who assembled The Band at Woodstock) was offered two ways of leaving Roulette Records' office: through the front door, immediately; through the window, if he continued to hang around demanding unpaid royalties.

When Weiss was owed money by Levy, however, it was one of the bodyguards who found himself being pushed out of the window, while Weiss yelled, "Where is my check? Give me my money." Levy, who knows a good man when he sees one, said, "He's crazy, he's crazy, give him what he wants."

Such escapades gave Weiss a reputation of his own—one that certainly intimidated young Seymour Stein. Before going to work for Syd Nathan in Cincinnati, Stein was briefly a compiler of charts for *Billboard* (his persistence in hand-copying the charts back to his birthday having finally been rewarded with a job). Weiss says Stein "promised to do something for me"—which was to rig *Billboard*'s chart to include a record Weiss was promoting. He waited three weeks for the promise to be fulfilled. When it was not, he banged on Stein's apartment door shouting, "Hey, open up, this is Hy Weiss." Stein, who was packing his suitcase for a trip to Houston, bolted out of the window and huddled on the ledge—which is where Weiss found him, wearing an overcoat and his pajamas.

Weiss started his own label, Old Town Records, while still working for Cosnat. (He called it Old Town because his brother worked for a carbon paper manufacturer of that name: "I used his letterheads so when I wrote a letter it looked nice but I didn't have to spend any money.") He obtained at least some of his artists by hijacking other labels' groups. "One time I saw five guys in front of Cosnat waiting to see Jerry Blaine [the owner of Cosnat and Jubilee Records]. I asked them who they were and they told me they were a group called the Five Crowns. They told me they were waiting to see Mr. Blaine. I said, 'Why are you waiting to see Mr. Blaine—I'm here.' And I grabbed them and I went into a studio that night and we cut some sides."

To save money Weiss would record three or four groups in one night using session musicians he literally picked up off the street. The sessions were distinctly lacking in finesse.

"Where is the music?" asked one of Weiss's itinerant keyboard players.

"There is no music," said Weiss, "just play."

"What key is it in?"

"We don't have no motherfucking key here, just play the song."

His relaxed approach to arranging music was often extended to the songwriting credits, which he shared, thereby entitling himself to a share of the royalties. "Well, I put in a few lines here and there but I actually didn't write [them]," he admits. "I may be a writer on the thing but it was just a few lines. In those days we all did that. It was part of life, part of history."

All in all, Hy Weiss did not think much of his artists: "Those illiterates, they would have ended up eating from pails in Delancey Street if it wasn't for us."

The stark contrast between the attitude of Atlantic Records toward its artists and the attitude of most of the other independents is well illustrated by a story told by Seymour Stein. It concerns Chess Records—one of the more important labels of the 1950s which recorded, among others, Chuck Berry, Bo Diddley, Muddy Waters, and Howlin' Wolf. One of its founders, Leonard Chess, was a Polish immigrant who ran the Macombo Lounge in a black ghetto of Chicago. According to his son, Marshall Chess, it was extremely wild—"a hangout for pimps, whores, dope dealers, jazz musicians. It was an all-night place—definitely for a certain kind of clientele." Marshall was in the club one night when gunfire broke out. He was five or six at the time, and remembers being passed like a football across the room until he reached safety under the bar.

Leonard Chess, and his brother Phil, did not establish Chess Records from any love of music. Their ambition, says Marshall, was simply to make money: "You have to remember that always, with all these kinds of guys. Ahmet and Nesuhi were different—the only ones I'd ever met who were different because they were rich. It was their hobby, it was their fun."

Eventually Leonard Chess made enough money from the record business to build a large house in Chicago and invited Syd Nathan of King Records to visit. According to Seymour Stein, Chess said to Nathan, "Syd, you got to come and see my new house, it is fabulous. It's not finished yet, but you got to see it."

When Nathan arrived there was a black workman painting the outside of the house and singing. "Do you know, you have a very nice voice and I like that song—real great blues," said

Nathan. "How would you like to come to Cincinnati and make a record?"

"I record for Mr. Chess," said the workman.

"Really, what's your name?"

"McKinley Morganfield, but I record under the name of Muddy Waters."

Nathan apologized for approaching Chess's legendary star, particularly since he was obviously a good friend of Leonard Chess. "Friend? I'm not a friend—but Mr. Chess says if I do a good job painting the house, we're going to eat tonight."

Muddy Waters' fortunes did not change even as his records grew more successful. When the Rolling Stones went to Chicago some years later to record, Muddy was still there painting—this time Chess's studio. "That was just the system," says Mick Jagger.

Little wonder then that internationally famous performers from the 1950s such as Little Richard (who nowadays insists on being called *the* innovator, *the* architect, *the* originator of rock and roll) temper their affection for most of the pioneers of the modern record industry with something close to loathing.

Little Richard is to be found in Los Angeles—not in a luxurious Beverly Hills villa, but at a modest hotel on a seedy section of Sunset Strip. Everything in his room—the bed, the walls, the carpet—is colored a monotonous beige. The only feature to distinguish it from any other hotel room is the tank of tropical fish built into the wall. Little Richard, tall, broad, dressed totally in black, is somehow reminiscent of a caged lion.

It was, he says, easy for the fast-talking entrepreneurs from New York to exploit performers in the 1950s, especially black artists from the South. "The artists back in that time, they didn't know business. The artists back there, they had to do something to make money because they were so poor . . .

When I was a little boy, people were very depressed. They didn't have anything because the racism was so heavy ... You could go to a water fountain and you couldn't drink no water because it was whites only. The white fountain would be a beautiful electric fountain with cold water. The black fountain would be an old fountain that whites used to have—that was run-down and rusty and had spit in it, flies in it."

Little Richard Penniman speaks from his experience of growing up as one of twelve children of a devout but poor family in Macon, Georgia. He was an enthusiastic gospel singer at church until, at age fourteen, he left home because of his father's disapproval of his homosexuality. He joined up with "Doctor Hudson"—a quack whose traveling Medicine Show went from town to town selling snake oil. Little Richard would sing to draw in gullible passersby.

In Fitzgerald, Georgia he became the protégé of a woman named Ethel Wayne who owned the Winsetta Patio club, where Little Richard sang with B. Brown and His Orchestra. Before long he was touring first Georgia and then all of the southern states, singing gospel and rhythm and blues. He had already developed a freakish stage personality, wearing his hair in an outrageous pompadour. He began making records in 1951, but with little success.

Then in 1955 Little Richard sent a demonstration tape of himself to Specialty Records, an independent label in Los Angeles, which was searching the country for a singer who might rival the success that Ray Charles was enjoying at Atlantic. The tape landed on the desk of "Bumps" Blackwell, a producer who was Specialty's chief talent scout. On his recommendation Specialty signed Little Richard. A songwriter was found to clean up Richard's lyrics, and on September 14, 1955, Little Richard went into a New Orleans recording studio to make musical history.

The first result of that session to be released was "Tutti Frutti." It was soon rising up the R&B charts but, initially at least, white radio stations refused to play the record. They preferred the smoother sound of the cover version of "Tutti

Frutti" recorded by Pat Boone. Although the white crooner's voice made the wild rock-and-roll lyrics sound ridiculous, Boone's version went gold. Little Richard was furious. "What they did was they took Pat Boone and threw me over instantly, to cover my music, to block my sales of 'Tutti Frutti,' so that he would become a hero . . . Oh, I couldn't stand him. I wanted to break his toes and his legs because, to me, he was stopping my success." (Jerry Wexler agrees that Boone is indebted to Little Richard: "Pat Boone should get down on his knees and kiss the ring and say, 'Thank you, Little Richard.' Because without Little Richard Pat Boone would have been—maybe—a minor league Conway Twitty.")

Nevertheless, Pat Boone's success helped to popularize the new sound—and, indeed, eventually helped sales of Little Richard's original version. Richard's "Tutti Frutti" went on to sell more than one million records and in the next two years he became a superstar, giving Specialty six more major hits including "Long Tall Sally," "Good Golly, Miss Molly," and "Rip It Up."

Richard's influence on modern music was incalculable—not least because in Liverpool, England, it inspired a teenaged boy named Paul McCartney. McCartney's first solo performance, at the age of fourteen at a holiday camp talent contest, was his rendition of "Long Tall Sally."

The owner of Specialty Records was Art Rupe, who has long since retired from the music business and is now a publicity-shy oil and property tycoon. Unlike the Erteguns and the Jerry Wexlers, Rupe's skills did not lie in producing records. "Art Rupe didn't know nothing about no rhythm," says Little Richard. "He'd stamp his feet off beat, he'd clap his hands out of time, and shake his butt off beat too . . . But he knows what he is doing when it comes to money. He knows how to run a record company—for himself and for his own profit. Art Rupe is a business wizard, he is a business genius. He makes sharp deals."

One of the sharp deals Rupe made was to assign all of Little Richard's songs to his own publishing company. For the publishing rights to "Tutti Frutti," bought *before* the record was released, Rupe paid $50. And, under the further terms of his deal with Specialty, Little Richard did not receive a standard two-cent royalty on every record sold for the "mechanical rights" to the song; he received a half-cent. "I had signed a bad deal with Specialty," he says in a classic understatement. "If you wanted to record, you signed on their terms or not at all . . . It didn't matter how many records you sold—if you were black."

Then in 1957, when Little Richard made his first, but not his last, renunciation of the evils of rock and roll, he sold all his rights to all his songs and recordings to Rupe for $10,000. Putting aside worldly things (and, some say, in order to avoid the attentions of the tax man) Little Richard turned to God and was ordained a minister in the Seventh Day Adventist Church. (Specialty attempted to keep his conversion a secret until it could release "Keep a Knockin'," pieced together from unfinished sessions.)

Years later Little Richard sued Rupe. He lost, but that did not prevent him making regular appearances on television talk shows, on which he would complain that Rupe had ripped him off. To put an end to this, Rupe offered a stick and a carrot: He threatened Little Richard with a four-million-dollar defamation suit if he continued, or $40,000 to keep his mouth shut. Finally Little Richard seems to have accepted what another West Coast record man said about the case: "If you sign away your rights, then you sign them away."

But the bitterness remains: "I didn't know anything about the business, I was very dumb . . . I was just like a sheep among a bunch of wolves that would devour me at any moment. I think I was taken advantage of because I was uneducated. I think I was used and abused and used again. I think I was treated inhumane . . . I think I was treated wrong and many people got rich out of the style of music I created. They are all millionaires writ many times, and nobody offered me nothing."

To which many, if not most, of his black musical contemporaries would answer, Amen.

Chapter 4
BOOZE, BRIBES, AND BROADS

The irascible Morris Levy once owned rock and roll—literally. In 1954, with characteristic smartness, Levy brought to New York—from Cleveland, Ohio—the man who invented "rock 'n' roll" as his catchphrase and together they claimed the copyright. For a while they even collected royalties from companies that used the name. It could not last, of course: As Levy says, with some regret, "It got too big and we lost control of the name."

Eventually Levy also lost control of his prodigy from Cleveland. His name was Alan Freed and although he neither made records nor produced them, he had more influence on the nascent industry than most of those who did. His power lay in the fact that he was among the first disc jockeys in the country to bring the black music recorded by Atlantic Records, King, Chess, Roulette, and other independent companies to a mass, white, teenage audience—and he did so with whoops of joy, and in utter defiance of the bigots who called him "nigger lover" in reports written for the files of the FBI.

The tragedy is, he became too powerful. After Morris Levy brought him to New York, Freed became the emperor of America's disc jockeys and he behaved like one. He held court at radio station WINS—the station he moved to the top of the ratings—and for those who wished to promote their records there was no choice but to attend. A veteran of that era remembers the scene late one night when, as usual, he stood in line at Freed's office to pay his respects, and ask for a favor: "I saw this guy in with Freed, and I'd never seen anyone like that before. He was young—maybe in his late twenties—but he was completely bald. He had on this coat, vicuña or some crap. He looked like a millionaire out on the town . . . and I thought, How did Freed get to know a class guy like that? Then it turned out this guy was a supplicant to Freed, just like me. I found out that I had seen Ahmet on his rounds."

Ahmet Ertegun paid court to Alan Freed like everybody else—and, like everybody else, he paid money to him. Freed did not invent "payola" but he was one of those who institutionalized it. In the end it destroyed his career while he destroyed himself. He died penniless and persecuted at the age of forty-two, abandoned by almost all of those who had once sat at his court. The story of the rise and fall of Alan Freed says a great deal about the record industry—and some of the people in it.

Alan Freed's father was a Jewish immigrant from Russia who changed his name in Germany while he waited for his chance to get to America. His choice of a new name was symbolic: "You have a name that means freedom," he told his children. They were brought up to believe that freedom was a precious gift to which all men were entitled, and Alan Freed never forgot it.

He was born in Johnstown, Pennsylvania, in 1922 and raised with two brothers in the small Ohio town of Salem (where there is now a street named after him). In high school he learned to play the trombone and led a jazz band called the Sultans of Swing. He served in the army (where he suffered a partial hearing loss) and afterward obtained a master's degree in engineering from Ohio State University. There was, however, never any doubt that Freed would become a broadcaster: Every evening he practiced voice delivery and timing by reading aloud the Salem *Journal* from cover to cover. His son Lance (now head of publishing for A&M Records) recalls the family being subjected to this ritual for years. "Thank God it was not the *New York Times.*"

Freed got his first job in radio as a sportscaster in New Castle, Pennsylvania, and then advanced his career by moving every few months to a larger station in a bigger city. By 1951 he had reached Cleveland and station WJW, where he read the news at the top of the hour. His determination was to be a disc jockey and he got his chance when he was asked to stand in for a sick colleague. He willingly took over the microphone but not the "playlist"—the selection of records he was supposed to broadcast. Instead Freed made a hurried visit to a store called the Record Rendezvous where he had been introduced to rhythm and blues. That night his Cleveland audience became the first mass market in America to hear the records put out by Chess, Modern, King, and Atlantic Records. The next day Freed was fired—not for ignoring the playlist but because the music he played was black.

But station WJW was overwhelmed with enthusiastic mail from listeners and Freed was rehired. Indeed, he was given his own program, albeit late on Saturday night—the "moondog" shift. Thus began the "Moondog Rock 'n' Roll Party," and if the management of WJW had hoped Freed's show would escape too much attention at such a late hour it was disappointed. Within eighteen months, "Moondog's Party" was rated the number one radio show in Cleveland. And when, in 1952, Freed inaugurated live concerts—"Moondog Balls"—25,000 people attempted to get into a hall that could hold only half that number.

Freed's ambition was to take his show to New York, and he applied three times for a job with the 50,000-watt "superstation" WINS. Three times he was turned down. But if WINS was slow to recognize Freed's remarkable appeal, Morris Levy was not. Levy had first met Freed when he took the acts from his club on the road for what he called the "Birdland Tours." At each venue he would hire a local disc jockey to act as announcer, and in the process built up a useful nationwide network of friendly radio announcers. Freed became part of that network—but stood out from it. Other disc jockeys had followed his example and begun to broadcast black music, but with no great enthusiasm. As Ahmet Ertegun says, they preferred the sounds of Dizzie Gillespie and Lester Young—"music that in their minds was sophisticated and brought dignity to the human race." Freed loved the much more raw music of LaVern Baker and Ray Charles and Little Richard; in fact he reveled in it. On air, with a rattle in one hand (and a bottle of whisky in the other), he yelled and screamed his enthusiasm. Moondog's parties were exactly that: noisy and boisterous—and the airwaves had never heard the like of it. In 1954 Morris Levy became Freed's manager and moved him to Manhattan where he wanted to be. In Ertegun's words, "Alan Freed hit New York like a ball of fire."

Under Levy's management Freed was finally hired by WINS and the station moved to the top of the ratings. There was only one small hiccup. New York already had a Moondog—a blind eccentric who, says Levy, "looked like Christ in Christ-like clothes," and who sold umbrellas from a stand at the corner of 54th Street and Sixth Avenue. This Moondog got fed up with being congratulated on "last night's show" and obtained a court injunction to stop Freed using his name.

From the distance of the family's new home in Connecticut, Lance Freed watched as his father became a mascot for American teenagers determined to throw off the shackles of their parents' rigid beliefs. "I think my dad defended everybody's right to have a good time with their music. He was committed to the kids. He was kind of their Pied Piper."

He had the ability to make each of his listeners believe he was talking directly to *them* and he cultivated that appeal by asking his audience to send him messages he could read on the air. Two women were employed to open the resulting sacks of mail and underline suitable excerpts with red crayon. And Freed did read them on air—"This is from Julie to Bobby: 'I hope you'll stop by my locker tomorrow, I'm not really mad at you' "—as though he had an intense familiarity with his listeners' lives, and his son, listening at home, finally understood the purpose of those interminable readings from the Salem *Journal.* Perhaps just as important: "He was a man who was really very much a kid at heart. I remember when the Good Humor ice-cream truck would pass our house on Sunday. Once he bought the whole truck. He had the guy back up and we emptied it. He loved ice cream. He was a kid."

Freed's success was consolidated when he began staging live shows in New York, much as he had done in Cleveland. "We announced two nights of dances at the St. Nicholas arena five weeks before the event," says Levy. "Within three days they were sold out. The place was so crowded, the ceilings were dripping water like rain—it was raining inside the arena." Moving to the larger Paramount Theater in Brooklyn, Freed attracted greater crowds than the Moonglows and Chuck Berry had done. Even a Frank Sinatra concert did not have the same pull.

The concerts were extremely lucrative thanks to a clever deal Levy struck. He agreed to forgo the normal "guaranteed take" paid to promoters (a predetermined share of possible ticket sales) in exchange for a much higher percentage of the actual takings—up to 90 percent. Freed was not enamored of this arrangement until the night of the first concert when—with two lines stretching around the block—Levy told him, "Alan, we'll cut up sixty or seventy thousand dollars." In the first ten days the take was over $240,000.

That represented almost pure profit for Freed, Levy, and WINS (which shared in the take) because Levy had a method of keeping costs as low as possible: He would deliberately book artists with new records that had not yet become hits (at correspondingly low prices)—and Freed would then build them up in time for the concert by heavily promoting their records on air. "I have no apology for that," says Levy, defying any suggestion that he should.

From that it was but a small step to payola. Freed had an enormous influence on record sales—and there was no shortage of people willing to pay him to misuse it.

The practice of bestowing "gifts" on radio disc jockeys is as old as the industry itself.

On one of their first promotional trips to Tennessee, Ahmet Ertegun and Jerry Wexler arrived in Memphis bearing a modest "gift" for Dewey Phillips, then one of the hottest disc jockeys in the South. Unfortunately Dewey had just received a visit from Leonard Chess, the co-founder of Chess Records, who had already filled Dewey's pockets—and he scorned Atlantic's meager offering. Dewey made Ertegun and Wexler sit in the broadcast studio while he played every record but theirs, and taunted them with announcements such as: "I've got two record thieves here from New York." (The story has a curious postscript. Dewey finally did play Atlantic's record and Ertegun and Wexler stayed on after the show. As Ertegun tells it: "Then some guys arrived from the Memphis State basketball team. We all went down to the gymnasium at Memphis State University, broke in, turned on the lights, and proceeded to play basketball." Ertegun bowed out of the game, but Dewey entered into it with a vengeance. "He jumped up and came crashing to the floor—and broke his leg," says Ertegun. "It was one of those strange southern evenings.")

Joe Smith (now president of Capitol Records) was a disc jockey in Boston in those halcyon days, and is frank about the perks of the job. "Of course there was payola!" says Smith. "It wasn't illegal at the time. Morris Levy used to send people checks. I used to get fifty dollars a month or something like that from 'Moishe' Levy." Smith got married during that period and was inundated with gifts. In industry circles Levy and Hy Weiss are credited with conceiving the "fifty-dollar handshake."

There was no lack of ingenuity in finding ways to reward

"friendly jocks." They might be given a songwriter's credit on a particular record and, thus, an inducement to promote it since they shared in the royalties. Some set up publishing companies to receive the copyright to the songs they plugged—with the same result. Joe Smith says he even received, along with Freed, shares in a record label from George Goldner, a legendary record entrepreneur who told him: "It's about time I did something for you guys, and you built something for your future." In this instance, however, the promise was greater than the reward: "He used to press our records on stuff that after three plays, the needle went straight through it." And if, by chance, "their" label did have a hit record, Goldner instantly reclaimed the song and reissued it on one of his own labels. (Nevertheless, Smith regarded Goldner as "wonderful"—an opinion widely shared in the industry. Goldner, a former teacher of ballroom dancing, became a highly respected record producer in the 1950s—and an irregular partner to Morris Levy. Theirs was a love-hate relationship complicated by the fact that Goldner was a "degenerate gambler." Time and again Goldner would leave Levy to set up in business on his own—only to return shamefaced when he had gambled away half his assets at the racetrack.)

What made the corruption of Alan Freed exceptional was the scale of it, and the degree of his conceit. As he became the top disc jockey in America, broadcasting to the largest market, his vanity grew to matching heights. "He was humble to begin with, and then he became a big shot and it went to his head," says Ertegun. "People realized that he was a center of profit, as well as a center of promotion . . . He had all the record companies at his feet." In Jerry Wexler's view Freed simply became greedy. He certainly became erratic.

Ertegun and Wexler sent a bulldozer to Freed's house to dig a hole for the swimming pool they bought him, complete with flagstones. Freed accepted the gift but did not respond, as he was meant to, by playing Atlantic's latest release. Ertegun complained to Levy, who confronted Freed: "Why are you doing this to Ahmet and Jerry? They're nice guys." More important, he added, it was not advisable to antagonize Atlantic.

"I just have to prove to them that they don't own me because they bought me a pool," said Freed.

In 1957 Atlantic ran into a temporary bad patch, when few of the company's releases became major sellers, and had difficulty meeting Freed's regular monthly payments. "It was a terrible year," says Wexler with his customary gloominess. "First of all we paid ourselves fifty dollars a week, then nothing. I used to have to meet [Freed] at the Brill Building to deliver the money. I was the bagman. We paid him six hundred a month . . . One day I met him and said, 'We can't keep up the payments. Can you carry us for a while?' He said, 'Gee, I'd love to—but it would be taking the bread out of my children's mouths.' " Yet when Jerry Blane of Jubilee Records asked the going rate for Freed's "hit of the week," was told "one thousand bucks," and wrote a check for $52,000 saying "I'll take the next fifty-two," Freed tore it up.

Morris Levy is certain it was vanity and not avarice that got the better of Freed: "Alan loved good things . . . He liked living good, but it was not the moving factor."

By this time Levy's relationship with Freed was on the rocks. As Freed's egotism spiraled, and his schemes became more and more grandiose, Levy would try to make him "see sense" and the two men would argue. One of their fights was over a new rock-and-roll show that Freed presented on ABC TV in 1957, of which Levy was the executive producer.

Freed insisted that every act on his show perform live, a demand that required the full-time employment of a twenty-piece band. Levy wanted to follow the example of *American Bandstand*—a rival television show hosted by Dick Clark, another influential disc jockey, based in Philadelphia—and avoid such expense by requiring guests to mime to their records. But Freed would not hear of it—or, as Levy says, "Alan

Freed wouldn't listen to economic sense." Freed's show was canned after thirteen weeks. (*American Bandstand* continues to this day.)

The final straw was Freed's decision to dispose of his share of 25 percent of the stock of Roulette Records which Levy had given him on the grounds, "What's the difference? He's family." Levy is very tight-lipped about what happened: "Alan sold his twenty-five percent to some tough guys who then came in and said they were my partners. I took back my stock." Who the tough guys were, and precisely how Levy wrested back his stock, he will not elaborate.

For Levy this incident underlined Freed's fundamental flaw: "One of the problems with Alan was that he had to be protected from people who would play up to him. He was a remarkable piece of talent but he did have his needs and his weaknesses. One of these was to be told how great he was. If people did that, they could get to him," says Levy.

And by all accounts Freed was "got to" by some very shadowy figures. Once Levy was out of the picture, the record companies found their path to the master of the airwaves obstinately blocked by hoodlums. "There were a lot of people who were around my father," says Lance Freed. "Guys like Johnny Brantley and Jack Hook, his so-called manager. I remember as a kid being outside, watching guys having to hand them money just to go into the door. This guy Johnny Brantley, who was always hanging around, would say, 'Hey, you want to see Alan? Give me a hundred and I'll get you in there.' "

Many of his father's patrons, as well as Lance, were astounded by this development. Lance says, "My father didn't operate that way. He operated on music. He loved music. He loved the shows. He loved the kids. I'm not making him out to be a perfect human being, but if his motivation was money he could have done a lot better than he did."

In the dark days that were to follow, Freed told his son he never played a record purely for money: If he did not like a song, he did not play it. (And Lance was a witness to succes-

sive Sunday sessions in Connecticut when his father listened
to the first ten bars of a hundred or more new releases. The
rejects, 95 percent of them, were hurled across the living
room like Frisbees—and Lance was paid twenty-five cents to
dispose of them with the trash.) And, certainly, Freed never
compromised his absolute opposition to racism. He simply
would not broadcast the bland white cover versions of black
artists' songs. "They're anti-Negro," he said, pointing his finger at the major record companies that released the cover
versions. "They excuse it on the grounds that the covers are
better quality, but I defy anyone to show me that the quality
of the original 'Tweedledee' [by LaVern Baker on Atlantic]
or 'Seven Days' [by Clyde McPhatter, also on Atlantic] is
poor."

Freed's integrity on this issue was a saving grace but it was
not sufficient to save him; indeed, it may have accelerated his
downfall. The very worldly Hy Weiss perfectly summarized
Freed's fate: "He loved black music and if he liked your record he *would* play it for nothing. But he was weak and he
allowed himself to be controlled by some bad guys. He hap
pened to be a nice guy—and nice guys always wind up that
way."

Alan Freed alienated almost all of his support in the record
industry at a time when he most needed friends.

Before it was dropped by the ABC network, his extravagant version of *American Bandstand* broadcast pictures to
the nation of Frankie Lymon, a black youth, dancing with a
white girl. Thirteen ABC affiliates canceled Freed's show and
from across the southern states there came ringing declarations of which this—from the White Citizens Council of Bir-
mingham, Alabama—was typical: "Rock 'n' roll is part of a
test to undermine the morals of the youth of our nation. It is
sexualistic, unmoralistic and . . . brings people of both races
together." When the members of the council failed in their
attempt to outlaw rock and roll in the state of Alabama, they

attended a performance given by Nat King Cole, pulled him from his piano stool, and gave him a thorough beating.

Freed disregarded this violent warning and, in May 1958, he staged one of his concerts in Boston, Massachusetts—despite the most fervent opposition of the district attorney, the chief of police, and the Catholic Church, which made its views known repeatedly, in writing. "The threats basically were he would be jailed," says Lance Freed. "The Catholic Church, the archdiocese, didn't want this filthy rock-and-roll stuff coming in. They didn't want niggers dancing with white women." The words Lance uses come from FBI memoranda, written at the time, which he has since obtained under the Freedom of Information Act.

"They were going to find some way to keep this rock and roll out of the city of Boston. And I think my father was the kind of guy who, the more you said no, the more he wanted to do something. But it was the beginning of the end when he took that show to Boston."

Joe Smith, then a disc jockey in Boston, agrees in retrospect that Freed was playing with fire in bringing what was a very volatile show to "a very uptight city." "You're talking about a very different kind of time back then. When I played Elvis Presley records I was accused of spreading venereal disease. It really was a bizarre time, especially in a very narrow city like Boston."

Smith was backstage on the night of the concert and remembers the tensions between some of the artists mirrored the growing chaos in the hall: "All during that tour, Chuck Berry and Jerry Lee Lewis had been going at it. You had a redneck [Lewis] and you had a wild militant [Berry] and they were getting down to it, they were going to kill each other—literally kill each other. Picture the scene: The curtain is drawn, we're about to start the show—and what we used to have at the start was everybody on stage and they'd all do a number . . . Jerry Lee Lewis's father has a gun pointed to Chuck Berry and Chuck Berry has a knife to Jerry Lee Lewis's neck. Now they were going to open the curtain with this going on there!" And in front of the curtain Freed was "stirring up the crowd pretty good."

Before the show could begin, however, the house lights came up and a posse of police streamed down the aisles to the front of the stage where they formed a barricade, their billy clubs at the ready. Freed repeatedly shouted, "What's the problem?" until the police commissioner told him: "Everybody must sit down *now* or this show is not going to go on." Freed then said something to the audience that he may later have regretted: "We're not going to let them get away with this, are we?" As the crowd yelled "No!" Freed was arrested for inciting a riot.

Lance Freed believes the Boston police greatly exaggerated what followed. "There was a group of very unhappy kids leaving the theater. A few people were beaten up. There was one stabbing. There were some rocks thrown . . . There wasn't a real riot. There was just no show."

Freed was charged under an old anarchy statute which forbade attempts to overthrow the government of Massachusetts and spent three days in jail. Other cities canceled his show. His contract with radio station WINS in New York was terminated; whether he left or was fired is a matter of dispute. "And then the rest of it started to fall," says Lance Freed—"the ax, I mean."

In the summer of 1958, while the shock waves from the Boston "riot" still reverberated, the disc jockeys' annual convention was held in the America Hotel in Miami Beach, Florida. Such events were largely an excuse to allow record companies to "entertain" disc jockeys, and that year in Miami they did so with what was essentially one continuous orgy of "Booze, Bribes and Broads"—as the *Miami Herald* succinctly described it in a headline.

The leading architect of such events was George Goldner, Morris Levy's irregular partner, who had developed the entertainment of disc jockeys into a fine art. Artie Ripp, who was then learning the trade as an apprentice to Goldner, remembers the impact when the George Goldner show hit town: "He was brilliant out on the road. He would rent entire floors of hotels and fill them up with girls. When we went into a city, nothing could follow us—unless you were going to bring in a freaks' circus." In between "being generous with gifts where guys had problems" and taking them gambling, the cry was "It's breakfast time. Have a shrimp cocktail—and two girls," says Ripp (and forty years on, the recollection still excites him).

The women would be well briefed. "There were fabulous instances where we would sit with the girls and prompt them, 'We really want to get this new Flamingos record on, so as you are fooling about with this fella, it's real important to convey how much you love the new Flamingos record.' By the time we left town we would have our record on the air, and everyone would be talking about the party for months."

They certainly talked about the party in Miami Beach. The sensational publicity surrounding the disc jockeys' convention would plant seeds of upheaval in the record industry.

Levy's company, Roulette Records, was at the heart of the celebrations. Roulette hosted a "Barbecue Breakfast with Basie"—an all-night party ending at 7 A.M., with music by Count Basie and Ronnie Hawkins and the Hawks. "That was terrific," says Joe Smith, as was the Roulette Suite, equipped with a roulette wheel, where the disc jockeys were given fake money to gamble with; afterward they exchanged their "winnings" for lavish gifts. "I was a little naive," says Smith. "I was betting blackjack and losing but they kept paying me. I said, 'But I lost—why are you giving me this stuff?' " And to complete the entertainment, Levy had prostitutes bussed into Miami Beach for the disc jockeys' pleasure.

Both the *New York Post* and the *Miami Herald* gave large headlines to stories about prostitutes and payola in Miami. The *Post*'s society editor, Doris Lilly, had met Don Ovens—Alan Freed's former music director from WINS—at a party and asked him about the convention. Ovens told her he had not been present in Miami but had heard much the same stories as she had. When Lilly quoted Ovens as the source of her story, he received an anonymous telephone call warning him to keep his mouth shut and to be careful when he went outside. In some panic Ovens went to see Levy to persuade him he had been misquoted by the *Post.* It was only later that Ovens discovered Lilly knew Levy. Her normal beat was the Vanderbilts and the Astors but "she wanted to know how the other half lived."

Levy was not unduly disturbed by the publicity. He dismissed it as sour grapes on the part of the *Miami Herald,* which owned a local radio station in direct competition with the one that had sponsored the convention. "So they rammed it to the whole industry," he said. But the damage had been done.

In New York City the district attorney began a formal investigation into corrupt practices within the music industry. There was no law prohibiting payola as such, but the city did have a law to deal with "commercial bribery"—originally framed to prevent employees in major department stores from accepting gratuities without their employer's knowledge.

Of more immediate concern to the industry was a second investigation, this one mounted by a subcommittee of the Committee on Interstate and Foreign Commerce of the House of Representatives in Washington. The subcommittee was already investigating the "Responsibilities of Broadcast Licensees"—namely, the manner in which television game shows such as *The $64,000 Question* were rigged—so when the committee turned its attention to radio, in light of the revelations from the Miami convention, its investigators had a head start.

Congressional investigators have great powers to compel testimony and the production of documents, and are generally not restrained by the Miranda laws, or the rules of evidence, or the need to prove a case beyond reasonable doubt. Jerry Wexler remembers his rising feelings of trepidation when the staff investigators, armed with subpoena powers, arrived at Atlantic's offices to search the business records. They found a check made out to Joe Smith by Ertegun, and evidence of some—though not all—of Atlantic's dealings with Alan Freed. "It was scary," says Wexler. Atlantic, like most of the record companies that were investigated, took the easy way out. It signed a consent judgment, which was not an admission of wrongdoing—but a promise not to do it again.

Roulette Records took a more robust approach. There was ample evidence of the company's financial relationship with Freed: For example, Jerry Blaine of Jubilee Records told the House investigators he had loaned Freed $11,000 in 1956— and then "sold" the loan to Levy; and Roulette held two mortgages on Freed's Connecticut house. "I thought, the last thing I need is a payola probe at this point in my life," says Levy, but he offered to meet with an investigator at a club named the Roundhouse ("On one condition," said the investigator—"I pay my check and you pay yours") and then telephoned his contacts to learn of the investigator's background. Told he was a former New York detective "who would arrest his grandmother," Levy decided the best strategy was one of attack.

Told by the investigator that he might be called to testify before the congressional subcommittee, Levy said, "What date are those hearings, because I want to be there." The investigator, not accustomed to willing witnesses, said, "You what?"

"Yes," Levy continued, "because I have got some questions for them. I want to know what all this is about. A little bribery! What is the difference between that and this guy Summerhill who got a job with Eisenhower because he put up a lot of money for Eisenhower's election; the hookers in the State Department; and the money the government gave to Brunei so that they would support U.S. policy at the U.N.?" Those were not exactly the words he used: "I did a lot of

swearing and 'fucking' and 'motherfucking.' I think I persuaded the guy I was completely crazy, a real nut, because I
never heard from them [again]. A week before the hearings I
called him and said, 'Do you want me to attend?' He said,
'No, no—*please* no!' So I was never called to the payola hearings."

But others were, and throughout the industry the hearings
were a cause of sleepless nights and near-hysteria. All over
America disc jockeys were fired or resigned or agreed to take
lie detector tests on television. In Boston, radio station WILD
said it had fired Joe Smith, although he contacted the press to
deny it.

The two most prominent witnesses to be called to the subcommittee's hearings were Alan Freed and Dick Clark—the
disc jockey from Philadelphia who hosted *American Bandstand,* a syndicated television show. The subcommittee's investigators had done a thorough job of analyzing Clark's business records and learned that an astonishingly high
percentage of the records broadcast on *American Bandstand*
were manufactured by companies in which Clark had an interest, or were songs published by companies he owned. The
investigators' report was written in a highly critical tone:
"Mr. Clark managed to keep an average of 4.1 records owned
by [his] publishing, manufacturing or artist management
firms in the charts every week between October 1957 and
November 1959 . . . Mr. Clark pushed songs in which he had
an interest . . . Mr. Clark manipulated these plays to the full-
est advantage."

At the hearings Clark's response to the catalogue of allegations against him was defiant. When, for example, it was put
to him that a record company in which he had shares paid a
bribe to Tony Mammarella, the producer of Clark's own television show, he shrugged it off. He said he did not feel that
"ownership of shares in a company making payments to disc
jockeys makes a person guilty of making payola payments."
He refused to admit he had done anything wrong, and he
emerged from the hearings with his reputation entirely in-

tact. Freed, on the other hand, looked as though he had been through a wringer. "I don't have any comment, fellas," he told the waiting reporters and television cameras. "I've always been honest with you guys but right now I'm just whipped from this thing."

Reading the official record of the proceedings provides few clues as to why Clark made such a good impression on the subcommittee—and Freed such a bad one. Reaching back into her memories of forty years ago, Elizabeth Paola, the fortuitously named secretary of the subcommittee, can suggest only: "Clark charmed everybody. Freed appeared to be more insidious . . . I don't believe they were ever able to pin on Dick Clark any payola, so to speak. He made enough money by establishing these companies—he didn't have to take from the wrong guys . . . He was nobody's fool."

The chairman of the subcommittee, Judge Oren Harris, shares that impression. His memory of Freed is now hazy but he recalls his "devious means" and "under-the-table payments." Of Clark he says, "He showed a lot of capacity and ability." At the time of the hearings Harris told Clark he was "an attractive and successful young man" who "took advantage of a unique opportunity to control too many elements in the popular music field."

Another member of the subcommittee, who does not wish to be named, hints there was a conspiracy to get Clark off the hook: "The interests in keeping him available were stronger." And within the industry there was widespread belief that Freed was set up—that the hearings were prompted by ASCAP, the body which represented the songwriters and publishers of *white* pop music, much of which Freed refused to play. Lance Freed says: "ASCAP was the original group that went to Congress and asked that the hearings be held. Their membership felt that these [black] songs were so bad, how else [except through payola] could they be hits?"

Whatever the explanation, there is no doubt the payola investigation was surrounded by hypocrisy. As Morris Levy points out, payola, by any other name, was the industry *norm.* To prove his point, he flourishes Freed's contract with WINS, signed in 1954 for ten years. It is a revealing document because it shows that Freed was paid $15,000 a year by WINS—not the $75,000 widely reported at the time. Levy says that Freed, like every other disc jockey, was expected to make the balance of his salary himself, and everybody in the industry knew perfectly well where it came from.

The House subcommittee could impose no formal punishment on Freed. It contented itself with framing legislation to make the giving or receiving of payola a federal crime, punishable by up to two years in jail. But in New York City a grand jury indicted Freed for accepting corrupt payments. He eventually pleaded guilty to two counts of commercial bribery. He was fined $300 and given a suspended sentence.

By then his career was over. Immediately after the congressional hearings he was fired by radio station WABC in New York (where he had taken his show after leaving WINS) for refusing to sign an affidavit stating his participation in bribes. "I'm not signing that stuff," he said. "It's not true." He went on air for the last time to say, "This is not goodbye, it's just so long." He said he was sorry to leave his fans but "I know a bunch of ASCAP publishers who will be glad I'm off the air."

Lance Freed thinks his father may have received bad legal advice. "Or he may have felt that he was an untouchable, in the sense he was such a popular phenomenon he could just say 'No' and he would be vindicated." Far from being vindicated, Freed was also fired by WNEW TV where he had a daily hour-long show. "It was an escalation of the Boston incident," says Lance. "It was just more publicity. People had started to get nervous about this guy."

There is no doubt Freed handled the growing scandal badly. Morris Levy—who had seen Freed rarely since their partnership broke up in 1957—was surprised to receive a telephone call from Freed at the height of the crisis, seeking Levy's advice. Levy told him: "Go home, don't talk to anybody—let's wait and see where the dust settles." That night

Levy was bemused to read the banner headline in an evening newspaper: EXCLUSIVE INTERVIEW WITH ALAN FREED.

Later Freed telephoned Levy and said: "Did you see the size of the type? There hasn't been such a big headline since the end of the World War." Levy said: "Alan, you're a sick man."

Still, Levy tried to help him. After Freed's criminal conviction in December 1962, Levy paid for the disgraced disc jockey to travel to Miami and live in a hotel, and helped him get a job with radio station WQAM. With his customary flair Freed moved the station from number seventeen in the ratings to number three in a matter of months. But Freed could not, or would not, accept the rigid rule introduced by all radio stations in the wake of the payola scandal, whereby the disc jockey had little or no say in what music was played. The playlist was (and is) compiled by the stations' "program directors," who were, supposedly, less susceptible to bribery. "He was used to picking the records himself," says Lance, "so he got fired"—on Thanksgiving Day 1963, by telegram.

Within a year he was dying. Some ten years earlier—before leaving Cleveland for New York—Freed was involved in an automobile accident which damaged most of his internal organs including his liver and spleen. He spent several months in a hospital and doctors told him he was lucky to survive. They also told him the damage to his liver was permanent, and his life might be curtailed—especially if he continued to drink alcohol. It was a warning he had never really heeded; now he disregarded it altogether.

"His liver problem was getting worse and worse," says Levy. "He couldn't last too long. When Alan was told to stop drinking even before the payola probe—when the doctor told him to stop drinking or he would die—instead of drinking one bottle a day, he would drink two bottles a day." But more serious than the drinking, says Levy, "his heart was broken."

That was because the people who had once flattered and feted Alan Freed turned their backs on him, almost to a man. "I think what crushed him the most was that people wouldn't call him back," says Lance Freed. "I remember our phone being disconnected in 1964 because of all the long-distance calls he had made to his friends, to try to reenter, to get back in the business—to ask somebody for some support, some help. And there were very few people who would call back."

To make matters worse, in March 1964 Freed was indicted on charges of tax evasion and the Internal Revenue Service seized his properties in Connecticut and Florida. He was left only with a homestead in Palm Springs, California (which the IRS could not seize because of the homestead exemption laws), and it was to there he retreated with his third wife and Lance. He stood it as long as he could before telling Lance: "Enough of this sitting around Palm Springs, rotting, watching lizards and getting suntanned. I may be bankrupt and we may be broke, but we're going to buy a yellow bus, a school-bus, and here's what we're going to do. We're going to drive across country. I'm going to drive that thing to New York and I'm going to get back on the air."

The reality was very different. When Freed reached New York he stayed with Artie Ripp, George Goldner's former apprentice in the glory days, who was also down on his luck. "He was broke, he had no place to stay, and no money," says Ripp, "so I told my wife Phyllis that Alan Freed was going to come and live with us. He lived with me for three months, looking for a job and looking to [say], 'Hey, remember me, remember what I did for you, I'm trying to pick up a couple of bucks'—and he was waking up every morning and drinking three ounces of scotch before he brushed his teeth."

Freed became more and more embittered. Some of his old friends were no longer around: Ahmet Ertegun, for example, was busy on the West Coast, nurturing new white acts who were beginning to supplant the music Freed had championed. And while George Goldner did the honorable thing, and gave him a contract to compile such albums as *Alan*

Freed's Memory Lane, and while an old stalwart like Hy Weiss would gladly invite Freed to his home, most other people froze him out. Ripp says: "He hated the fact that here were these guys sitting on top of the world with lots of money and they [would not] just say, 'Hey, I'm putting you on the payroll. You'll listen to records for me for a thousand dollars a year.' "

Ripp believes that Freed was spurned by almost everybody in the industry because they bitterly resented him. "When Alan was down and out the people he went to felt they'd had their pockets picked [by Freed] . . . 'You are responsible, you son of a bitch, you made me pay, when I put out a terrific record.' When they had the opportunity to degrade him and to make him crawl, make him grovel for a couple of bucks, they did."

After a few months of humiliation in New York, Freed returned to Palm Springs where he fell ill with uremia—a condition caused by retention in the body of poisons normally expelled in urine. That last Christmas, just before he died, he made a recording for Lance of himself reading aloud passages from *A Christmas Carol* by Charles Dickens; in that department at least, he had lost none of his skill. In January 1965, with his trial on tax evasion charges imminent, Freed was admitted to a hospital in Palm Springs where he died of cirrhosis of the liver.

The funeral was paid for by Randy Wood, of Vee Jay Records—another of the few who did not abandon Freed. Wood also paid for a suit for Lance, who was then sixteen, and an airline ticket so he could travel to New York to attend his father's memorial service.

Most of the tributes to Alan Freed that were undoubtedly paid at the service have not survived, but Lance has one of his own: "He burned like a meteor and he went and burned out fast. And he had a hell of a good time doing it. Some people live long lives of quiet desperation . . . He lived one that was rather short, but I think he passed several hundred in the joy he gave other people."

Chapter 5
ILL FEELINGS, BAD GRACE

hanks in part to Alan Freed, and to the energy of their own labors, Ahmet Ertegun and Jerry Wexler saw Atlantic Records go from strength to strength. In little more than one year, Bobby Darin's spectacular success with "Splish Splash" was repeated three times. In 1958 "Queen of the Hop" made it to the Top 10 of the pop charts, and the following year "Dream Lover" and "Mack the Knife" both achieved the status of "gold" records—meaning, at that time, they each earned at least $1 million at wholesale prices. "Mack the Knife" also earned Darin two Grammy awards—the record industry's equivalent of Oscars. They were still celebrating at Atlantic when Darin quit. He joined Capitol Records and took himself off to Hollywood to begin a movie career confident, he said, he would be "bigger than Sinatra."

That same year—1959—Atlantic released "What'd I Say" by Ray Charles, which had been recorded at the Atlantic studios on 234 West 56th Street in New York City. The song epitomized rhythm and blues at its most vital and it sold over one million copies. They were still celebrating at Atlantic when Charles quit—lured away to ABC Records by a better contract.

"We felt betrayed," says Miriam Abramson (who had by then remarried and become Miriam Bienstock). "It was a terrible thing." She deals with the subject of Ray Charles's departure in her characteristically tart way: "He thought he

would like to widen his horizons . . . It's an amazing thing that
blind people are not as benign as they are portrayed in literature. They're supposed to have this second sight, and they're
always supposed to be so God-like. But they're not: Because
they don't have sight, they're very, very suspicious, and
they're not always the most pleasant people to work with, in
my experience." (She adds, as an acerbic footnote, a comment on Al Hibbler, another blind rhythm-and-blues singer
who recorded for Atlantic in the 1950s: "I remember Duke
Ellington said about Al Hibbler, 'If he had sight, he'd be a
train robber.' ")

Ahmet Ertegun was devastated, according to Noreen
Woods, who was his secretary at the time. "Two of your biggest artists leaving in the same year—and Ahmet was friends
with both of them." Now a vice-president of Atlantic Records, Woods says she has since learned to expect an artist's
departure from the label that provides their first nurturance
and care: "It happens all the time—and it makes you feel
they have no loyalty. You build them up, and another record
company offers them two dollars more—and they leave."
(According to Peter Guralnick, writing in his book *Sweet Soul
Music:* "It was a deal that was much misunderstood at the
time . . . In addition to a far better royalty rate than Atlantic
was paying, ABC held out a production deal, profit-sharing,
and eventual ownership of his own masters—a contractual
point virtually unheard of at the time and a notable rarity
even today." Ertegun disputes this view, saying: "I don't believe that Ray got any profit-sharing outside of his royalty,
and he does not now own his masters. Furthermore, he was
earning a top royalty at Atlantic, so I doubt he got more than
a point or two increase.")

Jerry Wexler regarded the dual departures of Bobby Darin
and Ray Charles as nothing short of apocalyptic. "It was very
grim," he says. "I thought we were going to die."

Ertegun, as ever, took a more sanguine approach. Though
he may have been "devastated" by the almost simultaneous
loss of Atlantic's two biggest money earners, he did not lose

Bobby Darin as a friend and, "Somehow, I wasn't that concerned. I always figured that we were going to make another hit . . . When you lose big artists, you figure that you are going to lose a great deal of your billing, and the label is going to lose its glamour—but then new artists somehow magically appear."

Still, the episode was a watershed for Atlantic and it came at a time of great change in the music business. The payola scandal had signaled the end of the rock industry's buccaneering infancy and the start of its coming of age. Meanwhile, the arrival on the scene of Elvis Presley presaged an era when white rock and roll would eclipse black rhythm and blues. (Atlantic had attempted to sign Presley in 1955 but could afford to offer only $25,000. "It was all the money we had then," says Ertegun with a rare note of regret. The $45,000 demanded by Presley's manager, Colonel Parker, was paid by RCA. Ertegun adds, pointedly: "The president of RCA at the time had been extensively quoted in *Variety* damning R&B music as immoral. He soon stopped when RCA signed Elvis Presley.") It was a time of great uncertainty—and it would take more than a faith in "magic" for Atlantic to survive.

Ertegun faced the prospect with the buoyant optimism that is his trademark, and looked to the West Coast where he believed the immediate future of music lay. Wexler worried about impending bankruptcy and grew increasingly introspective.

Today Phil Spector lives the life of a rich, solitary eccentric on a large Beverly Hills estate—in contact with his long-suffering assistant and secretary only by intercom. He rarely sees anybody, but when he does he is reluctant to let them leave. One of his friends, Seymour Stein, is sparing with his visits ever since Spector locked him inside his twenty-three-room mansion for two days, apparently terrified of being left alone to his solitude. The Ramones, who worked with Spec-

tor in 1980, had the same experience. And a songwriter who
was ushered into a completely darkened room in Spector's
house waited uneasily for the next two hours. Suddenly, the
curtain moved slightly and allowed a tiny chink of light into
the room. As his eyes grew accustomed to the now only partial darkness, he was able to make out the shape of a man
sitting on the other side of the room. Spector had been there
all the time, silently waiting to be noticed.

Spector's eccentricities became apparent even before he
achieved enduring fame, and great wealth, with his "wall of
sound" productions, which employed layer upon layer of in-
strumental and vocal tracks and which produced twenty con-
secutive smash hits (including "Da Doo Ron Ron" and "Then
He Kissed Me," by the Crystals; "Be My Baby," by the Ron-
ettes; and "You've Lost That Lovin' Feeling," by the Righ-
teous Brothers). Sonny Bono—who with Cher would play an
important part in the revival of Atlantic's fortunes—once
worked for Spector as an assistant: "Philip was always a very
strange person," says Bono. "He always had a tough time
staying rational, a real tough time. I don't think it was any
reason you or I would know—you'd have to go back into his
family history and trace it. It was more than just his success
that was the crux of the problem. It traced all the way back.
His sister, his whole family was a turbulent family. His mom
would come to every session and drive us all nuts. He hated
his mom [and] we hated it when she came to the sessions. His
sister was committed [to an institution]—and sometimes I'd
have to go and give his sister money from him, and I'd have
to slip it under the door. It was a strange family."

But in 1959—when Atlantic was in crisis—Phil Spector arrived in New York from Los Angeles offering only enormous
promise.

He had been "discovered" a year earlier when he wrote,
produced, and sang one of the parts in the Teddy Bears' hit
record, "To Know Him Is to Love Him"—a title taken from
the gravestone of his father, who had died when Spector was
twelve. The Teddy Bears were unable to repeat their success

but Spector gained a mentor in Lester Sill, a leading independent producer in Los Angeles. Sill believed the "very quiet, serious . . . bashful" Spector, who was "anxious to learn," would benefit by working with the best songwriters in what was still the mecca, New York, and urged him to go there and work with Jerry Leiber and Mike Stoller—the songwriting and producing duo who had become Atlantic's most prolific "hit makers."

Leiber and Stoller were sympathetic to the young Spector. They had made the same coast-to-coast journey after early success in Los Angeles with such songs as "Hound Dog." They understood that New York was the "place to be" for any aspiring songwriter and, to make that possible for Spector, Jerry Leiber gave him a place to stay in his own apartment. Leiber and Stoller also got him work as a session musician (playing guitar) at Atlantic.

Though Leiber and Stoller were kind to their new protégé they did not like him. "He wasn't likeable," says Leiber. "He was funny, he was amusing—but he wasn't very nice." Indeed Spector endeared himself to almost nobody at Atlantic—with the exception of Ahmet Ertegun. Wexler simply had no time for him. For Miriam Bienstock, Spector was an administrative burden, and an irritating one at that: "I thought he was insane."

Miriam "hated" Spector because he never kept appointments. "My point of view was different," she says. "I didn't consider the fact he might be terribly talented . . . He'd always ask groups to show up, and there'd be two groups sitting there—we didn't have that much space, and they'd be waiting for him—and he wouldn't show up. He'd show up two days later. I just thought that he was a little cocky, and a little insane . . . I think now, in some sense, you would excuse it as . . . 'star quality.' But at the time he did it he was no star—he was just a pain in the neck."

Nevertheless, Leiber and Stoller continued to help Spector, however reluctantly, by securing for him production assignments from Atlantic. The most important of the label's artists for whom they wrote were the Drifters, and the group's new lead singer, Ben E. King—who, in 1959, was Atlantic's best hope as a replacement for Ray Charles. Thanks to Leiber and Stoller, Spector was therefore present at the Drifters' recording sessions, and the sessions at which King recorded his solo releases. Since Spector has subsequently been given much of the credit for the records that emerged from those sessions, that is an act of generosity Leiber and Stoller now regret.

In 1959, Leiber and Stoller conceived the notion of diluting the raw quality of rhythm and blues by adding an accompaniment of soaring strings. When Jerry Wexler heard the first result, "There Goes My Baby," he was simply appalled: "Get that out of here, I hate it. It's out of tune and it's phony, and it's shit, and get it out of here." But he was wrong—at least in commercial terms. "There Goes My Baby" became the Drifters' biggest hit to date, reaching number one in the pop chart and establishing a style that would become the group's trademark. "Save the Last Dance for Me," released in 1960, also reached number one. Then in midwinter of that year Ben E. King began his solo career by recording two considerable hits for Atlantic—"Spanish Harlem" and "Stand by Me."

Who did what at those memorable sessions will always be a matter of dispute. Mike Stoller accuses Spector of taking credit for "most of the things Jerry and I produced—including things that had been done before he even came to New York." But, perhaps, the truth is more subtle than that. "I'd say that Leiber and Stoller did ninety-five percent of the actual production," says Ben E. King. "They wrote up the string lines and they would come up with the format of the rhythm." Then, says King, they would "purposefully" leave it to Spector to add a touch of genius. "Spector was great for coming in with what we call 'hooks'—which are little key pieces to put in songs that you hear all through the record . . . It is like seeing you in a beautiful suit and saying, 'That suit is great but if you put on this tie you will really look fantastic.' So he had that genius about him."

Ahmet Ertegun also recognized the genius in Spector and told the young man, "We are going to produce a lot of records together." Despite their age difference (Spector was in his early twenties, Ertegun almost forty) they became friends—perhaps because "I was pretty wild in those days, and he was much wilder." They traveled to California together in search of new songs, and would drive around Hollywood in Spector's Thunderbird "going far in excess of the speed limit."

Long before the days of car stereo systems, Spector installed a record player in the Thunderbird and, says Ertegun, still laughing at the memory: "When publishers rang to try and sell us their songs, we'd say, 'Look, we listen to records in the car,' and we'd start whizzing round town—all the little streets—at ninety miles an hour. All these publishers, who were all old guys, would start screaming, 'Let me out of the car! You people are crazy! I don't care if you don't record the song.' "

Ertegun indulged his protégé, not seeming to care how much he antagonized other people. Once, but only once, he took Spector to meet Bobby Darin—by then a movie star and married to actress Sandra Dee—at the couple's lavish Hollywood home. While a butler served drinks, Darin sat with his feet dangling in the swimming pool, playing chords on a guitar and singing snatches of songs. Darin was never an accomplished guitarist but Ertegun, ever the diplomat, encouraged him, saying, "That's pretty nice. Have you got something else?" Spector looked at Ertegun in disbelief: "Are you crazy or am I crazy? You think those songs are any good? Those songs sound like shit." Darin threw him out of the house. (Some time later, when "wall of sound" productions were dominating the charts, Darin proposed making a record for Atlantic with the now-famous Phil Spector as producer. The look on Darin's face when Ertegun told him who Spector was is one that even Ertegun cannot adequately describe.)

In particular, Ertegun did not seem to care about the abrasive effect Spector was having on Leiber and Stoller, who grew increasingly resentful at the credit their former pupil received. Their insecurity was only heightened by the fact that they received little sympathy for their aggrieved feelings from either Miriam or Wexler.

Miriam had opposed Atlantic's hiring of Leiber and Stoller from the start. "Here were these people coming in who were rather brash—and I couldn't see why it was necessary to use them." In her customary acidic manner she questioned Leiber and Stoller's right to complain about Spector since they, she now hints, had themselves exploited other people's work.

Wexler, whose business acumen had always intimidated them—"He seemed awfully sure of himself in the office, dealing with contracts and money," says Leiber—was totally insensitive to their request for a producer's credit on record labels and sleeves. "What is a producer?" said Wexler. "You just sit in the studio and you say, 'Take one.'" When Leiber and Stoller pressed their case, they say, Wexler exploded: "What the hell do you want your name on the label for? Your name is on the label as writers. How many times do you want your names on the record? We tell everybody that you made the record, they all know."

Leiber and Stoller won this battle (and it became standard practice in the industry for producers to get credit—indeed, in Spector's case preeminent credit—on labels and album sleeves). To Atlantic's horror, Leiber and Stoller then went on to demand a producer's royalty. Miriam, in particular, was outraged: "At that time there weren't many producers—especially ones getting royalties. As a principal in the company, I just didn't want to pay it. That's the whole principle of capitalism—you take advantage of people! I just didn't see why Jerry or Ahmet or Herb couldn't do it."

Again, Leiber and Stoller won the argument. Atlantic began paying them a producer's royalty, in addition to a songwriter's royalty, but it was an informal agreement: Nobody bothered to draw up a proper contract setting down exact amounts and percentages, and written statements were neither sent nor demanded. All of which did not please Leiber and Stoller's accountant, who wanted a precise arrangement. And, since the team had been with Atlantic for about six years, he said it was about time for an audit of Atlantic's books to make sure the songwriters had been paid their due on every record sold. Leiber was worried that Ertegun would take offense but the accountant assured him it was "business as usual."

As soon as the proposed audit was announced to Atlantic, Wexler telephoned Leiber. "I'm really offended," he said. "Why are you doing an audit?" Leiber tried to explain that it was routine, but Wexler would not be placated. Over his objections the audit went ahead—and the accountant found that Leiber and Stoller had been underpaid $18,000. Feeling increasingly nervous at what they had set in motion, Leiber considered dropping the whole matter. After all, he says now, "everyone can make a mistake. There's always some seepage, some breakage, some leakage, or some slippage. In those days eighteen thousand dollars was a fair amount, but it was not a lot of money." Stoller, however, a stickler for the letter of the law, insisted on pressing for the money to be paid.

Stoller might since have had cause to regret his insistence. Leiber and Stoller presented their case at a meeting with Ertegun and Wexler in what they say was a "relaxed and friendly" way. Ertegun's reaction was, to them, surprising: "Fine, I'll pay the eighteen thousand, but I don't ever want to do business with you guys again." Wexler jumped in to spell out the full implications: "If you want to collect your money, fine, but that's the end of the relationship—and you can forget about the roster of artists." That roster consisted of the Drifters, Ben E. King, and the Coasters—and if Leiber and Stoller could not produce their records they were essentially out of business. Though "shocked" at Atlantic's unwillingness to pay what they were owed, they backed down.

If they expected that to end the matter they were wrong—
life at Atlantic Records was not that simple. One month later
the Drifters prepared to make their next record, which Leiber and Stoller assumed they would produce. "Forget it,"
said Ertegun and Wexler—and gave the job to Phil Spector.
"We had groomed our own competition," says Leiber. "It
was very galling," says Stoller.

Leiber and Stoller left Atlantic Records in 1961 to work for
United Artists. Their only consolation in the whole bitter affair was that the Coasters—a group they had brought to Atlantic from Los Angeles—quit the label too; that, and their
satisfaction that Phil Spector on his own did not produce one
hit record for Atlantic.

Almost twenty-five years later the acrimony lingers. Perched
on a large cream sofa in his opulent midtown Manhattan sitting room, Jerry Leiber, wearing jeans and a jaunty cap, describes how sharply wounded he and Stoller (an altogether
more staid character) felt about their unceremonious dump-
ing in favor of Spector. "They brought Phil in—who we had
groomed—to replace us. That was part of the bad feeling. We
thought that was not the proper thing to do, since we had
brought Phil to them, to help Phil out and to help Atlantic.
They used Phil as competition."

Curiously, although most of their fights at Atlantic directly
involved Wexler rather than Ertegun, and "the big falling-
out was really with Jerry," the more lasting rift has been with
Ertegun. "Ahmet took offense at a situation where *we* were
wronged. He has always been like that. I think he was offended because *he* was in the wrong, and I think he was
embarrassed. I don't think he has ever gotten over it," says
Leiber.

Asked whether *he* has recovered Leiber says, "Yeah, I
think so"—but after a few moments' reflection he decides,
"No, I haven't." He talks of a 1987 speech given by Ertegun
at the Rock-and-Roll Hall of Fame dinner in New York—a

glittering occasion, devised by Ertegun, where the architects of rock and roll are honored every year—in which "he thanked everybody at Atlantic down to the secretaries, and the receptionists and the mail clerks—but he never mentioned us."

The parting of the ways of Leiber and Stoller and Ertegun and Wexler was not the end of the story. There was one last chapter to be written, even more bitter—and, for Atlantic Records, the most important.

Some two years after leaving Atlantic, in the belief that they, too, could be entrepreneurs, Leiber and Stoller created two record labels of their own which they called Daisy and Tiger. Their timing was awful: They released their first records at the end of November 1963, the week President John F. Kennedy was assassinated, and nobody bought them. But even when there was no such national diversion the records flopped. Leiber describes how perplexed he felt when their releases (of all-girl groups) gained rapturous reviews in the music press but notched up pitifully low sales.

"We put these records out and they were hot picks, and none of them sold. Now at Atlantic, records sold before you knew it . . . We left the promotion up to our distributors. We gave our distributors [free] records to pay for our promotion costs because we were told that was all you had to do."

To which Ertegun and Wexler might have said, "Welcome to the real world." Leiber and Stoller's sheltered life in the recording studios at Atlantic had in no way prepared them for the perilous paths through independent distribution and record promotion. They simply had not realized that while they tinkered with kettle-drum parts for the Drifters, Ertegun and Wexler were getting on with manufacturing, design, distribution, marketing, and promotion, to ensure their records sold. And while some things changed after the payola scandal, they did not change very much.

"We were very naive about it," admits Leiber. "We didn't

know what we were doing. We knew how to make records but we didn't know how to promote them. We just told the pressing plants to mail them out to the disc jockeys. We thought that was all you had to do. But what you needed was more, a whole lot more: promotion men, sales force, money, dancing girls, dope . . . We were naive not because we were stupid but because we were isolated from the business."

Feeling at his lowest ebb—despondent at their lack of success and worried sick about money—Leiber went one night to Al & Dick's, a restaurant on Broadway where music moguls then congregated. He needed cheering up—and there was no one better qualified to do that than Hy Weiss, who was sitting at a table in the restaurant with George Goldner. Weiss whistled for Leiber to join them.

Weiss was smoking a large pungent cigar and blowing the smoke in Goldner's face. Goldner pleaded with him to "cut it out," but Weiss carried on anyway. "You know what, George, you know why I blow smoke in your face? Because you are a schmuck."

Weiss turned to Leiber and said: "Leiber, now isn't this guy a schmuck, doesn't he have to be a schmuck? Look at him. He started Gee, Rama, Gone, End, Roulette Records—all of them. Five record companies. You know who owns his record companies? Morris Levy owns them. You know how Morris Levy got them? Because this schmuck went to the track and lost the companies at the racetrack—right, schmuck?" And he blew more smoke into Goldner's face.

"Now, tell me, Leiber, would you give a schmuck three hundred and fifty dollars a week to go on the road and promote your records? Somebody that is so stupid he lost five record companies worth maybe fifteen million dollars? Would you trust a guy with three hundred and fifty dollars a week on the road? That is why I'm offering him *two* hundred and fifty dollars."

"Hy, I can't pay a fraction of my mortgage with two hundred and fifty dollars a week," said Goldner. "Two hundred and fifty a week I pay my pharmacist."

"That is the kind of bind you have got yourself into," said Weiss. "You are living in this big house in Scarsdale and you have lost all your companies at the track. I'll give you two-fifty a week and that's it—take it or leave it."

By now Goldner was looking utterly miserable, and Leiber had a flash of inspiration. "George, you want to go into the record business?" he said.

"Leiber and Stoller, right?" said George, perking up for the first time in the conversation. "You're not kidding me? I am feeling very sensitive these days. No jokes, you mean it?"

"Hey, wait a minute," said Weiss. "I ask you to my table for a drink and you are trying to steal my flunky from me."

"Hy, you haven't paid for the drink yet," said Goldner.

Leiber said, "I need a good promotion man and somebody who knows about sales."

Leiber and Goldner haggled over the deal with frequent interpolations from Weiss. Goldner asked Leiber how much money was left in the bank—and insisted that he would need every penny of it to go out on the road and promote records in his inimitable style. "Don't give it to him, Leiber, he's going to go to the track," said Weiss. "Leiber, don't give him the money."

Ignoring this sensible advice, Leiber said Goldner could take what was left of the company's capital in lieu of a regular salary—which Leiber and Stoller could not afford to pay. Leiber and Stoller would form a new label, Red Bird, and if Goldner made the first record a hit, he would become a partner.

"What's going on here?" said Weiss. "I want a piece of this for putting this deal together."

"You're not getting anything," said Leiber, trying to be firm.

Unperturbed, Weiss said: "Do you have a distributor in town? Well, my brother Sammy is distributing your records." Leiber agreed.

"And at that point," says Leiber, relishing the memory, "George Goldner goes into his inside pocket and he pulls out this very elegant, old Tiffany silver cigarette case. He takes out a long Pall-Mall cigarette, he lights it up and takes a deep breath, and goes over to Hy and blows the smoke in Hy's face . . . and says, 'You're going to see who the schmuck is.' "

George Goldner spent that night at the Brill Building, the epicenter of the music industry in the early 1960s, listening to the backlog of master recordings that Leiber and Stoller had accumulated. Leiber remembers, "I went in at eleven the next morning. He was sitting at my desk, not a hair out of place. He was like Dracula, shirt, tie—not a crease."

Goldner meant business. He immediately recruited to Red Bird Seymour Stein—thinking, perhaps, that Stein's experience of compiling the charts at *Billboard* could be helpful to the enterprise. The now ebullient head of Sire Records seemed a very self-effacing young man when he was introduced to Leiber and Stoller in 1963. "He was very apologetic," says Stoller. "As Jerry used to say, he was the only guy that entered the room by backing into it. He's changed."

But he was certainly knowledgeable on records. "The amazing thing about Seymour," says Stoller, "was that he knew every record that had ever been released, and what color label it was on, and what the serial number was—and he would stand to attention as he recited the number."

With Stein on board, the first decision to be made was which song should Red Bird bank on? Which of the records Leiber and Stoller had "in the can" should the remaining capital be spent on? The momentous decision was made in late 1963 at an uproarious listening session at Goldner's Scarsdale house. According to Stein: "We were listening to these records over and over again, and we couldn't make up our minds what to take, and all of a sudden [Goldner's] wife, who had a hot Latin temperament, came down the stairs and said, 'That's the one.' " The Goldners were legendary for their titanic rows (Stein claims that on the day they moved to Scarsdale they had such a fight their neighbors offered to buy them out) and Mrs. Goldner's unsolicited advice started a confrontation that entirely lived up to the billing. "What do you know about records?" Goldner shouted—and the battle was joined. But "Chapel of Love" by the Dixie Cups *was* the record selected as Red Bird's first release. "George probably beat her up for saying it," says Stein. "But in the end that was the record we went for."

Jerry Leiber hated the record—perhaps because the song was co-written by Phil Spector—but it hit the top of the charts. Red Bird then had a string of hits with the Dixie Cups, the Jellybeans, and the Shangri-Las (best remembered for "Leader of the Pack"). "And this was a very hot little company," says Stein. "Hotter even than Atlantic and Motown," says Leiber.

But the warning Hy Weiss had given Leiber at the start of Red Bird came back to haunt them. Leiber and Stoller discovered that Goldner was running a parallel business to Red Bird called George Goldner Enterprises. Every time Red Bird had a hit, up to 200,000 additional records would be pressed and shipped to California to be sold privately—for the benefit of George Goldner Enterprises. "George controlled the pressing plants in New Jersey," says Leiber. "George controlled the back door of the pressing plant. If he wanted to ship eighty thousand records to Los Angeles in the middle of the night, what were we going to do?"

They could not afford to lose Goldner's invaluable skills as a promotions man—and they could not afford to support his destructive addiction to the racetrack. The only solution Leiber and Stoller could see was to merge Red Bird with Atlantic and have Ertegun and Wexler in charge—or so they claim.

The caveat is necessary because that is only one of the explanations for an extraordinary luncheon that took place at the Plaza Hotel in Manhattan in 1964. Present were Ertegun, Wexler, Goldner, Leiber and Stoller, and their attorney Lee Eastman. So divisive and explosive were the issues at stake that, today, each party to the discussions has a completely different recollection of what happened.

. . .

The deterioration of a relationship that has once been intensely strong is rarely caused by a single event, but the attempted merger of Red Bird and Atlantic in 1964 was both the cause and the symptom of the rift between Ertegun and Wexler. Even Ertegun, who will rarely discuss the breakdown of their relationship, lets his habitual discretion slip for a moment when he admits, "That was the beginning of a break of faith between myself and Jerry."

Bluntly put, Ertegun believes there was a conspiracy to "steal" his company—and that Wexler was part of it. His sense of betrayal is still apparent. He felt it grossly unfair that Wexler should attempt to undermine his position when it was he, Ertegun, who had brought Wexler into the company in the first place, and when it was he, Ertegun, who had taught Wexler all he knew about creating records. "The reality is this," says Ertegun firmly. "Jerry Wexler in those days was just learning to produce records. He had never produced records before he came to Atlantic, and when most of the records were made, he was with me—and *I* produced the records. He was really much more involved with promotion and sales than I was." (Herb Abramson, of course, held very much the same sentiments when he returned to Atlantic from the army.)

As for Wexler, he simply does not want to discuss the subject of the Red Bird "merger," other than to say that it was "mishandled." But sitting one night in New York's University Club, over a glass of fine red wine, he looks melancholy and admits, "There are some things in life that you wish you could go back and do differently." To go any further, however, is too painful, too disquieting: "It's best not to go over this old ground, digging up the past."

Ertegun cannot remember who invited him to lunch at the Plaza Hotel—whether it was Goldner or Wexler—nor can he remember the supposed purpose: "It could have been about a number of things. We were always doing deals."

But he has a clear recollection of what happened: Leiber dropped the bombshell that he and Stoller, George Goldner, *and Wexler* had been talking amongst themselves and had decided to buy Ertegun out. "I think they tried to get the lawyer to explain to me how it would inure to my benefit," says Ertegun. "I said that it was out of the question." For Ertegun, Goldner was the only one who came out of the affair with honor. He looked embarrassed and said to Ertegun, "Man, it's not my idea."

Leiber and Stoller insist that Ertegun's recollection is wrong. They claim that what was proposed was a merger between Atlantic and Red Bird and both are adamant that buying Ertegun out was the last thing on their minds. "We wanted Ahmet to be in there because we respect him and we knew that he was the great ambassador in the music business," says Leiber. "We wanted him up-front for us. Who else was going to get us . . . I don't know . . . Joe Cocker? Who could go to get Joe Cocker? Hy Weiss! There were a hundred reasons we wanted to merge with them and keep Ahmet in the picture. It would have been to our detriment not to have him. He was the greatest emissary in the music business and we knew it."

In any case, Leiber and Stoller insist, the merger was not their idea in the first place—Atlantic had approached them. Atlantic was in the process of buying out Dr. Sabit, the Turkish dentist whose original investment had allowed Ertegun to go into business, and the proposal was for Leiber and Stoller to buy the dentist's shares, and for Red Bird to come under Atlantic's wing. "Ahmet certainly had no beef about that," says Leiber.

Leiber says that he and Stoller were enthusiastic about the idea because it made sense—as much for Atlantic as for Red Bird. "Atlantic was not calling us because we were needy," says Jerry Leiber. "At that period of time we were hotter than pistols. We were very hot, but very unstable. We had lots of singles but no album product. They [Atlantic] were going through a cold patch—everybody gets cold and then gets hot again—but they had a very stable and solid foundation, and they had great management."

To add weight to their declarations of innocence, Leiber and Stoller say their main objective was to limit George Goldner's sphere of influence. "The whole thing was to put George under Ahmet and Jerry's thumb because we couldn't control him," says Leiber.

But, by their version of events, Goldner was too smart for them. They claim, darkly, that Goldner deliberately sabotaged the proposed merger with Atlantic by manipulating the conversation at lunch in such a way that Ertegun was certain to be outraged. "George didn't want us to merge with Atlantic because George was running Red Bird, and doing exactly what he wanted to do, and if we merged with Atlantic he was going to have to contend with Ertegun and Wexler, and he would no longer be Number One Kingpin. He was going to have to answer to them and discuss things with them. He was running this like it was his own kingdom," says Leiber.

And at the lunch, says Stoller, "George Goldner was saying some rather high-handed untactful things about how he would like the merged company to be run." To which Leiber adds: "Can you imagine? George is like a beggar that came out of the gutter and all of a sudden he put on king's clothing, and was sitting at a table with Ahmet, who was the duke of Windsor—and all of a sudden this panhandler was making demands of the duke of Windsor. Goldner was saying, 'We'll do it this way and that way.' "

Ertegun found it intolerable, according to Leiber, and said he was washing his hands of the proposed merger. Wexler, who had as yet played a minor role in the conversation, now stepped in to try and salvage the deal but Ertegun was adamant—they could count him out.

Leiber's and Stoller's descriptions of these events tend to be long-winded and slightly contradictory but there is some evidence to support their contention that, to this point, there was genuine talk of a merger. Under pressure Wexler does admit "I did want to merge with Red Bird. But I wanted Ahmet to be a part of it."

However, it is what happened next that has remained firmly at the forefront of Ertegun's mind. According to Leiber, Wexler said that if Ertegun refused to go ahead, Wexler would do the deal without him.

"There was only one problem—it was my company," says Ertegun. "Jerry only had a small share; about twenty percent."

Ertegun does not believe a word of Leiber's and Stoller's protestations and remains convinced they plotted with Wexler to buy him out. He utterly denies their contention that Atlantic was going through a cool patch and says: "At that time Leiber and Stoller looked like the hottest writers and producers in R&B so they probably figured that with Jerry doing the administration and them making the records, and with George Goldner there too, it would be a great merger."

But he would never have agreed to consider such a merger, he says, because the number of partners would have made it implausible. Atlantic already had four partners— himself, Wexler, Nesuhi, and Miriam—and a merger with Red Bird would have brought three more. "There would always be someone else to be added; before you knew it, there would have been twelve. No, it was *never* suggested that we would do this—with my involvement."

"Ahmet is still angry with me," says Leiber. "He keeps accusing me of trying to steal his company. It's a shame that he's labored under that terrible idea all his life—but he has, I know it." Leiber recalls an evening in 1985 when he bumped into Ertegun at Elaine's restaurant in New York. "Ahmet got drunk and he started saying, 'Yeah, you and Wexler tried to buy me out.' He was going on and on."

It was the beginning of the end for Red Bird Records, and for George Goldner.

Neither Leiber nor Stoller cares to reminisce about the last days of Red Bird. Stoller says simply that they grew tired of recording all-girl groups and wanted to do something else. "Jerry and I lost interest in it. We were capable of producing that kind of music . . . but it wasn't the kind of music that really turned us on."

In 1966, Stoller turned to Leiber and said: "You know, if we get one more hot act, we could get stuck here." As they tell the story, they decided to sell their two-thirds of the company to George Goldner—for one dollar.

What they neglect to mention is the reason for their generosity, and for the unseemly haste with which they departed: Red Bird had been taken over by the Mob.

Mafia involvement in the record industry is a touchy subject. It has been rumored from the start, thanks mainly to Morris Levy and his connections—and, as we shall see, in Levy's case the suspicions are now more solid than rumor. As we shall also see, one of the six major record companies that dominate the market today has had a mobster on its payroll, and two other majors have been touched by Mafia-related scandal. There are those who believe the industry has been infiltrated by the Mob from top to bottom.

Miriam Bienstock says that is not true. "There isn't a Mob presence in the record business, like there is in a lot of other businesses. It's surprising. They could be on the fringes, like [record] piracy, but they don't come in and say, 'We're taking over your business.' "

This is a reassuring view but not entirely accurate. Jerry Wexler's appraisal is probably closer to the truth. "The Mafia would like to control the record industry, but they have never managed to. They're just on the fringes: selling cut-out records [records that have been deleted from catalogues], pressing, independent promotion." Nevertheless, he says, it requires great vigilance to keep the mobsters out. There are various mistakes that could make a record company vulnerable to a Mafia takeover, according to Wexler: borrowing money from dubious sources; asking for a "favor" from people "with connections"; and indulging in "careless talk" which the Mob might "overhear." Atlantic Records managed to stay out of the Mafia's grasp because, as Wexler says, "We were very, very careful not to do any of those things."

Other independent companies were less prudent. Florence Greenberg was one of the few women to own a label, Scepter Records, which thrived from 1959 through to the early 1970s with the Shirelles, Luther Dixon, and Dionne Warwick. It is not clear exactly how the Mob moved in on the formidable Florence and her team of ambitious young male assistants. It is believed the Mafia caught her ripping off cash from her own company and used this as a "handle" to take control.

In any event, having been taken over, Florence acquired bad habits. Scepter Records released a record made from the demo tapes of a band which had since become successful after signing with Morris Levy's Roulette Records. "I got her demos stopped," says Levy, chuckling at the thought of what happened next. "She paid some tough guys fifteen thousand dollars to get me." Unfortunately for Florence, "the guys took her money and then came to tell me the story."

It was an acquaintance of Morris Levy who headed one of the most outrageous attempted Mob takeovers in the music business of the 1960s. The victim was Kamasutra Productions, a production and record company based in Los Angeles, run by George Goldner's protégé Artie Ripp and his two partners, Hy Masrati and Phil Steinberg.

Kamasutra's initial financing had been dubious: $60,000 that Hy Masrati received as insurance money when his record store burned down. "Rumor has it that a fire sale was appropriate," says Ripp.

By the time he was invited to become a partner Kamasutra had already run out of that money. "Unbeknownst to me they had borrowed some other money from some friendly people from the other side of town," says Ripp with heavy sarcasm. "Some friendly loan sharks."

Oblivious to this, Ripp set to work making records with

groups such as the Shangri-Las and the Critturs. It was only after Kamasutra Productions had enjoyed five smash hits out of its first eight releases that Ripp had time to relax and look around. He didn't like what he saw. "What are these guys doing sitting in the office?" Ripp demanded of his partners. "They look like something out of *Guys and Dolls.*"

"Well, they're friends," his partners lamely replied.

"They're not friends of mine," said Ripp. "I haven't invited them here. Why are they here? Aside from that, they're pinching the girls' asses, they're trying to fuck the secretaries—anything that's breathing they're trying to nail. I didn't realize we're running a massage parlor or a whorehouse here."

The partners were shamed into confessing they had borrowed $10,000 from mobsters, and then greater amounts when that money ran out—in return for shares in the company. "It was rather disturbing," says Ripp. "I took it upon myself to figure out how I was going to get mercy from what was supposed to be a merciless group of people—people who now had a piece of this hot, happening rock-and-roll production company."

In fact the Mob owned only 10 percent of Kamasutra—but as Ripp says, "That's like being a little pregnant." Ripp got to know the leader of the group of men that haunted Kamasutra's offices, a man named Sonny Francesi, and, to his surprise, became quite fond of him. "This fellow was personable, lovable, supportive, warm, decisive, strong, and very, very empowered."

Ripp therefore decided to try a straightforward appeal for mercy to Francesi: "You know, you guys are terrific but I can't take this where it is supposed to go. Heaven's gates are open, and the problem besetting me is that I know that you've got the FBI, you've got the IRS, you've got gangbusters—you've got everybody watching you and everybody watching you in turn is watching me. And everybody who is watching me creatively is now saying, 'Aren't you the ones who are involved with the wise guys?' So, you got a chance to be able to do something good. You never believed that those two guys who borrowed the money would stand up for it. What was ten g's? You know, you write it off. Look, please give me a break, give me your blessing, give me a price and let me put it in a brown paper bag, and let me give it to whomever. Let's be friends but let's not have this relationship."

That night Francesi and Ripp went out together. "We went to the Copacabana or some place, and we got absolutely smashed. Sonny and I rode on the back of this El Dorado convertible, just screaming and drinking and riding through the streets. We hugged and kissed and he said, 'You got it.' So I put the money together, put it in a brown paper bag, gave it to a mutual friend, and that was that."

George Goldner and Red Bird Records were not so lucky. What appears to have happened is that Goldner borrowed money from Mafia loan sharks in order to pay off his gambling debts—using Red Bird as collateral. When he was unable to pay the debt, the gangsters moved into the company's offices, waiting for money to come in. Leiber and Stoller attempted to negotiate with the Mob but failed—and left Red Bird, and Goldner, to his new partners.

The story is not much talked about in the industry. Only Miriam Bienstock is prepared to spill the beans about what really happened to Red Bird, which—in her view—is that Leiber and Stoller got the comeuppance they deserved.

"May I quote Jerry Wexler about Leiber and Stoller?" she says. "His words for them were Mr. Lust and Mr. Greed. They were just ambitious for themselves—and they always messed up. They had delusions of glory. 'Why should we make money for somebody else when we can do it for ourselves?' So they went into partnership with George Goldner, he gambled away all their money, the Mafia came in—and all kinds of strange and terrible things happened. George was involved with bad people. Did Jerry [Leiber] tell you about his meetings with the Mafia? Jerry actually had a meeting with these people who said they wanted to take over, and he didn't know what to do."

After Leiber and Stoller departed (to become independent producers and begin a publishing empire), Goldner ran Red Bird into the ground. Few records were made, artists rarely got paid, and Goldner began to sell off the Red Bird masters—often three times over to three different companies. His gambling debts grew as his health failed.

The night before he died in 1970, Goldner had the mixed blessing of the company of Hy Weiss. "George was always putting his hand to his chest and complaining, 'I'm dying,' but on this occasion he really did look terrible."

Weiss says he told Goldner: "I think you're going to have a heart attack. You have been bullshitting for years but this time I believe you."

"Then why don't you take me to a hospital?" said Goldner.

"No, I don't believe you that much," said Weiss—and went off leaving George to make his own arrangements. Later that night, Weiss was watching a hockey game on television, when the telephone rang. It was Goldner. He said he had been discharged from the hospital and was watching the hockey on television, and "I want some of the action."

"I refuse to let you gamble while you are ill," said Weiss. "What if you should die in the morning and you lose the bet. How do I get the money?"

A wise decision, as things turned out.

There was never any possibility that Goldner's unfortunate death would stop people telling stories at his expense. Morris Levy, as his oldest friend and enemy, has the last word: "This is the funniest story I know about George Goldner. About three or four weeks after he died, his young Australian wife came to see me. She told me that George had lain on his deathbed mumbling, 'Sue this guy, sue that guy, sue Morris Levy.' Then about five minutes later he said to her, 'And if you ever need any help, go and see Morris Levy.' She said, 'But you just told me to sue him.' He said, 'Oh, that don't matter with Morris—one thing hasn't got anything to do with another.' " (According to Hy Weiss, Levy paid Goldner's widow a salary for a year: "If Morris likes you, he'll do anything for you.")

It was perhaps fitting that Goldner died when he did, for his time had passed. There was not much room left for an old-time promotions man. Increasingly disc jockeys were only allowed to play Top 40 hits, and new artists with new songs discovered by independent companies were difficult to get on the air. "It wasn't that you went to a city and there was a couple of powerful deejays there, whom you were friendly with," says Levy. "There was mass programming and program directors and it was computerized—it was what we called 'no-break radio' . . . [It] was very good for the majors but it eventually beat the hell out of a lot of independents of that period. Really, the last road trip I made with Goldner, it wasn't like it was. I really believe Goldner was beaten because the industry changed on him. His heart was broken."

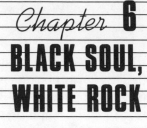

Chapter 6
BLACK SOUL, WHITE ROCK

"I t is a testament to my relationship with Jerry Wexler that we could continue to be on friendly terms," says Ahmet Ertegun, speaking of the aftermath of the failed attempt to "merge" Red Bird and Atlantic Records. Friendly, perhaps—but increasingly distant.

For one thing, Ertegun gained a wife and, with her, a lifestyle entirely different from that of any of his colleagues—some of whom, he suspects, resented it.

Mica Banu is in fact Ertegun's second wife, but his first marriage (to a Scandinavian who "looked like Greta Garbo") was so unmemorable that when he attended a party at which his former wife was present Ertegun did not know who she was—until *she* told him. The second Mrs. Ertegun would never be that easy to forget.

She was born the daughter of wealthy landowners in what was then the kingdom of Romania. She was not much more than a girl when she married the son of a "very, very good Romanian family" who was a member of the royal household. Unfortunately for the royal court, postwar elections in Romania resulted in a Communist-dominated government and in 1947 King Michael I abdicated. Mica and her husband left the country on the last train out "with just our suitcases." After a brief stint in Switzerland, and then in Paris (where she was a Dior model), the aristocratic refugee bought a farm near Montreal, Canada, where for the next eight years she milked the cows and mucked out the coops of 15,000 chickens. She would get up every morning at 4 A.M. to feed the livestock; even so, every evening she dressed for dinner and put candles on the table. It is not a period she cares much to talk about.

She was introduced to Ertegun in the late 1950s, while on a visit to New York, by the Turkish ambassador to the United States. Ertegun was in the throes of divorce, she still married. Nevertheless he launched an extravagant courtship which eventually led to her, too, seeking a divorce—and to their marriage in 1961. The couple bought a house on East 81st Street in Manhattan for $100,000, which required considerable interior renovation. To save money Mica did the design herself, and the startlingly beautiful result set her on a career that has since made her one of the most sought after interior designers in New York. She formed a partnership with Chessy Rayner (stepdaughter of the chairman of Condé Nast) and through that connection the Erteguns found themselves swept into the social whirl of Manhattan's high society. Mica's exotic background and impeccable taste, combined with Ertegun's irreverence toward everything and everybody, his inexhaustible supply of anecdotes, and his penchant for throwing spectacular parties, made the couple irresistible. Ertegun's social contact with his colleagues, never extensive, virtually ceased.

If Wexler therefore felt that Mica had come between him and Ertegun, he was not alone. Phil Spector and Ertegun had been, in Ertegun's words, "very, very close—we used to see each other every night." Once Mica was on the scene, however, "I think he realized I wasn't going to be hanging out with him every day." Spector quit Atlantic Records the day Ertegun was married.

In Wexler's case the breach was more subtle—and explained by him in different terms. "What happened was that [Atlantic] got big enough, and diversified enough, that we had to stop working together," he says. "I mean stop working together literally—being interfaced every day, on everything. Of course we still worked together, but now we each had a separate portmanteau of duties and artists. It was a big step, it was a milestone. It meant that each one had to go out without the support of the other, and make records."

They no longer had adjacent desks, rather adjoining offices separated by silk screens. But more often than not, and increasingly, Ahmet Ertegun and Jerry Wexler were separated by at least 3,000 miles—and in terms of the music they produced, were worlds apart.

On February 7, 1964, four young men from Liverpool landed at New York's John F. Kennedy Airport where they were met by a screaming mob. The Beatles' two television appearances on the *Ed Sullivan Show* were each watched by an estimated seventy million people. By April the group's records held the top five positions in *Billboard*'s pop chart. The record industry had never seen anything like it. As Wexler says, shaking his head at the memory, "If you didn't have the Beatles in 1964, you didn't have anything."

Unlike several other independents, Atlantic survived "Beatlemania" though, in Wexler's words, "it was a difficult year." That it did survive was due in large part to the substantial presence on the label of Solomon Burke—preacher, soul singer, and sometime mortician. After recording a string of hits for Atlantic between 1961 and 1964, Burke was proclaimed "King of Rock 'n' Soul" by radio station WEBB in Baltimore, Maryland, and, says Wexler, "Solomon kept us going." (Ever since then Burke—a performer of the utmost theatricality—has taken to the stage in robe and scepter. He continues to perform while still finding time to run a string of mortuaries, and act as spiritual father to the 40,000 parishioners of his House of God for All People. He is also the literal father of twenty-one children, and grandfather of fourteen. Burke remembers his days at Atlantic with great affection: "What Jerry Wexler and Ahmet Ertegun had in the 1960s was faith in the artists. This is what is rare today. The record companies don't have faith anymore, they have statistics.")

But it was obvious—to Ertegun at least—that if Atlantic was to do more than survive it would have to radically modify the musical output of the label. With the exception of Bobby Darin, all of Atlantic's hit makers had been black artists who did not now hold much appeal for the vast, new record-buying market of white teenagers who, in the main, preferred "white" music performed by white artists. Wexler had no liking for the "new" music, or for most of the people who made it. Ertegun, on the other hand, thoroughly embraced it. Leaving Wexler to mind the store he headed for California to secure Atlantic's future by signing to the label an unlikely duo named Salvatore Bono and Cherilyn Sarkasian LaPier— otherwise known, to their few fans, as Caesar and Cleo.

"Sonny" Bono had been trying to break into the music business for years—an ambition that prompted him to move from his native Detroit to Los Angeles where "just driving down Hollywood Boulevard" was exciting because "it meant movies, music, and all those things." For much longer than he had hoped, however, Bono traveled the boulevard in a meat truck making deliveries. He would "write a song, go in real fast to the markets and deliver the meat, and then stop off at the record companies and sing my song. I'd go in with a bloody apron, sing my song, and then run back to the truck." But some of Bono's songs were bought by Specialty Records (the label for which Little Richard recorded) and one of them, "High School Dance," reached number ninety on the pop chart. "They liked me and they liked my songs," says Bono. The singing meat delivery man was "doing pretty good."

Bono's next break came when he walked into Specialty's office one day during a slack period on his meat round to find Art Rupe, Specialty's irascible owner, in the midst of an argument with the label's producer, "Bumps" Blackwell. Rupe was furious that Blackwell had recorded one of the members of the Soul Stirrers, the label's most important gospel group, singing a secular pop song that was likely to offend most gospel fans. No matter that the singer was a young man named Sam Cooke who would go on to become one of the most widely imitated of all soul crooners. Rupe kicked Cooke off the label, and fired Bumps Blackwell—and Sonny Bono, standing in the office in his bloody apron, found himself appointed Specialty's new A&R man. "I was there, so I got hired on the spot," he says. (Dispensing of the services of Cooke and Blackwell was "a very bad move," as Bono says laconically. The two men persuaded an airplane parts manufacturer named Bob Keen to set up Keen Records and release "You Send Me," Cooke's debut under his own name. The record went to number one and sold 1.7 million copies, making it one of the most successful singles of its time.)

As Specialty's staff producer, Bono worked with Little Richard and Larry Williams (of "Bony Moronie" and "Dizzy Miss Lizzy" fame), and recorded songs himself under the name Don Christy—to no great success. These were days of change—of Elvis Presley, and Gene Vincent, and Ricky Nelson—and like so many other independent labels Specialty could not keep up. "We were really a black label and to switch over from black to rockabilly kind of confused us all," says Bono. "We didn't understand [the music] as well as they did in the South. The independent distributors wouldn't even work a black record because they wanted that new sound." Bono, like just about everybody else in the business, went in search of "a good, solid, white hit artist," but he could never pull one in. He says he simply did not have a feel for white pop music: "I liked black R&B."

Luckily for Bono, he had the opportunity to learn about pop music when he went to work for Philles Records, the label started by Phil Spector after he left Atlantic (in partnership with Lester Sill). Bono was, among other things, a session man for Spector and thus a contributor to the "wall of sound" that made Spector's productions so extraordinary. "I really wanted to work for him, because I wanted to know what the heck he was doing to create that incredible sound," says Bono. "He was the king—the king producer."

But for all his talent in the studio, and his commercial success, Spector still could not cope with personal relationships on anything but his own terms. Spector and Bono were close—until Bono acquired a girlfriend. Then, as had happened with Ertegun two years before, Spector turned decidedly sour. "He was just weird," says Bono. "When you wanted to be with your girlfriend and not him . . . I think that may have had something to do with [the tension]."

Bono's girlfriend was Cherilyn LaPier, whom he met when she sang backup vocals at one of Spector's recording sessions. Matters came to a head when Bono proposed moving Cher into the foreground and recording her as a solo artist. Inevitably, Spector refused. Bono quit Philles Records, married Cher, and started working as a promotion man for Atlantic's Los Angeles distributor, where he came to the attention of Nesuhi Ertegun. Atlantic signed the couple, who called themselves Caesar and Cleo on the grounds that Sonny supposedly had a martial look about him, and Cher resembled Cleopatra. Unfortunately, their first two singles flopped.

Undaunted, Bono borrowed $300 and independently recorded "Baby Don't Go." It was intended as a solo performance by Cher but "at that time she was real afraid to sing, so I sang with her."

The record was released on Reprise—a label then owned by Frank Sinatra and members of his family and run by Mo Ostin, Sinatra's extremely astute friend. It did sufficiently well on the West Coast that Reprise would have expected to record the duo again. But in what was for Ostin an uncharacteristic oversight, Reprise had neglected to place Sonny and Cher (as they now called themselves) under a binding contract. Enter Ahmet Ertegun. "We signed with Ahmet because he was such a personable guy and he made such a big pitch to get us on his label—and I guess that always flatters you," says Bono. "Usually as artists you have to go and pitch but here was someone coming and pitching for us."

"I Got You Babe," the syrupy lovers' duet which clearly defined the new sound of Los Angeles folk rock, was released on Atlantic's subsidiary label, Atco, in August 1965. The record went to number one, stayed there for three weeks, sold over one million copies, and launched Sonny and Cher as America's favorite young lovers. (Bono says he had to insist that "I Got You Babe" was released as the A side of the record. Ertegun, true to form, preferred "a funky blues thing" on the B side.) Together and individually Sonny and Cher went on to produce a string of Top 10 hits for Atlantic that firmly established the label in the pop market. "I think we turned their label white," says Bono. "Bobby Darin was before us but they didn't catch that roll with him like they did when we were on Atlantic."

There is a ring of exaggeration to Bono's claim for Atlantic had not yet abandoned the black music on which it had built its reputation and success. Indeed, thanks to a deal made by Wexler with Stax Records—a tiny outfit in Memphis, Tennessee—Atlantic began releasing records of black soul music, as raw as anything that had come before; what one music critic described as "the real thing." The music was highly successful; the deal, for Stax at least, decidedly less so.

The origins of Stax Records were almost as unlikely as those of Atlantic. Estelle Axton, a forty-one-year-old teller at the Union Planters Bank in Memphis, entered the record business in 1959 with her younger brother, Jim Stewart, an amateur fiddle player and a clerk at the same bank. They took over a disused cinema on East McLemore Street in a black neighborhood of the city. Converting the auditorium into a studio, and the popcorn and candy stand in the lobby into a tiny record shop, Stax declared itself to be "Soulsville USA" in giant plastic letters on the billboard outside.

It was an ambitious claim for, with only a couple of artists on the roster, and no staff other than the two partners and a sometime professional guitarist named Chips Moman (one of whose passions was gambling), Stax was a largely amateur outfit. For session musicians it relied on talented but inexperienced players such as Booker T. Jones, who says: "I did my first session at Stax when I was in the tenth or eleventh grade—when I was fourteen, maybe fifteen years old. I had learnt to play the sax, and I borrowed a sax from the school to play on . . .

"My first impressions of Jim Stewart were that he never pretended to be a record person. He was just carrying on a hobby, which was music. He was a fiddle player and he never pretended to be more than that. His profession was a bank teller and when we first started he was at the bank for most of the day and would come into Stax after about three o'clock."

Jones knew Estelle Axton better, at the beginning, through his visits to the tiny record shop she ran in the cinema lobby. "She was usually behind the counter so she and I became friends when I was a teenager," he says. "She loved music, and she knew all the records."

Soulsville USA first came to Jerry Wexler's attention in 1960 when Stax issued, as one of its early releases, "Cause I Love You" by singer Rufus Thomas, a fixture on the music scene in Memphis, and his eighteen-year-old daughter, Carla, who was on vacation from college. Atlantic's distributor in Memphis called Wexler to say the record was the hot new single in the city. Wexler quickly did a deal with Jim Stewart, obtaining the national distribution rights to "Cause I Love You" for a $1,000 advance and a small royalty on each copy sold. Wexler also obtained a five-year option on all other duets by Carla and Rufus Thomas—or so the Stax partners interpreted it. In fact Stewart and his sister had no idea what the finer points of the contract meant, nor at the time did they care. The $1,000 advance paid by Atlantic was the first money Stax had ever made. Steve Cropper, who started playing guitar for the fledgling company when he was still a teenager, says: "It was a terrible deal—Atlantic really used us. But we needed them badly, so we used them as well. We needed them because it's very hard for an independent to be heard anywhere outside of its own territory. We used to promote our own records. We'd get in a car with a trunkload of records and go to as many radio stations as we could in Tennessee, Mississippi, and Arkansas. It worked—but how far can you drive your car? We had to have national distribution and the only way to do it was with Atlantic. Jim Stewart and all of us were willing to take whatever Atlantic was willing to hand us to get our records out there."

The true nature of the deal Stax had made with Atlantic did not become apparent until Carla Thomas made her solo debut with "Gee Whiz (Look at His Eyes)" in 1961. According to Wexler, by that time he had pushed the deal to the back of his mind and forgotten who owned what. But as Carla Thomas began to attract national attention, Hy Weiss, the famed New York wheeler-dealer, went to Memphis to see if he could obtain the distribution rights to her record. While going through the papers at Stax's offices with Jim Stewart, Weiss discovered the contract with Atlantic—and read the fine print.

Says Wexler: "I got a call from Hy Weiss saying, 'Hey, schmuck, don't you know you got a hit with Carla Thomas on Stax?' I said, 'No kidding?' And he said, 'You own the records, schmuck.' So I went and checked the contract, and we did have the rights to the record." Not only that record but *all* Stax releases—a fact Wexler had somehow overlooked in the original negotiations. He explains he could not be expected to know every detail of every deal: "The lawyers did it and I didn't read every contract," he says.

"So I got in touch with Jim Stewart again, and there was no acrimony. Everything was fine and we picked up the record. Then we really rolled with Stax."

No acrimony perhaps, but Jim Stewart was always ambivalent about the deal with Atlantic and now wonders if Stax would have fared better if it had remained independent. Even Wexler will admit there was an economic imbalance to the relationship which, twenty-five years on, makes the subject uncomfortable for him to talk about. On the one hand he asserts: "It was a perfect relationship. They made a lot of dough, and we were happy with it." Yet in his very next sentence he concedes: "But it was certainly biased in our favor. We didn't pay for the masters [master recordings]. Jim paid for the masters and then he would send us a finished tape and we would just put it out. Our costs began at the production level—the pressing, and distribution, and promotion, and advertising."

Nevertheless, according to Al Bell—who was the first black partner to join Stax—the Atlantic deal was simply essential. He agrees the financial terms were bad but adds: "They had to have somebody and fortunately there was an Atlantic and a Jerry Wexler that had an appreciation for what Stax was doing, and was willing to bet on it. You remove Atlantic, no Stax."

Bell was a disc jockey who got his first job at the microphone when he was seventeen in his hometown of Little Rock, Arkansas. After attending leadership training classes organized by Martin Luther King's Southern Christian Leadership Conference in Georgia, Bell went to work for radio station WLOK in Memphis—which is where he first met Jim Stewart and heard Stax's music. In 1960 he moved to a radio station in Washington, D.C., simultaneously setting up his own independent label, Safice, in partnership with the soul singer Eddie Floyd. ("The advantage I had with Safice was that I was a radio announcer so I could play my own records," says Bell with a laugh.) He was still in Washington, married with a newborn son, and making about $50,000 a year when he was asked by Stewart and Wexler to take over the national promotion of Stax releases—for the princely salary of $200 a week. "My wife thought it was the height of stupidity to entertain such a proposition," says Bell. Nevertheless he agreed to work for Stax, "because I believed in the music."

What made the music—the "Memphis sound"—so distinctive was the session players Stax drew together. Of the four key musicians, two (Steve Cropper and Donald "Duck" Dunn) were white, two (Booker T. Jones and Al Jackson) were black, yet in that most segregated of cities there was in Stax's studios total integration. As Cropper, who grew up in the hills of Missouri, puts it: "I didn't even see a black person until I was nine years old and my family moved to Memphis, so I didn't know you were supposed to discriminate."

The results of their sessions were not authentic black "soul," though they were hailed as such. Rather, their music was, in Bell's words, "a cross-fertilization or co-mingling of the southern American cultures. The influences were country, blues, jazz, and some rock 'n' roll."

Or as Wexler says, what created the "Memphis sound" was not a fortuitous geographical location, or the bricks and mortars of the studio, but "country boys, who instead of proceeding down the country road and going to Nashville, made a left turn and arrived at the blues. Then you mix in black musicians—and get an unthinkably great band. They were southern Americans who learned the music live, not from imported phonograph players."

They soon became hit makers in their own right. Cropper and Duck Dunn, as leaders of the Mar-Keys, reached number two in the pop and R&B charts with "Last Night." The following year, 1962, a jam session between Cropper, Dunn, and Booker T. Jones led to the formation of Booker T. and the MGs (for Memphis Group) and to the recording of "Green Onions." Nobody anticipated the result. "I don't even know if I had planned to go into music professionally at that time," says Jones. "It had become my part-time job, instead of my paper round . . . And when we recorded 'Green Onions' I was just looking for something to put on the B side of a record—to finish the session and get the fifteen dollars [which is what Stax paid him for a session]. Steve Cropper and I had worked on that little song, and we liked it. But we just liked it for ourselves, as something to play in the clubs."

"Green Onions" earned more than one million dollars for Stax and Atlantic.

Booker T. and the MGs scored several more hits but perhaps their most important contribution to Stax was in providing the musical backup for a host of other artists, including Rufus and Carla Thomas, Sam and Dave, Eddie Floyd—and the singer who would become the backbone of the label, Otis Redding.

The success Stax achieved was extraordinary and there is no doubt Wexler played a significant role, as Al Bell is the first to acknowledge: "I learned a lot from Jerry Wexler, an awful lot. He was very creative, very perceptive, and sensitive to the desires of the marketplace. He really had his finger on the pulse of the black consumer." At times Wexler could be a demanding taskmaster: "I could expect to hear from Jerry just as I tried to get home on a Saturday or Sunday to steal a little rest. He had to know every part of the Atlantic operation, and every part of the Stax operation, and every part of the phonograph industry. That was Jerry Wexler. He had to be on top of it—it was an incessant desire. You could just feel it. It emanated from him at all times. He just had to be on top of everything—which was what, by and large, contributed to his success." And Wexler never tired of impressing on Bell what might be called the Atlantic creed: "You never refuse to answer the telephone, you never refuse to listen to a tape, you never refuse to listen to a record—because you never know where your next million-seller is coming from."

As Stax went from strength to strength—and recognizing the unique sound created in Soulsville USA—Wexler began taking Atlantic artists from New York down to the converted cinema to have the magic Memphis touch applied to their records. One of those was Don "Pretty Boy" Covay, a protégé of Little Richard. Another was Wilson Pickett, one of the greatest soul singers of his era, who had not had much success at Atlantic—until, in May 1965, in Memphis, he got together with Steve Cropper and wrote and recorded "In the Midnight Hour." For Al Bell, it was the recognition he had craved for the label, and a tremendous compliment to see relatively established singers traveling to Memphis in search of a hit: "You started seeing Don Covay recording at Stax in Memphis, Tennessee, you started seeing Wilson Pickett recording at Stax in Memphis, Tennessee . . ."

But there was a price to pay. The closer the two labels

came together, the more obvious became the vast gulf that separated the culture and manners of Memphis and New York. Tom Dowd (Atlantic's first producer) spent between fifteen and twenty weekends a year in Memphis recording albums in the Stax studios. He describes the Stax team as "very naive, pleasant, warm people" who worked together as though it were a cooperative. Dowd, an easygoing, good-humored man, found he could slip easily into their ways by concentrating on the music they were producing together. "We had an empathy," he says—but more than once he was told by Stax people they could not relate to "those New York types."

There was no more archetypal New Yorker than Jerry Wexler. According to Booker T. Jones: "Jerry was an executive, a New York executive to me. He was friendly and he was personable but he would sit in the control room, and there was no real connection . . . He wore a suit every day, and he was running the business of Atlantic Records." And Steve Cropper, while admiring Wexler's talent as a producer, found him "a funny little New York guy. He had the New York rap, four hundred words a second, talks like a stenographer."

The underlying tension between the two cultures finally boiled over at the end of 1965. According to some the immediate cause was a Wilson Pickett recording session in Memphis at which "The Wicked Pickett" more than lived up to his reputation as an explosive personality. Others thought the catalyst was "the incredibly intense" Don Covay. Says Cropper: "He [Covay] literally drove everybody crazy . . . He didn't really need to come to Memphis—he could have done what he did in New York. He was so intense he was running the session. That had never happened before at Stax. We always ran the session. We called all the shots. We called the songs, we called the groove, we called the key, we called the tempo."

In any event, Jim Stewart announced that no more Atlantic artists would be recorded at Stax. According to Cropper:

"He didn't want to burn out the guys recording other people's artists . . . It had become an assembly line and there was just too much of a workload. Anything you start overworking—a horse, a car, a person—there's going to be problems." Similarly, Jim Stewart's explanation is that Stax was simply too busy recording its own artists. But Tom Dowd saw the situation as being rather more complicated: "There came a time when we wanted to record [again] in Memphis and Jim Stewart said, 'No—you're going to steal my sound.' That made everybody a bit uptight."

Uptight is an understatement. The highly profitable distribution arrangement between Stax and Atlantic continued for a while, but Jerry Wexler would never again return to Soulsville USA.

While the relationship between Atlantic and Stax disintegrated, Ertegun attempted to consolidate Atlantic's move into white music by signing Buffalo Springfield—a group best known for the haste and manner of its own destruction. But during its brief, stormy existence Buffalo Springfield (named after a farm vehicle) did represent the start of a new era, bringing together all the strands of American music—folk, country, blues, and soul—to create a new sound that became known as "rock"—"not rock and roll, but rock," as Wexler says with a hint of disapproval.

The problem with Buffalo Springfield was that the members of the group did not much like each other. In particular, Neil Young and Stephen Stills, the joint leaders, constantly squabbled about the group's music and direction, and the tensions were only exacerbated by their heavy intake of drugs and their dissipated life-styles.

But as Ertegun recognized, there was great talent and enormous potential. "For What It's Worth," the group's first hit single, perfectly captured the mood of the times. Written by Stills after he had watched a television news report of truncheon-wielding Los Angeles police clearing the sidewalk of singing crowds (demonstrating against local businessmen who had refused to serve "hippie" customers), the song became an anthem of the protest movement. The group followed up with a succession of Neil Young's haunting compositions—including "Broken Arrow" and "I Am a Child"—and Ertegun did everything he could to keep them together. In vain. Added to the internal dissension, the portentous weight of the burden they carried as rock's newest icons simply proved too great. By the time the group's second album was released Young had quit, and Buffalo Springfield formally disbanded in May 1968.

Ertegun may have been the one most hurt by the breakup. "It disappointed me very, very much," he says. "As a matter of fact, I think I had tears in my eyes at the last meeting." Even so, Ertegun had no doubt that "white rock" represented the future and he had no hesitation in signing Crosby, Stills, and Nash—the group that emerged from the wreckage of Buffalo Springfield. Occasionally joined by Neil Young, the new group proved no less volatile than the old, disbanding and regrouping with bewildering frequency. But, on and off over the next fourteen years, Crosby, Stills, and Nash (and sometimes Young) would sell millions of albums for Atlantic and become one of the most widely imitated groups in America. They were, in their day, as hot as it was possible to be. *Déjà Vu*, released in 1970, took two months to record—an extraordinary amount of time for that period. Atlantic's reward for its patience was *advance* orders for more than two million copies.

In Ertegun's view, "white rock" was the natural progression from the rhythm and blues and soul music that had been Atlantic's staple fare and, he says, he would have been "deaf and blind" if he'd failed to recognize "there was a huge new wave coming—from England as well as America." His first important sighting of the English wave came at the Scotch Club in London where Ertegun hosted a party for Atlantic's star of soul, "Wicked" Wilson Pickett. "There were some people jamming on the stage. I was sitting with my back to them so I couldn't see who was playing, but when I heard this blues guitar solo, I turned to Wilson and said, 'That can only be your guitarist. Man, he sure can play the blues.' Wilson says to me, 'My guitar player is having a drink at the bar.' I turned around and I saw this beautiful kid with an angelic face playing the guitar like B. B. King and Albert King put together."

The angelic face belonged to a self-confessed "nasty kid"— one-time art student, sometime construction worker— named Eric Clapton whose virtuosity at guitar had already attracted a cult following in London, and led to widespread graffiti: "Clapton is God." He had played with the British group the Yardbirds until it abandoned "power blues" for "psychedelic pop," and then joined John Mayall's Blues- breakers—a purist blues group inspired by obscure black musicians that most people in Britain had never heard of. It is probably true that John Mayall discovered and nurtured more accomplished musicians than anybody in rock music and, under his influence, Clapton developed and refined the talent he was born with. As Ertegun says, "Clapton doesn't imitate. He swallowed the germ which makes the music come out."

Shortly after Ertegun first saw him at the Scotch Club, Clapton formed his own band, Cream, which made its stun- ning debut at the Windsor Festival in England. At Ertegun's suggestion, the group (made up of Clapton; Ginger Baker, formerly of the Graham Bond Organization; and Jack Bruce, formerly of Manfred Mann) was immediately signed up by Robert Stigwood, a maverick manager-cum-producer who then worked for Polygram, which distributed Atlantic's re- leases in Great Britain and which, in turn, was distributed by Atlantic in the United States. The arrangement was that Stig- wood would produce Cream's records in England, but it was short-lived. "When they made their first record, there wasn't enough blues on it for my taste," says Ertegun. "I remember I bawled out Robert for making too poppy a record. But, anyway, it was a hit and then we took over the production after that . . . Boy, did they play loud. They were the first power trio—I don't know how I never lost my hearing."

In three years Cream sold fifteen million records in America. Then, in repetition of what had happened to Buffalo Springfield, personal tensions and drugs (Clapton was addicted to heroin) caused the band to break up. The only consolation for Ertegun was that by then Atlantic had gained a reputation as the label that could break British groups in America. In Ertegun's words, "We got a shot at almost all of them," including two more of Robert Stigwood's discoveries, the Bee Gees and Yes—two groups that would enjoy phenomenal success, albeit for very different reasons. (By a nice irony, Yes made one of its first appearances at Cream's farewell concert in London. It was instantly hailed as the next "supergroup.") It seemed that things could hardly get better—until the Yardbirds fell apart and its lead guitarist, Jimmy Page, looked around for recruits for what he intended to call the New Yardbirds. The resulting quartet, which Jerry Wexler signed, was instead called Led Zeppelin and it struck America like a thunderclap. In time Led Zeppelin would become, by any commercial measure, the most popular rock band in the world.

Surrounded by success, Ertegun shuttled between New York, Los Angeles, and London, difficult to catch up with and almost impossible to tie down. "You could never have a proper meeting with him," says Brian Lane, the manager of Yes. An easygoing Londoner, Lane found the frenetic atmosphere of Atlantic's New York offices utterly perplexing. "I was new to rock music and I found them all a bit bizarre at Atlantic. I'd heard all about Ahmet—he had this huge reputation. He was always taking phone calls in the middle of a meeting and it was very difficult to get him to concentrate on any particular point."

Lane remembers a meeting with Ertegun to renegotiate the contract for Yes at which "Ahmet, as usual, was talking in twenty-one different languages on the phone." Finally Lane had "a brainwave," left the room, found another office, and made a telephone call—to Ertegun. "I said I had to talk to him in privacy," says Lane. Ertegun agreed to leave the maelstrom of the office and the two of them climbed into an Atlantic limousine.

"Ahmet said to me, 'You want privacy? I'll give you privacy.' So we got out to this seedy part of Broadway and into a shabby club where you paid a dime for a dance. Ahmet pulled out twenty dollars and bought dozens of tickets. All these horrible Puerto Rican women were sitting there eating tuna fish sandwiches. They jumped to attention and we started dancing with them, and renegotiated the contract. The only interruption was when Ahmet went over to the jukebox to play Atlantic records."

Despite Ertegun's bewildering methods of doing business Lane could not help but admire his shrewdness. "All the other labels at the time had pop acts," he says. "Ahmet Ertegun was astute enough to see a hole in the market, and fill it up with white rock."

Perhaps perversely, perhaps to underline the growing distance between the two partners, Jerry Wexler meanwhile looked for new studios in which to record the music *he* remained faithful to—and chose one even farther south than Memphis, in Muscle Shoals, Alabama.

Rick Hall, a local musician and songwriter, had set up Fame Studios in Muscle Shoals in 1961, and had begun building a nucleus of session musicians who were mainly southern whites, although they played rhythm and blues. Like Stax, Fame Studios produced its own unique sound, and by 1965 its reputation had reached as far as New York. In early 1966, Wexler decided to take Wilson Pickett to record at Fame.

For Pickett, who had escaped his southern childhood to become a super-cool city slicker, his first trip down to Muscle Shoals was a profound shock. "I looked down out the plane window," he told author Gerri Hirshey, "and I see black folks pickin' cotton, and I say 'Shit, turn this motherfuckin' plane around—ain't no way I'm goin' back there.'"

Even more perturbing was the sight of the large white man from Fame Studios who was waiting to meet him at the airport. "Looked just like the law. Looked mean. How did I know Jerry Wexler was gonna send me to some big white southern cat? Woulda never got on that plane"—which, as Pickett is the first to say, would have been the biggest mistake of his life. The "big white cat" was Rick Hall, who despite all appearances, had an exceptional feel for black soul music. In Pickett's words, Hall "made things grow down there. What happened was beautiful. I love Rick Hall—but I never would have believed any of it before it happened."

Pickett recorded two major hits for Atlantic in Muscle Shoals, and was followed there by a largely unknown soul singer named Percy Sledge who cut a song called "When a Man Loves a Woman"—and, practically overnight, scored a number-one hit in both the pop and R&B charts.

Then, in early 1967, Wexler took another new Atlantic signing to Muscle Shoals. Rick Hall did not know who she was, but he knew from Wexler's enthusiasm that something extraordinary was about to happen.

Aretha Franklin was born to the sound of gospel music. Her father was pastor of the New Bethel Baptist Church in Detroit and a nationally known gospel singer who recorded for Chess Records. After her mother deserted the family when Aretha was six years old, she was raised with the help of friends including legendary gospel singers Mahalia Jackson and Clara Ward. Singing—at home and in her father's church—was always part of Aretha's childhood. By the age of eight or nine she was singing solos in church, and at fourteen she made her first recording. By eighteen she had signed to Columbia Records in New York, and crossed over to secular music. But, having recognized her talent, the company had no real idea of what to do with it, keeping her soaring voice tightly leashed by Broadway show tunes and sentimental pop songs. In 1966 Columbia released Aretha from her disappointingly unsuccessful labor for them.

It was Jerry Wexler who knew exactly how to unleash her talent, and who moved quickly to sign her. He then took her to record in Muscle Shoals, where she arrived in January 1967 with her husband and manager, Ted White, who was taken aback to find that the band included white musicians. Initial unease quickly spilled over into loud arguments between White and Rick Hall but, despite the problems, the resulting session produced by Wexler created something electrifyingly exciting. Two weeks later Atlantic released the result: "I Never Loved a Man (the Way I Love You)." The record sold more than 250,000 copies within two weeks; shortly after it went gold. Franklin was instantly proclaimed Lady Soul and her second single, "Respect," reached number one—becoming an anthem for the rapidly growing black civil rights movement. She went on to make more than a dozen one-million sellers—more than any other woman in recording history.

But for all the euphoria surrounding Franklin's success, the relationship between Atlantic and Fame Studios ended on sour notes. After making her breakthrough record in Muscle Shoals, Franklin recorded all of her subsequent hits at Atlantic's studios, though sometimes with the aid of Fame Studio's horn section, which Wexler "borrowed" and transported to New York. Rick Hall regarded this appropriation of the Fame sound as a "betrayal" and it made him extremely angry. Meanwhile, Wexler angered Sonny Bono by insisting that Sonny and Cher drag down south to record in Muscle Shoals. "It was like a penicillin cure," says Bono. "We had to go to Muscle Shoals to get this rhythm section that could be discovered 'nowhere else on earth . . .' So we cut an album there and Jerry recorded it. It was horrible."

Looking back on this period—a period of turbulent transition for Atlantic—Wexler is fiercely (and rightly) proud of his achievements, and of the musical integrity he maintained. But there is a sour note for him, too: For all Wexler's efforts, for all the talent of his artists, despite the magic ingredients added by Stax and, later, Fame Studios, Atlantic never succeeded in breaking into the pop market on anything like the scale of Motown Records.

Throughout the 1960s Motown dominated popular soul music, producing more than 120 Top 20 hits. According to Wexler, that was because while Atlantic's black records appealed mainly to black adults, Motown—through "some unfathomable concatenation of circumstances"—sold, in enormous quantities, to both black and white teenagers. Motown's owner, Berry Gordy, Jr. (who founded the company in Detroit in 1959 with a $700 loan from his sister), churned out hits as proficiently as Detroit's assembly lines churned out cars.

And, for Wexler, there lies the rub. However superb the quality of the music he produced during that period, it was not his contribution that was crucial to Atlantic's success. As he says, in an argument he seems to go over and over in his mind, "Atlantic didn't get big on black music. It thrived on black music, and got healthy, but it didn't get large. It got large with rock—not rock and roll, but rock."

If the transition of Atlantic Records during the 1960s was uncomfortable for Wexler, for a singer like Ruth Brown it was humiliating.

These days Ruth Brown is a little more stout than she was when they called her "Miss Rhythm" but she is still winning new fans, and reminding old ones of her prowess, as she belts out songs in musicals based around newly fashionable R&B hits from thirty years ago. Backstage in New York's Lower East Side Theater, where she is rehearsing *Staggerlee*—in between recording a regular radio show—Brown recalls the day she realized the time had come for her to leave Atlantic: "Atlantic had moved to big offices in Columbus Circle [and] I sat out in the lobby waiting to see Ahmet. By that time it was a big conglomerate, and I sat outside for four hours. There were secretaries for secretaries, and you didn't get past the receptionist, and the door was closed, and everything was done on the intercom. Before, it was not that way: We went up in the little freight elevator, and opened the door and went in there, and sat down over a pizza to talk about what we were going to do . . . But I sat there for so long waiting, and people passed by, and I felt bruised . . . I may have been there that day to get money—very possibly. Things were not going so good at that time. I had my children and I was out on Long Island trying to raise them, and doing little jobs here and there. All of a sudden I thought, Well, they don't want to deal with me. And I realized that my days at Atlantic were numbered."

It is only with the passing of time that she has been able to rationalize what happened: "I realize now that it probably wasn't neglect; it was just they were plain busy. Atlantic had grown, and with that growth, their responsibilities overshadowed the time they had to give to me. Simple. And I was the oldest. So I guess they felt I was able to stand on my own—like in any family."

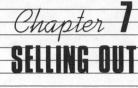

Chapter 7
SELLING OUT

J erry Wexler was determined to sell Atlantic Records. Ahmet Ertegun, on the other hand, had no desire whatsoever to sell. The discrepancy was as much due to the striking differences in the two men's characters as anything else. "I never think anything is going to work out—and I think that's better than being a smarmy optimist, walking around with a happy grin while the roof is falling in over your head," says Wexler. "Ravening fear was my motivator at Atlantic—that ran the engine for me." Ertegun, in total contrast, does not appear to know what fear is. As his old partner says, with a wry smile: "Ahmet had true courage and insouciance. You know, he's always been a devout practicing voluptuary. He really lived it—he gambled, took shots, and didn't worry about failure."

Wexler admits that his pessimism and deep-rooted insecurity were traits Ertegun simply could not understand. "Ahmet never had those feelings, or if he did he would never yield in the way I did," explains Wexler. "I had this feeling that a puff of wind could come along and blow us all away, instantly. All you had to do was make a succession of flop records, and you get blown away. The rewards were enormous—but so were the risks. [Atlantic was] like a little family corner store that used to be just plugging along with everybody very happy—it couldn't stay that way. It was either grow or disappear. And who's to predict? Everybody else disappeared."

Certainly, by the late 1960s, the future was looking extremely bleak for the few independent companies that still survived. In Chicago, Vee Jay Records had collapsed amid bitter litigation and Chess Records was in steep decline, while in New York Morris Levy had more or less retired—for now. "I bought a house in Miami Beach," says Levy laconically. "The most I had to do was walk round the pool, counting the times I walked round the pool, playing the stock market, fooling around with a few things. It got very boring."

Wexler, however, confesses that—his insecurity aside—he had a growing desire to enjoy the fruits of his labors. Walking around a pool and playing the stock market did not seem such a tedious prospect to him. "I wanted to sell because I wanted to cash in," says Wexler with a hint of defensiveness in his voice. "The American Dream—capital gains. It's a terrible thing for you to hear, right?"

As news of his inclination to sell began to filter through the industry Atlantic received various tentative approaches. It was all Ertegun could do to stop Wexler from accepting these offers instantly. "He wanted to sell it for half as much as we eventually sold it for," says Ertegun. "I mean, he just wanted to sell at almost any price because he was scared that doom was ahead. I don't know why he felt that. I guess he just wasn't confident that we could continue to make hits forever."

Wexler's fears were equally inexplicable to his assistant, Noreen Woods. "Ahmet did not want to sell the company, he absolutely did not want to sell. But Jerry Wexler wanted to. Isn't that amazing?—because the company was very successful. I think in his heart Jerry really thought that the company could collapse, that it would all just be gone. But there was no basis for that, no basis at all. We were on Fifty-seventh Street on the second floor, and we had just taken an extra floor of offices, and we had the studio. We were beginning to sign white artists and things were fine, absolutely fine."

According to the forthright Miriam Bienstock: "Jerry was always nervous. He was a worrier and he was hysterical." She says it was impossible for him to relax and simply enjoy the company's success. "It was doing well, but it was doing so well he thought it couldn't keep doing that well. And because it was doing well, we had increased our staff—we had sales managers, and secretaries, and people working in stock-rooms, and very big overheads. So he was afraid that if the record company went cold, all these overheads would re-main and everybody would be in a terrible situation. The only way he could perceive there would be any kind of secu-rity for him was to get a chunk of money and do something with it."

As far as Miriam was concerned, the last thing she wanted was for Atlantic to be sold. "I had a very big position at Atlan-tic, and I earned quite a lot of money for a woman at that time—unheard of. I felt if we sold to a large company they wouldn't need me. First of all, it would be integrated into whatever they were doing, which was beginning to get com-puterized. While Jerry and Ahmet would be essential to the company because they produced records, I was not in that situation—and I would be out."

But the fourth partner, Ahmet's brother Nesuhi Ertegun, eventually sided with Wexler and agreed that Atlantic should be sold. A calm, level-headed businessman, Nesuhi later ac-cepted that Atlantic would have survived as an independent company: "I think we would have got bigger and bigger, quite honestly," he said. But at the time he had "mixed feel-ings, very mixed feelings," and eventually found himself un-able to resist Wexler's arguments, however strenuously Ahmet objected. Since Wexler and Nesuhi between them held more stock in the company than Ahmet, Ertegun had no alternative but to capitulate. (Miriam had been bought out some three years before. "I was a minority shareholder," she says, "and as a minority shareholder there's really noth-ing much you can do. If somebody wants to buy you out, you make the best deal you possibly can.")

With the minority shareholders out of the way, the three remaining partners entered into complex negotiations with a number of suitors and, in October 1967, Atlantic Records was sold for $17.5 million. It was, in retrospect, a terrible deal.

First, as Sonny Bono puts it, "they sold the label way too cheap." Or, in Miriam Bienstock's words: "They didn't ask for enough. It was ridiculous, just ridiculous." She puts the primary blame on Wexler: "Jerry Wexler never could make a deal. He would always turn it over to the accountant and say, 'Is this a good deal, will this work out?' He never did it for himself and I think that was part of the reason they really did not do the best deal for themselves."

There appears to be some truth in that claim because Wexler—even now sounding disconsolate when he talks about that long-ago deal—says: "We had some Wall Street big shots come in to represent us and they did a horrible job. We wound up selling for about half what we should have got. Now how do you ever prove such a thing? You can't—but it's just a feeling I have that we should have held on. We sold it for seventeen and a half million when it was worth thirty-five million . . . I just have a feeling that our main negotiator was of a very low order of intelligence." It did not take long for the partners to realize they had sold themselves short. In the year after the takeover Atlantic achieved gross earnings of $45 million—thanks, in part, to the enormous success of Aretha Franklin's first album. In light of that, Wexler and Ertegun went to the new owners and offered $40 million to buy back Atlantic. Unsurprisingly, they were refused point-blank.

But, money aside, what made the takeover of Atlantic so extraordinary were the character and antecedents of the new owners, a Los Angeles–based company called Warner Seven-Arts. It might have looked respectable on paper but this Warner corporation was no longer the legendary Hollywood enterprise it had once been—nor was it yet the vast entertainment conglomerate it would become.

The movie studios of Warner Brothers had been in decline for the best part of a decade when Jack Warner, the last surviving founder, elected to sell his once-mighty empire to Seven-Arts, a small film distribution company. Joe Smith, then head of promotion for Warner Brothers Records, remembers the outrage and dismay he and his colleagues felt at the sale: "Seven-Arts! It was ridiculous. It was like the candy store buying the factory." It did not help matters that Seven-Arts was tainted by supposed links to the Mafia—because one of its original directors, Lew Chesler, was associated with mobster Meyer Lansky. Nor did it help that Seven-Arts' management knew nothing about the business of making movies and records, nor did it care. In Smith's words: "They were only in there to milk the company, only in there to get the stock price up and sell it." Few people could understand why, under those circumstances, Jack Warner had accepted the deal. Smith has a simple explanation: "Jack Warner was a very impulsive, egotistical man who decided one day that he was going to sell his company to the first guy who came along that could put together the financing. The man had to be over the hill to have made that decision."

The Seven-Arts management did not interfere with the Warner record division, though Smith still found it "kind of demeaning" working for "these people who didn't know or care much." The Warner film division was not so fortunate. "They destroyed the movie company; terrible deals," says Smith. Seven-Arts also refused to release Nicolas Roeg's film *Performance,* starring Mick Jagger as a reclusive rock star, apparently because the wife of one of the company's executives saw the movie at an early screening—and was appalled by it.

All of which made Seven-Arts a most unlikely candidate to take over Atlantic Records, which Ertegun and Wexler had built into one of the most respected labels in the industry. Ertegun certainly had no illusions about his new masters, or the company's chief executive, Elliot Hyman—whom Ertegun describes as "a businessman and wheeler-dealer of

The Ertegun brothers (Nesuhi *left,* Ahmet *center*) circa 1940, when they staged informal jazz concerts at the Turkish embassy in Washington, D.C. *(Courtesy of the Estate of Nesuhi Ertegun.)*

"Miss Rhythm," Ruth Brown, Atlantic's first female artist. *(Courtesy of Atlantic Records.)*

LaVern Baker, Atlantic R&B star of the 1950s. *(Courtesy of Atlantic Records.)*

Ray Charles, one of the originators of soul music, signed with Atlantic in 1952. *(Courtesy of Atlantic Records.)*

(Above left) Morris Levy at Birdland in the 1950s. *(Courtesy of Morris Levy.)*

(Above right) Ahmet Ertegun with his original partner in Atlantic Records, Herb Abramson, in the recording studio. *(Courtesy of Atlantic Records.)*

(Left to right) Jerry Wexler, Nesuhi Ertegun, Bobby Darin, and Ahmet Ertegun: Atlantic's three partners with their first white pop star. *(Courtesy of Atlantic Records.)*

Solomon Burke, the "King of Rock and
Soul," preacher, mortician, and Atlantic
star of the 1960s. *(Courtesy of Atlantic
Records.)*

Otis Redding, the Stax recording star who died in 1967. *(Courtesy
of Atlantic Records.)*

Jimmy Page, lead guitarist of Led Zeppelin, the highly successful rock group signed by Ertegun and Wexler in 1968. *(Courtesy of Atlantic Records.)*

The Rolling Stones, the "Greatest Rock-and-Roll Band in the World." *(Courtesy of Atlantic Records.)*

Genesis in the studio, after the departure of Peter Gabriel in 1974. *(Courtesy of Atlantic Records.)*

Foreigner, whose first album sold 5 million records worldwide for Atlantic in 1977. *(Courtesy of Atlantic Records.)*

(Above) Ertegun and Phil Collins, "one of the really good people," on the 1986/1987 Genesis tour. *(Courtesy of Atlantic Records.)*

(Right) Ertegun and Atlantic's first pop diva, Laura Branigan. *(Courtesy of Atlantic Records.)*

(Below) Ben E. King, lead singer of the Drifters in the 1960s and then solo artist who made a recent comeback with "Stand by Me." *(Courtesy of Atlantic Records.)*

Ertegun and Warner chairman Steve Ross *(right)* with their hero, the soccer player Pele. *(Courtesy of Atlantic Records.)*

Ertegun chats with Robert Plant—the former lead singer of Led Zeppelin—in 1988, Atlantic's fortieth anniversary. *(Courtesy of Atlantic Records.)*

Hard rock: Ertegun with AC/DC in 1988. *(Courtesy of Atlantic Records.)*

Ertegun with Michael Hutchence, the lead singer of Australian million-selling rock group INXS—one of Atlantic's most successful acts of the 1980s. *(Courtesy of Atlantic Records.)*

Ahmet Ertegun. *(Courtesy of Atlantic Records.)*

questionable reputation." Seven-Arts succeeded simply because it made the best offer. "There was nothing about Warner Seven-Arts that enchanted us," says Ertegun.

But, having lost the battle to prevent the takeover, Ertegun, with his customary sanguinity, determined to make the best of it. After less than two years he told Warner Seven-Arts that he and the rest of Atlantic's management would leave the company unless the original deal were renegotiated. "And, as the company did not have very much value without the management," says Ertegun calmly, "they had to re-sweeten the deal, so to speak." In effect, he explains with a certain understated glee, Seven-Arts virtually had to buy Atlantic all over again: "We almost sold it a second time."

Even so, Ertegun had no long-term plans to stay with Atlantic. "If Elliot Hyman had continued as head of the company, I probably wouldn't have stayed on," he says. In late 1968, however, it was Hyman and not Ertegun who quit. "He made his bunch," says Ertegun, pausing to choose his words carefully. Then: "How shall I put it? He ran off into the night."

The new owner of Warner Seven-Arts, and of Atlantic Records, was the Kinney Corporation—an enterprise that, in some ways, seemed no better qualified, and no more enchanting, than Seven-Arts. Kinney was the product of a merger between a string of New York funeral homes and a company that owned parking lots in Manhattan and it, too, had dubious past associations: The parking-lot business had been established by the son of a reputed mobster. Kinney's chief executive, however, was of a very different breed than Elliot Hyman.

Steve Ross, who was raised in Brooklyn and Manhattan, appears to have enjoyed an unremarkable childhood. He excelled at nothing in his high school years other than mathematics and football. After two years in the navy, he studied liberal arts at an obscure junior college in upstate New York and it was not until he married at the age of twenty that his life took on any clear direction. His wife, Carol Rosenthal, came from a Jewish family that owned the Riverside Memorial Chapel and several other funeral parlors, and Ross's father-in-law persuaded him to join the business. As he found the day-to-day work of funeral parlors an unappealing occupation, Ross concentrated on developing an offshoot of the business—the rental of the company's limousines to those other than mourners. Having made this a substantially profitable operation, Ross then did a deal with the Kinney System—New York's largest operator of parking lots—that resulted in the merger of the funeral parlors with the car rental and parking businesses, and he added an office-cleaning company run by another member of his wife's family. In June 1962 Ross took Kinney public and some of its shares were offered for sale on the New York Stock Exchange.

By 1966 Ross had acquired another cleaning contractor, and then expanded Kinney in new directions, buying a magazine distributor (National Periodical Publications) and a talent agency (Ashley-Famous). By this time, says Ross, "we had looked at many industries—and we decided that the entertainment industry really had a tremendous future."

A tall, silver-haired man, Ross looks less like a dynamic— and, some say, ruthless—corporate head than a friendly next-door neighbor who cooks barbecues on Sundays and takes his kids to the park to play softball. As he describes his company's rise to success, he takes the most laid-back position available to him in the plush office suite at the top of the Warner Communications tower in New York: Leaning back in his chair so far he is in danger of toppling over, Ross stretches out even further by putting his feet up on the gleaming mahogany boardroom table. The entertainment company he had set his heart on was Warner Seven-Arts but contrary to popular belief, he explains, it was the record companies that attracted him rather than the film division. "As a matter of fact, in the late sixties the movie industry was in dire straits," he says. "It was really in a terrible shape and we weren't sure if there was a business called the motion picture business." The Warner film library, and valuable real estate the company owned, made the asking price for Warner Seven-Arts reasonable—*if* Kinney could gain complete control of the Warner record division, and *if* Ahmet Ertegun could be persuaded to remain on board at Atlantic.

The problem facing Ross at the Warner record division was a legacy left by Jack Warner who, in 1963, had bought two-thirds of Frank Sinatra's Reprise Records—and sold Sinatra one-third of Warner Brothers Records. The negotiations to unscramble that deal were, says Ross, "unbelievable." He laughs when he remembers the deal-making at its Machiavellian height: "In the middle of the discussions with Sinatra I met his financial adviser—a wonderful lawyer named Mickey Rudin—and in the middle of my negotiations with Mickey he developed total laryngitis, and I was afraid that he was taking advantage of me. We entered La Reine [a Los Angeles restaurant] and we were negotiating the deal in a private room, and we were passing paper napkins back and forth to each other. Neither one of us had a pad, and Mickey would write on a paper napkin. I didn't want him to have an advantage over me in time to think so I would respond on a paper napkin. Those paper napkins are part of our files."

Having clinched the paper napkin deal, by agreeing on terms to buy out Sinatra, Ross then faced the task of persuading Ertegun to stay on as head of Atlantic—a task that promised to be much more formidable. "I knew they had a great roster," says Ross, "but my homework said they had fantastic management, especially Ahmet Ertegun—he was a star." The trouble was, Ertegun had had enough of running a company owned by other people who knew nothing about music. As Ross himself admits: "I certainly didn't understand the music of that time—not that I pretend to understand all of it today—but I certainly didn't understand any of it then."

As Ross became more determined to acquire Warner Seven-Arts, Ertegun—who had not yet met the Kinney executives—became all the more adamant he was going to leave.

"Then while we were trying to close the deal, friends of mine came to visit me and they brought their young son," says Ross. "I guess he was around eleven or twelve years old, and he said, 'Gee, Steve, I think it's great you're acquiring Warner Seven-Arts. You know it has a record company called Atlantic Records. They're really fantastic, and it's run by Ahmet Ertegun, a fantastic fellow. Have you met him?' I said 'No,' and he said, 'Well you've got to meet him because they've just put together a group called Blind Faith. That's Stevie Winwood on the organ, plus the old Cream, and they haven't cut a record yet, but they've sold out Madison Square Garden. Isn't that fantastic?' I didn't have the faintest idea what the kid was talking about, but I said, 'Yes, yes, fantastic.'

"Then a couple of weeks pass and I get word on the grapevine that Ahmet Ertegun really wants to quit—how could someone from a totally foreign business ever understand his business? So he didn't want any part of it—he'd just as soon quit. And when I heard that, I said, 'Gee, if he quits I don't want the company.' We really didn't want to go ahead with the acquisition unless he was staying. I didn't want a record company without management—that was the last thing we needed.

"So, to make a long story short, I called Ahmet and introduced myself to him over the phone and said would he have dinner with Ted Ashley, my associate, and me? He said, 'I'd be glad to, but I want you to know that I'm really not interested in going ahead with the deal.'" The dinner took place at a fashionable Manhattan restaurant, 21, but however congenial the surroundings, after almost six hours of attempted persuasion Ross had got no closer to convincing Ertegun to stay on.

"We'd been discussing how I would let him do his thing," says Ross. "I wouldn't interfere with him, and I wouldn't expect him to interfere with me. We could—please excuse the pun—make beautiful music together if we both stuck to that rule. I told him I had no desire to pick artists—I don't want to self-destruct. That's why I want him to do his thing and he can be left alone, and I'll be busy trying to turn around the motion picture company—if that's possible—and doing ten other things. But apparently that's what the Seven-Arts people had told him too—and that didn't work out too well. At any event, it's now about quarter to one, and Ahmet said, 'Let me just show you how you don't, or never will be able to, understand our business. We have a group called Blind Faith . . .'

"I think: Oh my God, Ross, if you can think, think now— what did that kid tell you? And I say, 'You mean Stevie Winwood on the organ, plus the old Cream, and you haven't got a record but you've sold out Madison Square Garden?'

"And Ahmet says, 'Yeah, yeah—that's it.' And Ted Ashley almost goes over his chair in a dead faint. I say, 'I think that's fantastic,' and Ahmet says, 'You're really good.' I say, 'Well, there it is.'

"So we made the deal right there. That was it. Needless to say, our young fellow who told me about Blind Faith has been on our mailing list for records ever since. And it took me about three or four years to tell Ahmet the truth. Naturally, he just roared with laughter." But in the interim, while the myth was still maintained, Ertegun would often telephone Ross to tell him of exciting groups he was about to sign: "I would say, 'Hold on, Ahmet, I've got to call you back, I'm on a long-distance call'—and then I'd try to find my kids to fill me in and tell me about the group."

In the twenty years since then Ross has remained extravagantly admiring of Ertegun, describing his decision to stay on as head of Atlantic as "one of the luckiest days of my life." Though he may not always understand what Ertegun is doing twenty-seven floors below him in the Warner Communications tower—in the somewhat shabby Atlantic offices where old-time Broadway hustlers mingle with long-haired heavy metal enthusiasts—Ross obviously trusts him implicitly. "I think it's been a wonderful association," says Ross. "We both stayed true to our word: I did my thing and he did his. We believe in strict autonomy."

Ertegun, who is usually less given to such high praise than Ross, returns the tribute: "The only reason I'm here is because of Steve Ross, because I would have been long gone with the previous group. But Steve Ross has lived up to everything he ever said, and has given me total autonomy. Of all the people I have ever worked with I have not known anyone that is as true to his word as Steve Ross. Ross has never criticized. We have made errors where the company lost money and I waited to hear from upstairs—but nothing. But whenever we did something good, I got a terrific telephone call or a visit from Steve to congratulate me. He has always been very supportive—whenever I needed help he has always been there."

Despite this mutual and unbridled enthusiasm for the new setup, there were some people at Atlantic who were far more ambivalent about the label's absorption into what would become the Warner Communications conglomerate. Francine Wakschal, who had joined the company as its first employee in 1949, found the changes more than a little disturbing. She had left the office in 1960 to raise her family but continued working from home, until she returned nine years later, just after the Kinney takeover, to work in the rapidly expanding foreign royalties department. Having previously been used to chatting to artists as they wandered in and out of Atlantic's small offices, she found no trace of that cozy intimacy at Warner Communications: The business affairs of the company were now kept strictly separate from the creative side, and security men and receptionists ensured that everyone was kept in their proper place. "When I came back in 1969 it was like a different company," she says, sitting in her windowless office in the Warner Communications tower block in Rockefeller Plaza. "It was strange. They had really grown . . . It didn't make a difference that it was owned by somebody else, change was inevitable. It was too big to have the same kind of closeness."

The ebullient soul singer Solomon Burke also felt the cold wind of change in the Atlantic corridors—and he left the label in 1969. "It was the age of computers and the age of fancy bookkeepers. The system changed. And when the system changes, the spirit changes. And when the spirit changes . . . it's very, very simple. It wasn't a family affair anymore. That family feeling wasn't there."

For Jerry Wexler the changes at Atlantic were even more confusing. Wexler soon discovered the sale he had pushed so hard for did not make him happy. "I'd be the first to admit that after we sold the company a lot of the steam went out of me, especially as regards the business part," he says. Yet, though he desperately wanted to stop worrying about the business, and unwind, he found he simply could not bear to relinquish all of his control over Atlantic.

Miriam Bienstock was not in the least surprised that Wexler found the experience traumatic: "Jerry was a very compulsive person. He'd be on the telephone day and night, talking to people night and day—disc jockeys and distributors, talk, talk, talk. It was such an extreme. He just could not stop doing it."

And according to Jerry Greenberg, who was hired as an assistant to Wexler in 1967: "This man was a workaholic. He was in there at eight in the morning until nine at night. I was a young boy but I used to think, I don't know how this guy does it. He would get in first thing in the morning, do his desk work until one, and then go down to the studio, which was right down the hall, and he would have the whole rhythm section flown up from Memphis, record Aretha Franklin until seven or eight at night, come out at eight, finish making his calls, go through his mail, and then go home at ten—and then start all over again.

"I told people that working next to him was like going to the best law school if you wanted to be a lawyer, or to the best medical school if you wanted to be a doctor. I used to say it was like going to Parris Island and joining the U.S. Marines: You either lived and you came out a man and you were a sergeant—or they found you floating in the alligator swamps somewhere because you were dead."

Wexler himself admits—with characteristic self-aware-ness—that when he was building Atlantic into a powerful independent company, work came before anything else in his life. "It probably ruined my marriage—I was a rotten fa-ther and a bad husband—but I was obsessed, totally obsessed with making it. I was committed to the company, I had an obligation to my partners and, furthermore, it was red hot and I loved it."

Once Atlantic had been sold, and Wexler could afford to relax, he was caught in a trap of his own making: Having thought he wanted to let go, he was irked to discover that the company had become too big for him to control. That realiza-tion was very hard for him to accept, given his dominance in the past. "We ran the company as the utmost despots," says Wexler. "We were absolutely despotic. We had to be into everything—especially me. I had to know everything that was going on. I had to know everybody's job—what they were doing, and how they were doing it.

"And it got to the point when that couldn't be done any-more because we had a larger and larger staff. I don't think I was cut out to be a really great executive because I never had any reliance on delegating authority. In other words, my mo-tivation is the exact opposite to what you read in books on the successful executive. Mine was based on the divine disbelief of everybody but me. I either had to do it myself, or check on it to see if they did it correctly—which was my way.

"Where it got to the point where that obviously couldn't work anymore, where it didn't wash, it got so big—then I think I just lost the handle. I couldn't believe that meetings were going on with staff personnel making decisions—for ex-ample, on advertising disbursements, or promotional budg-ets, or tour support—that I didn't have my thumbprint on. And I started seeing people in the halls whose names I didn't know. It was sort of the beginning of the end for me."

The increasing anonymity of the company was bad

enough, but Wexler was also alienated by the white rock acts that were more and more the basis of Atlantic's profits and success. He appears to have regarded them, at best, as a necessary evil. So, for example, though Wexler did sign Led Zeppelin to the label, "I didn't go into the studio with them. I never went into the studio with anyone I didn't like." To make matters even worse, the artists he *did* like, such as Ben E. King and Solomon Burke, left Atlantic as their record sales slowed to a trickle. King remained philosophical, going out onto the cabaret circuit to make a living by playing to faithful fans in small clubs and hotels. "It was just a sign of the times really," he says. "You cannot take it oh-so-seriously. You have to accept that you are not going to stay on top forever." But for Solomon Burke, the King of Rock and Soul, it was an outrageous insult to be pushed out of the charts—and, indeed, out of Atlantic—by scruffy young boys from England who played a watered-down version of R&B. "To walk on stage in a pair of sneakers and a pair of jeans with a hole in them, and a T-shirt, and get seventy-five thousand dollars a night—it takes me a very long time to understand that," says Burke, who takes great care to look resplendent at all times.

Similarly, Wexler found the success of Atlantic's new white artists both irritating and inexplicable, and dubbed them "the rockoids." A rockoid, he says dismissively, is "a creature who originally had hair down to his ass and an out-of-tune guitar, and for some reason got himself a million dollars by twanging away on the guitar. Suddenly, he's affected with delusions of mediocrity. Ahmet can put up with the antics of the rockoids—but I can't handle the rockoids. I'm just not geared that way. Ahmet would always go to the concerts, but I would never go. He'd say, 'Yes is at Madison Square Garden,' or 'Show up at the Zeppelin concert.' I'd just say, 'Ahmet, you go, and I'll stay with the people I'm handling.' "

To some onlookers, a certain confusion became apparent in Wexler's demeanor. According to Sonny Bono: "He went from being the administrator at the label to being this hippie A&R man." In the end, Wexler decided the best thing to do was get away from New York, with all its conflicts and tensions, and move to Miami. "The idea was I could go south and have a boat in my backyard," he explains. "It was time to go—we didn't own the company anymore." Nevertheless, he still expected to run the business, though quite how was unclear: "I don't know what I had in mind—I thought I could phone it in."

For those who knew him, Wexler's departure from New York was a startling decision. Solomon Burke thought it "unbelievable" and Noreen Woods, Wexler's personal assistant, was just as taken aback: "He was involved in every facet of this business. He had to know everything that was going on—and he did at one point. That's why it was such a shock when he just picked up and went to Florida. There were times when you couldn't even get him on the phone."

Perhaps just as surprising was the fact that once Wexler left New York, Ertegun—who had always studiously avoided the day-to-day running of the business—firmly took over the reins of control. As Sonny Bono remarks laconically, "Ahmet always could switch grooves."

It is difficult to know whether Wexler resented this dramatic change in the status quo because his attitude toward Ertegun is a very ambivalent one. Miriam Bienstock believes Wexler—whether consciously or not—had used his control and knowledge of the day-to-day affairs of Atlantic as a weapon against Ertegun whenever it came to disagreements between the two of them. Wexler himself remains reticent on the subject, merely pointing out that Ertegun's increasing involvement in the company's business was a remarkable volte-face: "It's not that Ahmet didn't contribute before—he did more than contribute. It's just that I'd be there during the daytime, and then Ahmet would come in—and we'd both be there at night making records." But Wexler does admit there was, in reality, no way he could continue to run the company once he moved to Florida: "I imagined I could phone it in; it didn't work. Somehow, Ahmet picked up the thing. He jumped in, and made a complete turnaround . . . He got totally into the daily affairs of the company."

With Wexler in Florida, and Miriam Bienstock gone from the company, there were few people left from the early days of Atlantic to witness at firsthand the changes caused by the takeover. Perhaps the most observant of the survivors was Tom Dowd, the producer, who had been with the label even longer than Wexler. He, too, had ambivalent feelings about the sale of the company, and about the inevitable changes that followed. On the one hand, he maintains that Atlantic remained as creative as it ever was. But he also says: "A year after the Warner deal went through I said to my staff, 'In ten years' time it's going to be like working for a library here, or being in a public school with beige walls everywhere.' The minute it became institutionalized, you could see institutionalism set in."

But Dowd only fully realized the profound nature of what had happened the day he waited for an elevator with Ertegun. "Atlantic is going to change," said Dowd. "Tom," replied Ertegun, "Atlantic has got so big it wouldn't matter if you and I died—there would still be an Atlantic."

Chapter 8
MAYHEM IN MIAMI, MURDER IN MEMPHIS

Jerry Wexler's dream of peace and tranquility in Florida—balmy days spent fishing and messing about in his boat, a reward for the years of toil in New York—was short-lived. Soon after his move to an airy house on an island off Miami Beach, events took place which not only disturbed the peaceful tenor of his life but profoundly changed his relationship with the record business. And in far-reaching ways, the record business itself was transformed. It was a rude awakening for all concerned.

In August 1968 disc jockeys, promotion men, and record company executives from all over America attended a convention in Miami. Ostensibly it was just another conference in the endless round of junkets that punctuate the music industry year: eagerly awaited occasions to eat and drink, do deals, and swap tall tales. Organized by the National Association of Television and Radio Announcers (NATRA), this convention, held at the Sheraton Four Ambassadors Hotel, was designed specifically to promote contact between black radio announcers and the rest of the industry.

A large contingent from Atlantic Records was in attendance, including Wexler; Dickie Kline, Wexler's new protégé in Atlantic's promotion department; Juggie Gales, a tiny but tough promotion man—who at the age of eighty is still a regular sight at conventions, with a rucksack of records slung over his shoulder; and Atlantic artists such as Aretha Franklin and King Curtis. Stax and Motown, the two largest black record companies of the era, were each the hosts of sumptuous parties.

Leaders from the black civil rights movement, such as Jesse Jackson and Coretta Scott King (widow of Martin Luther King), were in attendance, underlining the close existing links between soul music and the followers of King, who had been assassinated in Memphis just four months before. Their particular interest in the gathering lay in one of the stated aims of NATRA: to promote jobs for black people in a white-dominated industry which nevertheless depended on black artistry for its inspiration—and, some would say, for its very existence. Jesse Jackson already had extensive links with the music business. He had become friendly with the Ertegun brothers when he canvassed Atlantic to donate money and clout to help the black community. The Erteguns, who had espoused liberal causes since the days when they organized the first nonsegregated jazz concerts in Washington, D.C., usually complied. "Jesse Jackson had made a lot of demands that we should do more for the community, which I think was quite right," says Ahmet. "We've given money to PUSH [People United to Serve Humanity, Jackson's charitable organization in Chicago], to the United Negro College Fund, and to various other black organizations. Jesse Jackson has been very supportive and very fair."

On the first night of the convention, Wexler arrived at the Bayfront Auditorium to attend a dinner at which he was to receive two awards for his achievements as an R&B producer at Atlantic Records. But before the ceremony could begin, Wexler was given an urgent and chilling message: A man had turned up with a gun, at the auditorium, saying, "I'm looking for Wexler." Wexler was quickly hustled out of the building by King Curtis, who took him home to Miami Beach. Shirley Wexler, his wife, remembers pacing up and down anxiously that night as Jerry kept insisting he should go to the convention hotel to look for Aretha Franklin, who was drinking heavily and causing Wexler concern.

Marshall Sehorn, an R&B entrepreneur from New Orleans and the first white partner in a black record company (Fury Records, based in New York), had an even more frightening experience. Having gone up to his nineteenth-floor suite at the Sheraton Hotel for a wash before dinner, Sehorn bolted the suite door and went into the bathroom to take a shower. He was careful to leave the gun he thought it necessary to carry in its holster on a chair in the bedroom, in such a position that he could see it from the shower. He was washing himself when he looked at the chair and saw to his horror that the gun was no longer there. Desperately wondering what to do, he remained in the shower for a few moments, as if nothing had happened.

When Sehorn finally stepped out, he said, "What can I help you fellows with?" Four men came into the bathroom "looking like big brutes and grizzly bears," says Sehorn. One of them told him, "You have robbed your last black man. We don't want any more white niggers." Walking up to him, another grabbed Sehorn's testicles and twisted them, saying, "This is for all the black girls you ever screwed." A considerable beating followed and Sehorn was left lying unconscious on the floor.

The next thing he remembers is coming to in a hospital bed. It was apparent to Sehorn that his assailants did not want him to attend the awards ceremony (which was, effectively, the same message delivered to Wexler). But as Sehorn lay in bed he received a telephone call from someone he will describe only as "an anonymous person in New York," telling him there were two men outside his door waiting to accompany him to the awards ceremony. Many of those who were party to these events say the call was made by Morris Levy. Whoever it was, they were sufficiently powerful to ensure Sehorn's safety.

Sehorn arrived at the awards ceremony, flanked by "two Italian buddies," to find that his fellow dinner guests gathering in the auditorium were doing their best to ignore the subtly menacing atmosphere of the event. Dickie Kline of

Atlantic decided the best thing to do was "just look straight in front of you and mind your own business." But he found it impossible to ignore the signs of confrontation that night: "There was blood on the floor in certain places. I was told the place was inundated with FBI who had been called because of the threats. Security was very heavy."

The veneer of normality gave the evening's proceedings a surreal air. "The night went off very well—everything went the way it was supposed to," says Kline. "But you could cut the air with a knife, it was so thick. It was a very heavy event."

At first nobody was sure what was happening, but, as the evening progressed, it emerged that a group of blacks loosely related to the music business, who called themselves the Fairplay Committee, had decided to take over the function from NATRA. By all accounts the Fairplay Committee had commendable aims—to get a better deal for blacks in the music business—but it was made up of an intimidating group of people. According to Kline: "Someone said that if they weren't allowed to speak that night there were going to be guns going off. And there were a lot of guns at the hotel that night, and there were a lot of guns at the Bayfront Auditorium." Interlopers thronged the platform at the awards ceremony and the bona-fide organizers of the convention were pushed aside by their more militant brethren. "I don't think Del Shields [the organizer of NATRA] was there anymore," says Kline. "Del tried to put up a fight and was definitely pushed into a corner."

A regional promotion man from Atlantic named Leroy Little, Sr., collected the award on Wexler's behalf. But the fact that Leroy Little was black did not satisfy the Fairplay Committee. One of its members said, "Anyone that works for Atlantic Records is not welcome at any black radio station." As the night's celebrations continued, Wexler was hanged in effigy.

The next day the atmosphere of fear grew worse. Marshall Sehorn fled to New Orleans, accompanied by an FBI agent.

And rumor spread throughout the convention hall that Al Bell—the personable one-time deejay who was reviving the fortunes of Stax Records—had been beaten, "kidnapped," and taken out to sea in a boat; being black, it seemed, did not make him immune from the attentions of the Fairplay Committee. Nothing was heard or seen of Bell for several weeks. Those who knew him speculated that during his disappearance Bell was threatened with awful repercussions by the Fairplay Committee unless he bent to its will. Today, Bell laughs long and heartily at this suggestion: He had, he says, merely stayed out of the way in another hotel in Miami Beach—relaxing, fishing, and listening to music. He asserts that nobody would dare to strong-arm Al Bell: "I'm not one— if you look at my stature and if you listen to me—I'm not one you'd really want to apply pressure to unless you were prepared to defend your position. I may be soft-spoken and all that, but it doesn't mean that I'm a cream puff."

But Bell's associates from Stax Records say that he is dissimulating—that even today he does not want to reveal what really happened to him. "We saved Al Bell's life," says Steve Cropper (the Stax session guitarist who was one of the most important contributors to the "Memphis sound"). "He got major threats on his life. We had to hide him out on the ocean for a while." Cropper's perception is that Stax, and Atlantic, were the major targets of the threats. Booker T. Jones (Cropper's musical collaborator at Stax) was warned by the Fairplay Committee he should not be playing in a mixed black and white band. All of Stax's principal players who were at the Miami convention were forced into hiding. Security guards were hired to stand sentry at the doors of empty hotel rooms, in some attempt to confuse the hoodlums.

Although the major protagonists in these events are reluctant to talk about them, even twenty years later, speculation about the identity and motivation of the members of the Fairplay Committee is still a matter of lively interest in the industry.

According to Wexler: "The people who came to the fore

were con men, street-smart guys, extortionists, and rack-eteers." According to Dickie Kline: "It was a street gang, moved out of Harlem. They had picked up on all Del Shield's good causes—Del Shield was a good man and his organiza-tion had a viable reason to exist. There were things happen-ing that had to be corrected—jockeys that were underpaid and should have had some sort of relationship going with other people so they could move from market to market. And there was definitely room for interplay between music people and disc jockeys; there was room to have a party, and a dinner, and discussion, and not feel intimidated in any way."

Marshall Schorn ventures that the main aim of the Fair-play Committee was to become the prime collector of payola for all black disc jockeys. If, for example, Atlantic wanted its records played on all the black radio stations in the country, Wexler would have to hand over the cash to an appointed Fairplay Committee member—or else see Atlantic boycot-ted by all the black stations. Sehorn believes he earned his beating by standing up at a meeting and telling the commit-tee members their plan was crazy and would never work: A typical deejay in New York received more payola than one in Pittsburgh, and he would never agree to have his earnings pooled. At the end of the day, says Sehorn, "their plan back-fired."

Did it? And who were the members of the Fairplay Com-mittee who, for a while, captured the complete attention of the movers and shakers of the music industry?

Dino "Boom Boom" Woodward now lives a life of seclusion as an "associate minister" of the Baptist Abyssinian Church, an obscure institution tucked away in a Harlem side street. Arriving for the day's work with an egg sandwich and a plas-tic cup of coffee, Boom Boom seems a most unorthodox minister. He wears a fedora angled over one eye, a smart double-breasted suit, and scuffed shoes. His fingers are as wide as sausages, and his face bears all the traces of his former career—sparring partner to the one-time world boxing champion Sugar Ray Robinson. Punch drunk, he often loses grasp of a word he is searching for and replaces it with "Boom!" or "Zap, hey, boom!"

These days Boom Boom is studying for his master's degree in divinity but he still looks forward to the time when he will once again take up cudgels for black artists in the music business. Boom Boom says that, as Jesus demonstrated when he threw the moneylenders out of the temple and kicked over their tables, physical force in a good cause is justifiable, even for a man of the cloth.

Boom Boom was one of the founding members of the Fairplay Committee, along with his great and late friend, Johnny Baylor, who set up the committee in 1959. Baylor, like other members of this vigilante group, had no direct involvement in the music business at the time but he and Boom Boom used to hang out at Sugar Ray's nightclub and made friends with several black disc jockeys and artists who complained about their treatment at the hands of record companies. Jazz trumpeter Miles Davis was one such friend; Boom Boom used to box with him every day at the Broadway Gym, with Davis wearing a special face guard in the ring to protect his valuable lips.

At first Baylor and Boom Boom ran an informal system of help for black artists. "Like if people had a problem, we would try to stand up for them," says Boom Boom proudly. "We would go to certain radio stations who refused to play R&B records, and demand that they be played." Boom Boom also worked as security guard for a famous R&B disc jockey named Reggie LaVaughn, but he is unclear how Baylor earned his living. "He would just advise people. And he had some funds coming in to him. I guess for part of his life he could have been a gambler, you know what I mean?"

The Fairplay Committee brought thirty or forty people together in New York, and in other parts of the country, to systematically fight black exploitation in the record business. Boom Boom suggests they were trying to form a black "family" who would oppose the "families" he claims already controlled the music business. "You talk about the established families . . . say, Frankie Mavaratti [an alleged New York mobster]. He picks up the phone and makes his connection to big guys in Washington and sorts things out, boom! We felt we had got to be able to speak up for our people and demand certain things and make sure they happened," says Boom Boom, who is endearingly frank.

Inevitably, the original "families" did not like the new family and hurried meetings were held at the Turf Club on Broadway in New York City to seek some accommodation between them. It suited both sides to come to an arrangement, according to Boom Boom: "They didn't want no action, because it was going to reveal their hole-card. The same way as they had killers, other people had killers, too. So nobody wanted to cause a war."

Morris Levy—who had abandoned the idle life in Florida, and whose fortunes in the record business had been revived by the success of Tommy James and the Shondells—was one of those who objected to visits from Fairplay Committee members complaining about his cavalier treatment of black artists both past and present. Today Levy shrugs off the threat as pitiful: "They never bothered me. They didn't threaten me. They knew how I would react." But at the time Levy recruited to the payroll of Roulette Records Nat McCalla, one of the first blacks ever to be admitted to the ranks of the Italian Mafia—just in case the new upstart "family" decided to get smart.

According to Boom Boom, Atlantic Records—the main target of the intimidation in Miami—took the more conservative route of acceding to the Fairplay Committee's financial demands. "At least Ertegun and Wexler came up with some funds to help out with some things," says Boom Boom. Part of the money was used to keep the Fairplay Committee on the road, "to help us to stay around, so we could travel around," says Boom Boom, smiling happily at the memory of such munificence.

According to a black record producer who was present at the Miami convention, the committee's demands were sometimes hard to satisfy: "The first check Wexler gave them, they wouldn't accept. I think they made him tear it up and write another one. I think they made him keep on writing until the third check [and] they were satisfied with the amount." Demands for money were also made to Al Bell of Stax. Nobody knows whether or not he complied (and he will not say), but many at Stax believe the Fairplay Committee had a powerful hold on Bell.

The attitude of black artists to their self-proclaimed saviors was mixed. Booker T. Jones simply shrugged off the warnings he received about not playing with white musicians. To Jerry Williams—a black singer, writer, and producer who now goes by the more colorful name of Swamp Dogg—the activities of the Fairplay Committee posed a dilemma. White entrepreneurs might have been united in their condemnation of the militant language and unbridled violence unleashed at Miami but Swamp Dogg, like many others, was in sympathy with the committee's aims—even if he was ambivalent about its methods. He describes the disruption of the Miami convention as "a great idea that was rowdy and disorganized."

But, as Swamp Dogg admits, the Fairplay Committee's very existence was useful to him and other black artists. After years of feeling exploited by the record companies, and being powerless to fight back, black singers and songwriters suddenly had some leverage. As a result many black artists ignored their own doubts about the committee's methods and jumped onto the bandwagon. "One thing it did, it made a lot of blacks in the record industry end up with five dollars when they would have ended up with only one," says Swamp Dogg. "There were a lot of record companies that were hanging on to money. And then the Fairplay Committee showed up, and Johnny Baylor started passing the word around and started visiting distributors and so forth, and the distributors' attitude was 'I would rather overpay than underpay.' Another thing they did: You could mention the name and all of a sudden the doors would swing open. You could say, 'I'll get the Fairplay Committee to come up here and then we will see . . .' Right away it would be, 'Now come on, sit down, let's see what we can do.' "

Eventually Swamp Dogg decided this sort of coercion could do as much harm as good. "Right away everybody became a junior bully. It was bad. It didn't really help," he says, as though regretting some instance of youthful excess.

In this time of upheaval in the record industry, Atlantic Records in particular came onto the firing line as a company that had built its success on black music. While its executives—the Turkish Erteguns and the distinctly Jewish Wexler—could never be accused of being rednecks (as a Southerner like Marshall Sehorn could be and was), nevertheless they were white and most of their producers were white. Swamp Dogg says: "Atlantic Records was getting a lot of hits off black artists, and they started getting pressure from black groups because everything was black *except* Jerry, Nesuhi, and Ahmet. They didn't have a black staff producer."

Anxious to avoid this unwelcome focus on their company—particularly after the events in Miami—Wexler and Ertegun decided to hire Swamp Dogg. He was under no illusions that his appointment came about as a result of his own eccentric talents (which the world later witnessed on idiosyncratic albums such as *Rat On,* whose cover featured the artist astride a large white rat). He believes he was hired as a direct result of pressure from the Fairplay Committee. "That kind of pressure would make you hire someone—it would make you marry someone black," says Swamp Dogg.

Accordingly, when Swamp Dogg arrived at Atlantic to take up his new post as a staff producer, it was not long before he discovered he was little more than a "token black." He went in fired with enthusiasm for the chance to record some of the label's legendary R&B acts. Choosing Patti LaBelle, Sea and the Shells, and a few others from a long list Atlantic presented to him, he was horrified to discover that the remaining acts on the list were then dropped from Atlantic; Swamp Dogg had been given the "drop roster."

Further disillusionment came swiftly. Once Swamp Dogg had recorded the first batch of artists, there was little else for him to do. "I recorded them very fast. I had so much creativity in me and it was gushing out, and I would look around and I didn't have anything to do. I was running around asking all these questions: 'Why can't I do anything? Why are you paying me? Don't you want me here?' " So, when Wexler asked him if he wanted to record Aretha Franklin, he was more than delighted—but knew there had to be a catch. There was. Swamp Dogg learned he would not be entitled to the by-now-customary producer's royalty of 1 percent. Why not? Because Aretha Franklin was "guaranteed sales." Swamp Dogg decided to salvage his pride, he says, and forgo the chance to produce the legendary singer.

Swamp Dogg never felt welcome at Atlantic. Perhaps that stemmed from his own restless individualism (he has recorded for nearly every record label and never stayed put for long). Perhaps it was, as he suggests, the cutthroat office politics of Atlantic. Either way, it did not help matters that he used to stand in the lobby waiting to be buzzed in, and was never given his own desk and chair.

"They were all right to work for, it was just I wasn't ready for office politics. I didn't know that I was supposed to go in and back-stab, and do all kinds of things. I found myself caught up in it and all of a sudden, after about four months, I was given the honor of having my own restroom key. Before that, I'd used Tom Dowd's. It was almost like you wore your restroom key as a badge of merit."

Atlantic's hothouse atmosphere soon took its toll on Swamp Dogg's nerves. He began to overspend on his recording budgets, driving Cadillacs and living lavishly at the most expensive hotels. Eventually, and to his relief, he was fired by

Atlantic's financial controller, Sheldon Vogel (an extremely tough accountant brought into the company by Ertegun; Vogel relaxes on weekends by indulging in dangerous pastimes such as shooting rapids). Swamp Dogg later learned from Wexler that it was he who had instigated Swamp Dogg's dismissal, as a favor. "Man, I told Sheldon to fire you because it was the greatest thing for you," said Wexler. "And it was," says Swamp Dogg. "I would have turned into an alcoholic there because I found all I had to do was go downstairs and drink martinis, and go back up and talk shit—and nobody really cared when I was up there and when I was gone. I was just a pawn there . . . to keep off the black pressure groups."

To this day Jerry Wexler can hardly bear to talk about the treatment meted out to him by the Fairplay Committee. Instead of being lauded for a lifetime's achievement in the field of black music, he was branded as an exploiter who used and abused black musicians. Dickie Kline, who was close to Wexler at the time, remembers the pain these events caused: "Jerry was crushed because he was one of the most liberal of people. He was a free-thinking man who believed so much in equality, he was crushed this could happen to him in black music, which was his whole life at the time. He was a man who fought for equality for all men . . . and now he was singled out as an Uncle Tom, so to speak, for using people. Wexler did not use people. Jerry tried to work with the people, to help the people."

Kline believes what happened at the Miami convention had a direct and damaging effect on the record industry because it provoked new segregation in music. After Miami the industry slowly returned to the Dark Ages of before Alan Freed, when white radio played only pop music and black radio played only black music. In response to the demands of the Fairplay Committee, and more moderate groups such as the National Association for the Advancement of Colored People, record companies set up separate R&B departments, employing black promotion men to deal with black disc jockeys at black radio stations. In the pop department, which usually commanded far more money and resources, white promotion men spoke to white disc jockeys at white radio stations.

Atlantic Records, according to Ertegun, did not intend to segregate black and white music within the company but, gradually, a black department evolved as a result of demands made by Atlantic's black staff—demands fueled by the Fairplay Committee. Ertegun says, "It was partly a cause for all these departments becoming black and, of course, civil rights people say that's a good thing because it gave a lot of black people jobs. I think that's a shortsighted view because our ultimate aim is to have black people in 'white' jobs, and white people in 'black' jobs—to have no discrimination of any kind. That might be an ideal that is not around the corner—although I think we're not far from it; we're approaching it." As things were, however, segregation became re-entrenched, sometimes with unexpected results. At Atlantic, for example, Henry Allen—a black who was in charge of publicizing Atlantic's pop records—decided he should no longer be involved in "white promotion."

Swamp Dogg, like many other blacks in the industry, thought black departments were a necessary evil. "They were making money off the black acts but there was no black identification in any of the companies. Some blacks were making money, but there were no black departments and black departments were needed for development." He dismisses the heart-searching on the part of liberal white executives about the resulting segregation of the industry: "It was segregated in the first place. Black artists would always be on one label, pop artists would be on another—and never the twain would meet."

Nevertheless, the trauma felt by white independent companies seems to have been genuine. "I think it affected everyone very badly," says Ertegun. "In a probably stupid way, we all thought of ourselves as pioneers for black people. We were the ones who made the original black records that were covered by white artists—and we were the ones who fought to get the black artists on the air. When I say 'we' I mean not only the white independents, but also Vee Jay and Motown, which were black independents. We were all in the same boat." Ertegun was particularly upset that the Fairplay Committee was indiscriminate in choosing targets. "They were taking it out against whites like Marshall Sehorn, who has always been a champion of black artists and black music. To pick on a little guy like him, who never made any money from it and who has fought for it all his life, and struggled to keep alive, is patently unfair. When things like that happen, you lose your appetite for continuing on this thing—when the people you think are your allies . . ."

Checking his ire, Ertegun says he refrained from becoming too embittered himself. "I felt it to a certain extent but I knew this wasn't the wide majority of blacks, it was just some proselytizers and some loud speakers who were able to get the emotions of the people up. The real black rights leaders are not violent."

Jerry Wexler, Ertegun recalls, was affected very badly indeed. He carried on producing R&B records but with an increasing sense of disillusionment. Much of the roster he had built up was crumbling—partly through his own doing, partly through chance and the relentless ebb and flow of musical taste and fashions. And the once fruitful relationship between Stax and Atlantic had finally ended, with much bitterness and many recriminations—and with most of the anger directed at Wexler.

Wexler did his best to persuade Jim Stewart to bring Stax Records into the Warner group. "I said, 'Jim, come on in. We'll buy you with Warner's money.'" Stewart was attracted by the idea but Warner offered him a sum he considered to be little more than an insult. "We couldn't agree on a price," says Wexler, shaking his gray head regretfully. "Warner wasn't that interested in picking him up because [Stax] was R&B. They didn't care, so they let it go."

Steve Cropper and other long-standing members of the Stax family believed then (and still believe today) that Atlantic simply deserted them. "We thought, Guys, we've kept your record label above water, from sinking, for six years. Atlantic Records couldn't buy a hit. Every single artist they had was having trouble on radio until they came down to Stax. Jim felt, and we all felt, we deserved a little more than a pat on the back and 'Thanks fellows, we'll see you later.' "

The insult perceived in the miserly offer from Warner triggered off a series of complaints against Atlantic that were already rumbling under the surface. Steve Cropper believed (and believes to this day) that he and others at Stax had not received all the royalties they were owed by Atlantic. "I always had a feeling that Atlantic was keeping two sets of books on us—and now I have some information that makes me think they were keeping *three* sets of books on us." Cropper found his suspicions hard to bear. "I hated to think this because I loved Jerry Wexler so much. I respected Ahmet. I loved Nesuhi. Tom Dowd was like my blood brother—we were family-close. So, when I would hear stories they were stealing from us, I just couldn't believe it. It was like someone telling me my dad was stealing from me."

Worse was to come. As Jim Stewart negotiated his company's release from the Stax-Atlantic deal, his lawyers discovered a clause concerning ownership of the Stax catalogue—the backlist of records previously released but still available. Hidden away in a section on another subject, the clause stated that all of Stax's master tapes—everything that had ever been recorded on the label—belonged to Atlantic Records. Stewart and his team in Memphis now had no doubts they had been duped by the slick businessmen from New York City.

Wexler swears he was as shocked as Stewart at this news: "There was a clause in the agreement I didn't know about, until we sold the company, that was very hard on Jim Stewart—that all the masters we were distributing, that he had produced and paid for, we acquired ownership of them. I can only explain—and this sounds really mealy-mouthed—I really was shocked at this thing and I tried to give the masters back to Jim Stewart. But I couldn't do it. That would have been a corporate conflict of interest. I couldn't give those damn records back."

Al Bell, who had risen to second-in-command at Stax—thus fulfilling his ambition to emulate Wexler in all things—accepts Wexler's explanation: "That was just the norm. We were not, as an industry, that sophisticated at that time. You just pulled the contracts out, everybody signed them, and nobody read them. There was no conspiracy."

What perturbed Al Bell much more than the ownership of Stax's masters was the departure from Stax of the label's most popular singers, Sam and Dave, whose record "Hold On, I'm Coming" had established Stax in the pop market. Their contract, it turned out, was with Atlantic, not Stax. "As far as Sam and Dave were concerned, I hated the loss," says Bell. "That hurt, that penetrated. I loved them as two human beings and I loved what they were doing. They, at that time, were an extension of Isaac Hayes and David Porter, who were the two dominant writers. For a moment it left Hayes and Porter in limbo. We had to bear that."

Jim Stewart was livid. As far as he was concerned, Wexler had given Sam and Dave to Stax; to take them back seemed like a petty act of spite. It caused the final rift between Stewart and Wexler. It "inflamed him emotionally in his feelings about Jerry at the time," says Bell. "There were some abrasive moments between Jim and Jerry. I got the distinct impression that all was not well . . . like in any divorce."

The gods were surely angry with Stax. For in the midst of this acrimonious divorce, Otis Redding died. Flying from Cleveland to Madison (despite warnings of inclement weather), his chartered plane crashed into Lake Monona, Wisconsin, killing Redding and four members of his backup band, the Bar-Kays. The already stunned people at Stax now went into a state of total shock.

Redding's death, at the age of twenty-six, only increased the ill feeling against Atlantic. Even as his colleagues at Stax mourned him, rumors circulated that Redding had been about to sign a deal with Wexler to join Atlantic, rather than stay with Stax. Al Bell, convinced this was not true, prefers to gloss over the suggestion of further treachery and instead recall the grief everybody at Stax felt: "It took us a while to rebound from that, and I don't think any of us have totally recovered to this day. He was the cornerstone. Otis played the most dominant role in influencing and developing the Stax sound. [His death] really was a knock to sink us in the water—had it not been for a desire to prove that we could go on in his name. It was a great loss but it was also a motivating factor that pushed us to another level. So his death hurt—and it helped."

Bell, Stewart, and the others now had to summon up all their forces to rebuild Stax from scratch. The first decision they faced was whether to go it alone, or try to find a new partner to replace Atlantic. There were many anguished meetings in Memphis until Gulf & Western—a large entertainment conglomerate—arrived on the scene, eager to buy into the profitable record industry. Gulf & Western had recently acquired ABC-Paramount Records and, in May 1968, it paid $4.3 million to secure Stax as a wholly owned subsidiary, while allowing it to function as an independent record company.

From this secure base Stax rebounded from its almost insurmountable difficulties. The label hired new staff for sales, promotion, and accounting, expanded the offices, and built a new studio. Before long a rejuvenated Stax could do no wrong. It became more extravagantly successful than ever, selling more records than it had during the Atlantic period. The first single released after the Gulf & Western deal— "Soul Limbo" by Booker T. and the MGs—went high up the charts, as did million-selling records by Eddie Floyd, William

Bell, Judy Clay, Carla Thomas, and Johnny Taylor.

All of which made the company's subsequent downfall the more painful and prolonged. It is not easy to identify who killed Stax Records—who, or what, silenced the "Memphis sound"—but high on the list of suspects is a name: the Fairplay Committee.

Increasingly it seemed as though Jim Stewart had handed over the reins of Stax to Al Bell. In 1970 Bell became a full-fledged partner in the company, which was repurchased from Gulf & Western, and it was his name the outside world associated with the label. "I became the outside man while Jim was the inside man. I had the relationships, I had the contacts, he didn't." But even to insiders, Bell seemed the dominant partner. Despite the commercial success he brought to the company, his reign was divisive and destructive—with the "old guard" and Bell's new regime locked in mutual distrust.

Many Stax veterans, including Booker T. Jones, were reluctant to see their small, cozy enclave—which had survived happily enough under Atlantic's protective wing—transformed into a powerful "soul" conglomerate. Jones, Steve Cropper, and other cornerstones of the label who had thrived under Jim Stewart now began to lose their perks and privileged positions—much to the satisfaction of other artists and producers who thought themselves overlooked. Black artists such as Isaac Hayes (who had been with Stax since the mid-1960s) suddenly became extremely powerful in the company. His position was enhanced when his elaborately arranged *Hot Buttered Soul* album, containing only four tracks, made him into a superstar.

The divisions within Stax were exacerbated by the events at the Miami convention. "After that it was very hairy for a while," says Cropper. "There were stories of pistol whippings in the hall." The central focus of these complaints was Johnny Baylor, who, along with Boom Boom Woodward, was invited to Memphis by Al Bell a few months after the Fairplay Committee's takeover of the Miami convention.

The supposed reason for their presence in Memphis was a record deal: In 1964 Baylor had set up his own label, Koko Records, for an artist he had "discovered," named Luther Ingram, and Bell now agreed to distribute Koko's releases. But the more important purpose of their visit was to help Bell deal with threats of extortion from "thugs on the corner." In the aftermath of Martin Luther King's assassination, Stax—which was located in "the bowels of the ghetto"—became a target for black street gangs who took to hanging around McLemore Street, waiting to harass and intimidate Stax's white employees. Using Dr. King's death as an excuse, the thugs also demanded "protection" money from Stax in exchange for a license to operate. Ignoring the irony that the Fairplay Committee had extorted money from other record companies, Baylor and Boom Boom soon put an end to that. As Boom Boom tells it, with pride: "We were able to meet the little thugs and talk to them and let them know it was do or die. After meeting them a couple of times, they began to pull away."

Baylor and Boom Boom did not go away, however, and were soon firmly ensconced at Stax where they concentrated on their real aim—to consolidate black power at the company. "We really took our interests at heart, to be with Al—Al the Man," says Boom Boom. "We took to him because we knew, hey man, that Afro-Americans could run this business, and that's what we were there for. Johnny and I were always ready to die for our cause and what we believed in."

Baylor and Boom Boom set out to eradicate the racism they saw at Stax. White secretaries were being paid more than black secretaries, so they helped organize a strike. White producers such as Steve Cropper were receiving an "unfair" percentage from the producers' pool of royalties, it seemed, so Baylor and Boom Boom encouraged black producers to demand a bigger share.

As can be imagined, Steve Cropper was not sympathetic to

this rise of black consciousness at Stax. "People were coming in and brainwashing our secretaries, the girlfriends of our musicians—even the maids were being brainwashed." He saw no reason for whites at Stax to feel any sense of guilt: "If any black man walking this planet has something against white people having a business, then he doesn't need to be on this planet. They can look at history. If it hadn't been for white record companies there would never have been such a thing as successful black artists."

The last straw for Cropper was when he and the black saxophonist Booker T. Jones were put under pressure to play backup at recording sessions they had already declined. "You don't stick a gun in Steve Cropper's back and say, 'You're going to play on this record'—that's not the way you do business," says Cropper. "I don't play with guns—that's stupid—and neither did Booker." In 1970 both Cropper and Jones quit Stax. They were not sorry to leave: As they saw it, Al Bell also had a gun at his head and was no longer in control.

Johnny Baylor's power at Stax was consolidated over the next three years. His artist, Luther Ingram, had a major hit with "If Loving You Is Wrong, I Don't Want to Be Right." More important, Baylor was enlisted by Bell in a fight against a new threat to Stax: white-collar crime. The crime consisted, in Bell's words, of "fraud, theft, theft by deception, which involved bootlegging our records—not counterfeiting them but bootlegging them—selling our records without the knowledge of the company." The informant who told Bell that such crime existed at Stax was, of course, Johnny Baylor.

Bell says, "We were distributing his label and he and his guys were out in the field the whole time. They never had a place they called home base except New York . . . He and Dino [Boom Boom], and Jay Motedo [a fellow member of the Fairplay Committee], would go from city to city like some nomads across the country. They'd go into a city and one would go to radio stations, another would deal with retail outlets, and another would go to the distributors. They were out there, and then Johnny came in and said, 'Man, they're bootlegging your records.' "

Armed with this information, Bell hired a detective agency called Jaspen and Associates to conduct an undercover investigation into everybody who worked for and with Stax. After a year, according to Bell, Jaspen and Associates shocked Bell and Jim Stewart with a report implicating in the alleged thefts many of their closest colleagues. "We didn't know we were losing as much money as we were losing," says Bell. Instead of prosecuting the suspects, most of whom were sales and promotion men, Bell sacked them. That arbitrary action would later lead to severe criticism of Bell in federal court but he stoutly defends what he did, albeit with contorted and rather pious logic.

"It was important to preserve human life. If you allow a child to be disobedient, as the parent you ultimately have to take responsibility for the child. You really have to be careful, because a lot of innocent people can get destroyed. In an investigation that's that thorough, you reveal things you just might not want to know. We chose to do it that way purposely—just clean up the garbage and move on. We were criticized—a federal judge criticized us harshly for that, and stated we had obstructed justice. I didn't think so. We got our money back, and everything the government should have got the Internal Revenue Service received. So how had we obstructed justice? Because we were humanitarians?"

Jim Stewart was sickened by the whole business. "Man, I'm tired," he told Bell. "I'm forty and I want out of it . . . Let's sell the company."

Bell took this opportunity to enmesh Johnny Baylor even more firmly into the day-to-day running of Stax. He told Baylor he was trying to sell the company and, in the interim, did not want to employ new promotion people to replace those he had fired. Instead, "I asked Johnny and his staff of guys— because he had his own promotion people for his label—to

handle all the promotional responsibilities for Stax." In return Bell offered to distribute Baylor's Koko releases for
nothing.

After ninety days of knocking on doors, from RCA to 20th
Century Fox, Bell had still not managed to sell Stax. So he
begged Baylor to stay on, this time offering as the inducement lucrative publishing copyrights. And to run Stax's sales
department, to do on his own what four people had done
before, Bell recruited that legendary and ubiquitous hustler,
Hy Weiss. "Hy Weiss is someone I have a profound respect
for," says Bell. "I think he's probably one of the most knowledgeable record men in America, and I have always maintained a consultant relationship with Weiss."

Another factor that may have encouraged the recruitment
of Weiss was that he and Baylor were old friends from a distant period in New York—a period that Weiss prefers to keep
shrouded in mystery, giving out just enough hints to whet the
appetite for more. "Johnny Baylor was one of my closest
friends. He was a fighter originally and . . . I don't want to get
into his history. Johnny Baylor was a gentleman, a class guy,
and I still take care of his son. My son and myself were the
only two white guys at Johnny's funeral. I was probably the
only white guy that was part of that crew in Harlem. I could
walk through Harlem at four or five in the morning. Ahmet
[Ertegun] went to Harlem but he didn't go where I went. I
used to be with the people. He never hit with the people, the
street guys. I did because I am a street guy."

Weiss has fond if exaggerated memories of his time at Stax.
He points to a photograph on the wall of his Long Island
home, showing himself and Isaac Hayes receiving an award
for Hayes's double album *Shaft* (which included the theme
from that movie; the theme song won both an Academy
Award and a Grammy), and does not understate his contribution to the company: "I was taking care of their whole business. I started to pick the records to come out with—ten out
of eleven, I shipped over a million singles. I hit on every one.
Everyone I picked was a winner. They fought with me. I said,

'You just listen to me and keep your mouths shut.' We made everything legitimate. I fired about forty people. I put them back into shape. Johnny Baylor was my main man. We had our own crew and we did all right, we took care of business; it was all legitimately run."

That last claim does not coincide with the impressions of some of those from the Atlantic days who still remained at Stax. There were dark mutterings about dangerous gangsters and a takeover of Stax by a black mafia led by Baylor, of elaborate security systems, and so-called security guards, and "guns wherever you looked."

Al Bell, who can be disarmingly persuasive, dismisses all this as nonsense. He laughs at the suggestion there was anything sinister in the new security arrangements at McLemore Street. They resulted, he says, from the investigation and on the advice of Jaspen and Associates: "We had millions of dollars—master tapes worth thirty-two million dollars—and we'd been walking around here with them loose, where anybody could walk in, get one, and take it to a pressing plant, and make a record."

Bell also laughs at the accusations against Baylor. "You know, I've heard a lot of things about Baylor . . . that in Memphis, Tennessee, the 'mafia' and gangsters did all kinds of stuff. It's a bunch of nonsense, absolute insanity." By Bell's account, Baylor was a much misunderstood man: "Johnny Baylor lived on the streets of New York. If you go back—and put that time in perspective, and can live those moments—everything that went on here in that time was normal. He was a tough guy. As a personality he was a very firm, outspoken person, and a no-nonsense person, like Hy Weiss—except Hy Weiss, in some instances, can put charm into his frankness and forthrightness. And if you look at a guy like that who's frank, and has a firm voice, he could be intimidating. He was a muscular guy and he said, 'I think you're lying'—not 'I think you might be misrepresenting.' You see a guy who gets down on the floor and does a hundred press-ups and then jumps up without even being out of breath—I guess that can be intimidating to people."

Bell points out that after the murder of Martin Luther King, and the extortion attempts on McLemore Street, he and Baylor, and many others at Stax, took to carrying guns whenever they moved through the ghetto, especially if they were carrying money. "Now, I suppose someone not understanding that, and not appreciating that era, would say, 'He carried a gun—there's a bad guy.' But you have to look at the whole picture."

Nevertheless, the rumors that Stax had been taken over by a black mafia refused to die down in the record industry (and survive to this day). Swamp Dogg, who knows Al Bell—and almost everybody else in the black record business—very well, laughs at the suggestion that the heavy characters lurking around Stax were security guards: "You could call them Cosa Nostra security."

And whatever their affiliations, the antics of Baylor and his men earned Stax great resentment. "Johnny Baylor frightened a lot of record distributors round the country," says Swamp Dogg. "They were going in with guns to collect their money: 'We're going to be there Thursday and we want our check.' You had men who had been in the record business for a long time and they did not want to be treated like that." So the distributors banded together, he says, and considered how to put Stax out of business.

This deep well of ill feeling coincided, according to Swamp Dogg, with a general distaste on the part of the white establishment for an independent company that was so defiantly black. In 1972, for example, Bell and Jesse Jackson, firm friends since their days as followers of Martin Luther King, organized a summer music festival in Los Angeles called "Wattstax"—designed to commemorate the Watts uprising seven years earlier.

The fact that this sharply political, allegedly gangster-controlled company was also highly successful made it more than a minor irritant to the rest of the industry. Stax was running neck-and-neck with Motown in the contest to sell black albums, and Swamp Dogg, for one, has no doubt this contributed to Stax's final downfall: "Stax had too much of a foothold—not just a toehold, in fact they had a bodyhold on the record industry in the United States. Stax had set the mood for the music, the trends. Stax was selling millions of records. Stax was black, super-black. And whitey had never intended for that to be."

There are several versions of the death of Stax, which closed its doors in 1976 after three years of federal investigations and trials. The bald facts are: Early in 1973 Johnny Baylor was stopped by police at the Memphis airport with a brief-case containing thousands of dollars in cash. As a result, a grand jury investigated alleged kickbacks and other malprac-tices at Stax, and the Internal Revenue Service probed the company's finances. In 1975 Al Bell was indicted, along with an officer of the Union Planters National Bank in Memphis, for "conspiring to obtain more than $18 million in fraudulent bank loans." The indictment claimed that between 1969 and 1974 the Union Planters officer lent money to Stax based on fraudulent guarantees by Bell, receiving in return $700,000 in kickbacks. The bank official admitted embezzling money from the bank, but refused to implicate Bell, saying he had acted alone. Bell was exonerated. A year later Bell was also cleared by the IRS. By then it was too late to save Stax, which was declared bankrupt.

For Steve Cropper, though he was no longer with the com-pany, the reason for the catastrophe was abundantly clear. "Al Bell destroyed Stax because of his power-hungriness. We thought Al Bell was the greatest guy in the world, until he wanted to take over. He wanted to play President of the World, he wanted to be an Ahmet Ertegun. No, Al, you weren't born to be an Ahmet Ertegun. Al Bell, bless his heart, was not equipped to run a major company."

It seemed to Cropper that Bell expanded Stax too quickly—creating new divisions of the company to publish books, market basketballs, and make movies—and that however fast the money poured in, it poured out faster, "like through an open sieve." Cropper says Stax borrowed too much money and finally the Union Planters Bank "just cut the water off—like any bank would."

Al Bell, however, is passionate in his pleas that Stax was not a bankrupt company. Stax, he argues most cogently, was victimized by the white establishment in Memphis in order to save the Union Planters Bank. The bank had made serious losses in the real estate market and might have been closed down unless it came up with sizable amounts of money. The bank's solution, says Bell, was to file a claim with a bonding company for the $18.9 million it claims it was owed by Stax. (Bell disputes the amount of the debt, saying Stax had repaid part of the loan.)

Allied to the pressing need to save the bank, says Bell, was the prejudice directed against a defiantly black record company based in the cotton-picking capital of the South. He may have a point: At Bell's trial a witness testified that the agent of the bank who sought an involuntary bankruptcy petition against Stax told him, "We just took over their publishing company and we are going to take over the record company, put all those niggers out, and put that head nigger in jail."

Al Bell did not go to jail, of course. But although he was cleared on every count, his career and his reputation were ruined. "It was the end of a life for me," says Bell. "Dr. King was killed with a bullet in Memphis. I was killed economically in Memphis."

Another casualty of this affair was black music itself. Other black record companies—chiefly Motown and Philadelphia International—and several black radio stations found themselves being probed by federal investigators for evidence of graft and corruption. Only two record company executives—neither of them from Motown—were eventually charged, but the resulting aura of scandal surrounding black music had the effect of scaring off major record companies, including Atlantic, which concentrated increasingly on comparatively "safe" white pop and rock music.

For Jerry Wexler, the ignominious demise of the company he had nurtured through its infancy, and the declining popularity of the music he loved, brought to an end the few comfortable illusions he still harbored.

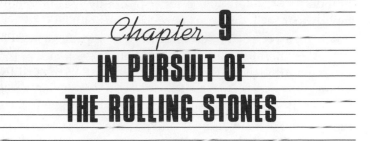

While Stax descended into chaos, Atlantic Records thrived. Jerry Wexler's move to Florida did not appear to have harmed the success of the company, and Ertegun seemed perfectly capable of directing the business more or less on his own. And whatever fears there had been about the wisdom of selling Atlantic in 1967, the label was now perceived by many people to embody the best of both worlds: It had the charm and creativity of an independent record company, backed by the muscle of a major corporation. It was this perception that brought to Atlantic one of the most prestigious groups the label could hope for—a group that would consolidate the company's preeminence in white music for the next decade.

The Rolling Stones combined a talent for white rhythm and blues with a prodigious flair for publicity. By the time the British band and Ahmet Ertegun got together—and, in a way, fulfilled each other's destinies—the Stones had successfully caused enormous outrage in England by urinating in public; started a riot in Chicago; had their version of "Little Red Rooster" banned in the United States because of its objectionable lyrics; been threatened with censorship again unless Mick Jagger mumbled the title line of "Let's Spend the Night Together"; and, during a concert in California, seen a member of their audience stabbed to death by Hell's Angels hired by the Stones as security guards. Jagger had been branded a "Lucifer" figure for supposedly encouraging Satanism with such songs as "Sympathy for the Devil." He had also been arrested and sentenced for drug possession, as had two other members of the group. And Brian Jones, perhaps the most gifted of the Stones, was dead at the age of twenty-seven.

It was an alluringly provocative history. By the end of the sixties there were few who would dispute the Stones' description of themselves as the "Greatest Rock-and-Roll Band in the World," and few record companies that would not have given the earth to sign them. Ertegun never imagined Atlantic would get the chance—nor, if it did, that the label could afford them.

He was, by his own account, roaring drunk when he first learned the Stones wanted to join Atlantic, and, according to Mick Jagger, he was no more sober when he finally signed them. In between, Ertegun pursued an exhausting courtship that must have nearly killed him. It seemed entirely worthwhile because the capture of the Rolling Stones firmly established Atlantic as the preeminent record label in America—a distinction that previously belonged to CBS Records, which Warner Communications saw as its great rival, and was determined to overtake. (There was, no doubt, much satisfaction felt in the Warner boardroom when the competition to sign the Stones came down to a two-horse race—and it was CBS that lost to Ertegun in the final straight.) But wooing and winning the Stones was only the beginning of Ertegun's task: Having won them, he devoted exceptional amounts of his time and energy to "masterminding" their records—and to the not inconsiderable problems their music sometimes created.

Today, as a wealthy rock aristocrat, Mick Jagger lives (from time to time) in an elegant brownstone on the Upper West Side of Manhattan. The house looks ordinary enough from the outside, with individual bells and mailboxes still remaining from less grand days when it was divided into apartments. But inside it is a New York version of a beautiful eighteenth-century English country house, with gilt moldings, embossed plaster walls, and polished parquet floors. A wide staircase leads to the first-floor living room where straight-backed leather chairs are softened by paisley cushions adorned with a design of fox hunters and horses. Marble pillars line the high-ceilinged room, offset by pictures of classical youths, and logs are piled by the fireplace as if in readiness for a welcoming fire to warm the master of the house when he returns from a bracing country walk.

There are a few anachronisms: the over-large matte-black television and video system, and Calico, an affectionate Texas farm cat. And when the master returns from his excursion—cycling in Central Park—smiling and disheveled, he is dressed not in tweeds but in a blue tracksuit. Nevertheless, English tea is served with due decorum in fine china and Mick Jagger (as gracious a host as one could wish for) settles down to reminisce about less comfortable days.

As Jagger explains, by 1969 the Rolling Stones—for all their success—were in a precarious position. "We couldn't have been in a worse situation than we were," he says. "We needed the money." Part of the reason for that was the Stones' traumatic relationship with their manager, Allen Klein, a New York accountant and one of the toughest wheeler-dealers in the music business. Klein had come to them in 1966 promising he would extract unpaid royalties from Decca. "That was his specialty," says Jagger, "and he did get a lot from Decca, because they didn't pay us, you see. This is the industry: The record companies don't pay, so you have to get someone to go and collect it for you." Unfortunately, though Klein collected the unpaid royalties from Decca with the utmost efficiency, he did not necessarily pass all of the money on to the Stones—a problem that led to angry disputes and litigation.

Meanwhile, the group's recording contract with the British label Decca Records was coming to a bitter and acrimonious end. The Stones were infuriated by what they saw as Decca's total inability to meet their artistic needs. According to Bill Wyman, the Stones' bass player, "Decca were useless. All we ever did with them was have continuous arguments about covers and records and what should be the single. They were atrocious."

Jo Bergman, the Stones' long-suffering personal assistant at the time, says the band and their record company were equally exasperated by each other. "It was a time when record companies didn't understand rock and roll. The Beatles were okay, because they were clean and positive—which the Rolling Stones clearly were not. They were perceived as being troublemakers, and they were troublemakers. It was a situation where record companies—particularly Decca—having made the huge mistake of not signing the Beatles, were obviously not going to make the same mistake with the Rolling Stones. But they kind of felt they were suffering for it—and they did rather take it out on the Stones."

In an attempt to save themselves, the Stones handed their business affairs over to Prince Rupert Lowenstein, a suavely intimidating German who acts as a financial consultant (to the very rich) in London. The contract with Decca was terminated and, with Prince Rupert's help, the Stones looked for a new label. The question was, which one? "The Rolling Stones were just a bit too much to handle for most people," says Jagger with a faint air of surprise as he sips another cup of tea. "It's hard to put your mind back to those days, but the Rolling Stones were a kind of nightmare for a record company to deal with—or at least they thought it was."

In contrast to Decca, and its staid caution, Ahmet Ertegun and Atlantic Records seemed very alluring. "We all knew that Ahmet was a good record person," says Jagger. "He was someone who was very involved in the music and he had the authenticity other record people don't have. The thing about Ahmet is, he is actually a guy who is a producer. He's an all-round record man." Jagger still recalls the occasion he saw Ertegun produce a blues artist in Chicago: "He was just great, with these black people, in this whole other world."

Ertegun's qualifications also attracted the other Stones, particularly when they compared him to Sir Edward Lewis, the sedate English head of Decca. "Ahmet loves to hang out with the musicians and go to recording sessions," says Bill Wyman approvingly. "He loves music. The whole company is like that—it goes right the way through from the top to the bottom. Other companies weren't the same. They didn't have any executives who could produce and write records." Moreover, as white English boys who loved black R&B with all the zeal of the converted, the natural home for the Stones was Atlantic because of its distinguished musical history. "All the people we loved were on Atlantic—all the people we had done cover versions of when we started out," says Wyman. That factor "was more important than money"—at least to him. Jo Bergman adds a touch of realism: "They knew that Ahmet cared about the music . . . There was a true history, and affection, and concern. That was a really important factor—money aside, which was a whole other issue."

Ertegun had by this time met the Stones a few times at parties ("He was always at every party," says Jagger approvingly) and had got on well with them. But he knew nothing about the affection in which he and his company were held, and nothing about the Stones' ambition to record for Atlantic. So, when the Stones went to Los Angeles to make their last album for Decca, and Ertegun happened to be in town, and when Mick Jagger sent one of the band's "roadies" to call on Ertegun and invite him to the studio on Sunset Boulevard, Ertegun thought it was nothing more than a friendly gesture. "I said thank you very much, I would try to make it, and it was very nice of them to invite me. I had a dinner and other things to do but I would try to pop in. As it was, I had a lot to do that night. I had to see some of my other artists. I thought it was just a social invitation, which I was quite touched by, but I couldn't go. The next day the roadie came back and said, 'Listen, Mick really would like you to come by. Can you come by tonight?' "

Still not catching on, "I went by the studio without any idea—just to say hello. They played me a couple of the tracks." As Ertegun was leaving the studio Jagger casually suggested they meet later that night, at around midnight, at the Whisky-a-Go-Go nightclub where Chuck Berry was playing.

But before then, Ertegun wanted to see an old friend, an extremely important radio program director named Bill Drake. Aside from any use Drake could be to Atlantic (which was considerable) Ertegun and he liked to go drinking together—which is precisely what they did that night. "He put out this big bottle of bourbon, and we finished that off, and we had more drinks, and so on," says Ertegun. "Then we went to some restaurant to have dinner." After finishing off the meal with yet more alcohol, Ertegun and Drake set off for the meeting with Jagger, with two girls in tow. (Ertegun always has girls in tow—the more the merrier and the prettier the better.)

"The place was jammed, and we sat there at a table in the corner, and we had another couple of drinks, and Mick arrived. The music was playing very loud and I don't think I've ever drunk as much as I had that night—because Bill Drake was proving to these idiots that I could out-drink anybody, and he could too. So Mick said to me, 'Listen, we're leaving our label.' I said, 'What did you say?'—because the music was very loud. He said, 'We're leaving our label, and we've decided we want to go on Atlantic.'

"At that point—the music was so loud, and it was so noisy and crowded there; he was telling me that they wanted to go on Atlantic, and while he was talking and everything—I fell asleep. I just couldn't stand it—the noise, the drink, everything. And I remember this girl I was with shaking me, saying, 'Wake up, wake up. Mick is talking to you.' And I just said, 'Oohh,' " says Ertegun, giving a convincing imitation of a drunken groan.

"Well, I tell you, that did it—because Mick is the kind of person who hates pushy people. He hates anybody who wants him to do anything, or wants anything from him. I think the fact I fell asleep while he was telling me they wanted to go on Atlantic absolutely solidified the deal because in his mind he thought, 'This is a guy who doesn't give a shit.' "

In fact Ertegun cared very much about winning the fickle hearts of the Rolling Stones, so that their style and reputation might grace his label. And although he now says the Stones joined Atlantic without him having to try very hard, the Los Angeles encounter was only the start of a long, uphill struggle: Onlookers remember Ertegun's subsequent courtship of the group to have been a protracted one, conducted with all the delicacy befitting major diplomatic negotiations. For when Mick Jagger said he wanted to be on Atlantic, he neglected to add *if* the price was right—and, perhaps more important, *only* when Ertegun realized just how lucky he was to sign the Greatest Rock-and-Roll Band in the World. Jerry Wexler watched the subsequent negotiations from the sidelines with the faintest of amusement. "Ahmet was the perfect person to do it," says Wexler. "There's no other record person who could have come close to Ahmet in engaging the admiration and the respect of Mick and Keith [Richards]." (In a different age, Wexler adds, "Ahmet would be the squire and Mick would be the equerry. Sub specie aeternitatis, Ahmet out-stars Mick—but they're both masters of pop irony.")

There is no doubt the competition to sign the Stones was intense. The Beatles had split up, and the Stones' tour of America in 1969 had established them as the most charismatic of rock groups. Difficult, and impossible to pin down, the Rolling Stones were nevertheless at the top of every music mogul's shopping list. "A lot of people wanted to sign them," says Jo Bergman. "Everybody was about. There were visitations."

Jack Holzman, the head of Elektra Records (another inde-

pendent label that had just become part of the Warner empire), saw Ertegun in London during this period. They met at
9 A.M. at a hotel to discuss whether Warner's music division
should record the upcoming Isle of Wight pop festival—but
Ertegun's thoughts were on other, more pressing matters. "I
got to the door and there was Ahmet reading an Arabic newspaper, but I could see his mind was preoccupied," says Holzman. "He had been out all night with Mick Jagger and he was
paying very little attention to what I was saying. Suddenly he
picked up the phone and said, 'Got to make a call.' He called
Mick and said, 'Wasn't that a wonderful time we had last
night?'—and Mick on the other end apparently agreed.
Ahmet had been courting and wooing the Stones for about a
year by then, and he said to Mick, 'It's probably time for you
and me and Prince Rupert to sit down and make a deal.' And
Mick said, 'Well, Ahmet, I'll be happy to sit down and talk
about a deal with you—just as soon as I've spoken to Clive
Davis at CBS.'

"All the color drained out of Ahmet's face. He looked old at
that moment: He was tired, and he had been up all night, and
God knows what he had done to his system over the year,
being pals with Mick. He got off the phone, and I could see it
was futile to continue our discussion.

"He waited about a minute, said nothing, then picked up
the phone and said to Mick, 'I've been thinking, and I understand what you're saying about wanting to talk to Clive
Davis. But look, I can only sign one major act this year, one
act of Rolling Stones caliber. So I want you to know unless I
get an answer in a hurry, it is going to be Paul Revere and the
Raiders.' And then he hung up. Twenty seconds later the
phone rings. Ahmet doesn't pick it up. The phone rang con-
sistently for forty-five minutes while we finished the rest of
our meeting . . . That was the biggest demonstration of cool I
had ever seen—before or since."

That incident may have clinched it, although Clive
Davis—then the president of CBS Records—says Jagger was
still prepared to negotiate a few days before the group was

supposed to sign with Atlantic. "With record companies, until the ink is dried there is no contract," observes Prince Rupert. "We wanted to go to Atlantic so long as the commercial terms were not less good than anywhere else."

In the end a compromise was reached. The Stones turned down higher cash offers (what Bill Wyman laconically describes as "a few million dollars higher") and signed with Atlantic in return for being given their own subsidiary label, Rolling Stones Records.

In grand celebration a glamorous party—one still talked about in an industry that is generally blasé about parties— was thrown by Atlantic Records in the South of France in April 1971. The rich and the famous and the powerful all converged on Cannes Yacht Club, where they were written about and photographed in great detail by the world's press. Fortunately, the actual signing of the contract was a more private affair, so Ertegun's drunkenness—due, no doubt, to his relief at closing the Byzantine and lengthy negotiations— was not publicly recorded. "Ahmet fell off the back of a chair," recalls Jagger. "It was in my house in London, and he'd drunk so much bourbon that when we actually shook hands on the deal, the chair fell back and he fell over."

In a long profile of Ertegun, published in the *New Yorker* in 1978, George Trow perfectly summed up the significance of it all:

The convergence of Ahmet Ertegun and the Rolling Stones had its resonance. This was not entirely due to the eminence of the Rolling Stones. By 1971, the Rolling Stones had recorded 18 albums . . . and for nearly a decade they had made the most powerful mock-black music of their times. But Ahmet Ertegun, informed men knew, had done at least as much. He had founded a small record company; he had turned a small record company into a major record company; he had superintended the careers of celebrated people and had superintended for himself a success of unrivaled longevity; he had owned a Rolls-Royce for more than five years; he had dressed extremely well; and he had, at one or two important moments, applied his own aesthetic to the talents of certain singers and musicians in a way that had influenced the whole of the music. In a business in which entrepreneurs and executives, however success- ful, were overshadowed, as they saw it, by hippies, druggies, spics, spades, transvestites, and Englishmen, Ahmet Ertegun was an exception. He had stature in his line of work that Irving Thalberg and Louis B. Mayer had had in theirs. By 1971, Ahmet Ertegun (jaunty, well-dressed, bald, forty-seven years old, and of very recent Turkish extraction) was the Greatest Rock-and- Roll Mogul in the World.

When Michael Phillip Jagger was merely a pupil at Dartford Grammar School in Kent, England, his consuming passion was for the great blues artists who recorded for Chess Rec- ords in Chicago: Howlin' Wolf, Muddy Waters, and, in partic- ular, Chuck Berry. Their work was not widely available in Britain at the time so Jagger would write letters to Chess in Chicago where they would be opened by young Marshall Chess, son of the label's founder, who, as a young man, worked in the mailroom. According to Marshall, he, in reply, mailed Jagger the latest Chess releases—and thus contrib- uted to the influences that guided and shaped the Greatest Rock-and-Roll Band in the World. "The Stones understand the essence of Chess Records," says Marshall. "They copied it, and they made it into something even more. They started by trying to mimic it and they couldn't. It came out as some- thing else that was their thing but it contained the essence: It's like Chess Records was garlic, and the Stones had garlic, but they had pepper and salt too." (Jagger remembers his first contact with Chess somewhat differently: "I did use to write to Chess—but they never replied. I used to have to buy the records from mail order shops that advertised in *NME* [*New Musical Express*] and *Melody Maker*. They would say,

'Blues records—send for list,' and you'd send your postal order, and three or four months later the thing would come.")

In July 1964 an adolescent dream came true for Jagger and the rest of the Stones when they recorded at the Chess studio in Chicago during their first American tour. As they arrived at 2120 South Michigan Boulevard they met their hero Muddy Waters, who—much to their awe—helped them carry their equipment inside. (The fact that Waters then continued to paint the walls of the studio while the Stones set up their equipment was not the only indication that Chess Records treated its resident artists with something less than respect. Jagger noticed a blackboard at the end of the studio, upon which was inscribed: "Best song for Sugar Pie Desanto wanted by next Monday—$50." As Jagger exclaims: "So you didn't get any royalties, you got fifty dollars—if you were lucky. And that was if you had the best song. What happened to the other ten songs? They got copyrighted, and you got nothing for them.")

"It was the first American studio we had worked in," says Bill Wyman, a former clerk who joined the Stones at the end of 1962 having changed his name from plain William Perks. "We wanted to get an American sound instead of a thin English sound—we wanted to have a big fat sound, like an R&B band." But it was the memories and the past associations that made the visit so evocative for the Stones; as Jagger puts it, that it was in *this* studio all those records he had sent away for had been made. "We went down to the dusty, cobwebby basement, and there all the singles were."

How appropriate, then, that when Rolling Stones Records was formed, and the Stones and Ertegun were seeking somebody to run it, the first person to apply for the job was Marshall Chess. By 1971 Chess Records had been taken over, and barely existed in any recognizable form, and Marshall Chess quit. The Stones "were and are my favorite white band," so "I said, if I was going to work with anyone, I was going to work with them. I told Mick on the phone I had quit Chess

Records, and I'd heard on the grapevine they were also looking to start their own thing, and I thought maybe it would be
a good marriage. He said, 'Great, man.' "

There was just one problem. Jagger said he would like to fly
to America to talk to Chess but he could not: "I can't leave
England. They've taken my passport because I was busted
for amphetamines." Instead, two weeks later, Chess flew to
London for his first taste of what life with the Rolling Stones
was going to be like. Today, leaning back on the Indian floor
cushions that decorate his rambling Manhattan apartment—
where nothing appears to have changed since the 1960s—he
recalls that bizarre encounter: "He was playing 'Black Snake
Blues' and the whole time we were rapping, for the whole
side of the record, he danced. He was probably nervous—and
I was too. You have to remember, I was a suit-and-tie kind of
guy then, I was a nine-to-five guy, a businessman."

Nevertheless, Jagger decided Marshall was the natural
choice to run Rolling Stones Records, and Ertegun—who had
attended Marshall's barmitzvah with his brother Nesuhi a
few years earlier—installed the young man in an office in
Atlantic's New York headquarters. "I loved it," says Chess.
"They were like family to me, they are to me still. I think it
was a fabulous deal. We all made money on it, we all had fun,
great times. I learned a lot of things, good and bad."

The bad things inevitably arose from the life-style Chess
adopted. He quickly ceased to be a straightforward Chicago
executive. "As well as hanging out all night with them, I was
doing business in the day, and I started taking a lot of heavy
drugs. I think at the end I was hooked on five or six at the
same time—Valiums, Quaaludes, everything." Chess did not
cope well with drugs. One senior Atlantic executive remembers a period when Marshall came into the office stoned
every day, with plans that ranged from the inventively bizarre to the completely unworkable. One of his ideas was for
an album cover that contained not only the record but also a
toy bird; when the cover was opened, the bird flew away.

Chess's erratic management style did not matter too much

because, whatever the paperwork might say, there was no doubt who was really in charge of Rolling Stones Records. Prince Rupert says Ertegun was always involved, "down to the smallest detail, down to the last cent. I always dealt with Ahmet, on any important point." Even when Ertegun was away from the office—a frequent occurrence—his involvement was intense. "Ahmet not being present did not mean that he was not at the end of the telephone within ten seconds," says Prince Rupert. "He had a lot to say about the records, he discussed them with Mick and other members of the band, he came to the concerts, and he certainly was involved with the running of the contract. He masterminded the whole thing." Or as Mick Jagger says: "He still kept his hand on the wheel. He was still very accessible."

The reason for his care and attention was not simply that the Rolling Stones were important figureheads for Atlantic, and significant contributors to the company's revenue. Ertegun was, first, an ardent fan of the Stones. And, unlikely as it may seem, the urbane son of the Turkish ambassador and the defiant "bad boy" of rock developed a close personal friendship. They shared a passion for soccer, a proclivity toward decadence, and a taste for the high life—a fact that became clear when Jagger married the Nicaraguan fashion model Bianca Pérez Morena de Macías, and (to the despair of some of his fans) joined Ertegun as a high-ranking member of the international jet set.

Ertegun and Jagger understood each other very well. The Rolling Stones signed with Atlantic because they believed Ertegun would understand and indulge their needs—which, for the most part, is what he did. The Stones' first album for Atlantic, *Sticky Fingers,* gave some hint of what that indulgence might produce: The sleeve, designed by Andy Warhol, showed a denim-clad crotch—its fly a real zip fastener opening to reveal Jagger's lascivious lips and tongue.

But Ertegun is a consummate diplomat who knows when to bend with the wind, and Jagger is not. Ertegun has certain sensitivities, and Jagger does not. Above all, Ertegun, unlike

Jagger, does sometimes care what other people think. The results of these differences were always certain to be interesting.

By 1973 the mood in America was hardening against what was seen as the depraved record industry, mired in blatant sexuality and a sea of illegal drugs. It was also seen as corrupt. Clive Davis, the head of CBS Records, had been fired in a sensational scandal concerning allegedly false expense claims. (He was supposed to have used company money to pay for, among other things, his son's barmitzvah. He was eventually exonerated.) And various investigations were under way into yet more supposed links between the industry and organized crime. Ertegun was astute enough to realize a certain tact was called for in Atlantic's public relations; this was not the time to further rock the boat.

The Rolling Stones chose this moment to write a song called "Starfucker." And not only that, they elected to go on tour with a forty-foot-long rubber penis for a stage prop. There were lengthy and anguished negotiations before Ertegun could persuade the Stones to modify the song's title to "Star Star," and to partially disguise the highly libelous lyrics, which were about the sexual activities of various well-known personalities. (Even so, before the song was released, an assurance had to be obtained from Steve McQueen that he would not sue Atlantic for libel.)

"I think the only time Ahmet was upset was about 'Starfucker,' " says Prince Rupert in his precise, clipped voice that cuts through other people's vagueness and indecision like a knife through butter. "That upset him terribly."

Or as Mick Jagger puts it, more prosaically, "Ahmet was in a real tizz." Jagger could see no rational reason for Ertegun— normally the most imperturbable of men—to worry. "It really disillusioned me, especially as no one else gave a shit at that point," says Jagger. "The day was past and gone when you had to worry about things like that." It was simply a sign, he says somewhat disapprovingly, that Ertegun had gone over to the other side, to the Establishment: "Respectability is something that even Ahmet and people like that realized they wanted to have. They want to have it all. They want to be the funky guy, yet they don't want to lose their social standing or their moral high ground."

The episode was soon forgotten, and it proved to be a mere dress rehearsal for what happened when the Stones produced what was to be their best-selling album so far, *Some Girls*. The album's title song included the line "Black girls like to fuck all night"—a supposedly ironic reflection on racial stereotyping. Ertegun said that whether the line was ironic or not, it sounded discriminatory and was likely to cause extreme offense—and he would not release the album unless the words were changed. Jagger was furious and refused to even consider rewriting the song. Their argument ended in total deadlock.

"Well of course we had absolutely no sympathy, there was no discrimination imaginable," says Prince Rupert dismissively. "Ahmet knew perfectly well that Mick Jagger was not anti-Negro or anti-woman, he just said what he felt like saying." The prince did, however, admit "everybody has their censorship threshold. Sir Edward Lewis of Decca was worried about obscenity, but wouldn't have worried about racism. Ahmet wouldn't have worried about obscenity, but minded about racism. I would mind about neither obscenity nor racism, but I would mind about blasphemy."

In the end it was Mica Ertegun—who had become a close friend of Jagger—who persuaded her husband to release the album with the words unchanged. For almost a year nothing happened, leading Ertegun to say, somewhat huffily, "It just showed me the Stones had no black following." The first indication of an approaching storm came when Hal Jackson, a powerful and influential black New York disc jockey, called Ertegun to complain about the lyrics. Ertegun did his best to be conciliatory but within a week of that call Atlantic's offices were being picketed by angry black groups. "Everybody you could possibly think of was there," says Ertegun. "Even the Abyssinian Church."

Jagger declares he simply could not understand, either then or now, what all the fuss was about: "There was lots of things in that tune—and it was only one tune, you have to remember—and you didn't have the Italian embassy phoning up saying it was a slur on Italian women, or the French or the English or the Chinese. There was no problem—except with black people. Of course, it's a great political hobbyhorse. Some people make a living out of that, whether or not they actually think it's a real slur. It's hypocrisy really."

Hypocrisy or not, the clamor grew louder. Jesse Jackson joined the fray, calling Ertegun to say, "Man, you're in trouble." Ertegun responded by asking for the black leader's help and Jackson promised he would try to sort things out.

Thus it was that Ertegun was summoned to Chicago, Jackson's base, to meet with all the community groups expressing outrage at Jagger's lyrics. Jackson told Ertegun to come alone except for his black assistant, Noreen Woods—who, in Ertegun's words, is "afraid of her own shadow."

Ertegun and Woods duly arrived in Chicago both feeling a certain amount of trepidation but Jackson assured them before the meeting got under way to trust his judgment, and leave everything to him. Then, when the meeting started, and to Ertegun's absolute horror, Jackson launched a bitter attack against him, denouncing him in a fiery preacher's tirade. So savage was the attack, says Ertegun, "I thought that I was going to be lynched. I was the only white person in the hall—and it was very scary." It occurred to Ertegun he had been set up by Jackson as some sort of scapegoat to bear the brunt of the black community's grievances. "But then after a while, Jesse went that bit too far in working up the crowd, until they began to feel sorry for me," says Ertegun. At that point, with his immaculate sense of timing, Jackson began to tell the crowd how much money and support Ertegun and Atlantic had given to black causes. It was a masterful performance by the preacher and it resulted not in

Ertegun's lynching but in a friendly lunch and forgiveness. "That man saved my life," says Ertegun, and he means it. Perhaps because of that he will always defend Jesse Jackson to the hilt, whatever the issue.

There was, however, one man of importance who still had to be placated: Hal Jackson, the New York disc jockey. Ertegun asked him if there was anything—anything at all—he could do to heal the rift caused by "Some Girls." Jackson thought for a while and then named his price: He was one of the organizers of the Miss Black American Teenage Pageant, held annually in Los Angeles, and, he said, he would forgive and forget Mick Jagger's slur if Jagger agreed to attend the pageant and present the prizes.

Ertegun should, perhaps, have known better. But so relieved was he by the prospect of peace, he broke his own cardinal rule of never being "pushy" with Jagger, of never asking him for anything, and persuaded Jagger to comply. The arrangements were made with meticulous care. And to make absolutely certain that nothing could go wrong, Ertegun himself went to Los Angeles and, on the day before the great event, telephoned Jagger to remind him of his duty, impressing on him the importance of the occasion. Fine, said Jagger. He would be there.

But he was not. Ertegun was about to have lunch with Brooke Hayward, the author of *Haywire,* a best-selling memoir at the time, when he received a frantic telephone call from Hal Jackson. Jackson said he was at Jagger's hotel, as agreed in the schedule, to collect Jagger—but Jagger was asleep and could not be awakened. Pausing only to pick up his lunch date, and attempting to stay calm, Ertegun rushed to the slumbering rock star's hotel to head off impending disaster.

But when Ertegun arrived at the hotel suite at noon he was told by one of the entourage that Jagger had been up all night, "partying"—and had only retired to bed one hour before. "I shouted at him, I threw water at him, but nothing would wake him up," says Ertegun. He eventually had to admit defeat and trailed downstairs to the hotel lobby to tell Hal Jackson the bad news. Jackson was furious. He told Ertegun, in no uncertain terms, he must unearth some other celebrity to make a speech at the pageant, and hand out the prizes—or there would be "big trouble."

Which is how Brooke Hayward—at that moment sitting patiently in the back of Ertegun's limousine, waiting for a nice quiet lunch—suddenly found herself cast into the limelight. Ertegun did not tell her what had happened, or what he had in store for her, because she had previously told him she was exhausted from her labors. Stalling for time, he pretended they were lunching in downtown L.A., discreetly directed his chauffeur to drive to the pageant, and, when they arrived, ushered her unsuspecting into a hall where, as he puts it, "there were a thousand expectant black teenage girls waiting for Mick Jagger."

She rose to the occasion, as Ertegun knew she would, giving a magnificent off-the-cuff speech on the hopes and aspirations of young women. Ertegun meanwhile managed to persuade his shy and much-put-upon assistant, Noreen Woods, to follow Hayward onto the platform and describe how she, as a black woman, had risen through the ranks of Atlantic to become an executive. "It was all very moving," says Ertegun. "Hal Jackson was delighted, and all the teenagers seemed to have a good time."

They did not seem to mind that the World's Greatest Rock-and-Roll Singer did not even turn up. Jagger confines himself to remarking it would have been "another disaster" if he had made the presentation.

Unfortunately for Ertegun, not all the problems surrounding the Rolling Stones could be solved so easily. By 1976 it was clear to everybody including Marshall Chess that Marshall Chess would have to leave Rolling Stones Records. As Ertegun describes it: "They [the Stones] decided not to continue with Marshall Chess, who was there in name but not in person—you know what I mean? He was nowhere to be seen, he was out of it."

Chess—who now resides in his country house (where he spends several hours a day in a flotation tank), or in his Upper West Side apartment filled with relics from the sixties—admits that keeping up with the Stones proved too much for him. "It's the same as if you have a love affair with someone, and it's real hot and it's fabulous, right? And I had that with the Stones. And you know how it is when you have a love affair that ends?

"What happens is, you get a little bored, and pretty soon you know you have to end it. It's exactly like that. It became a very good part of my life but after five years I started getting discontented, and saying, 'Where am I going, what am I doing? I'm sick of the drugs, I'm sick of the planes, the hotels . . . it's all bullshit.' I didn't really like my life. I wasn't a Rolling Stone but you sort of think you are in that position, because I was going on the private jets, and hanging out with them . . .

"Of course, I was raised with stars; I don't have any problems with stars at all. I got along fabulously with the Rolling Stones, we never had a fight. Maybe we had a few words when I quit—you know, it would be like telling a girl who thought everything was great, 'Look, I don't like it anymore.' It was a very demanding thing, it was a passionate thing—like a love affair. I really loved it, and put everything into it, and then it tapered off. It got boring, and it was wearing on my health, too. It took me years—five years—to really get myself totally back."

Chess's replacement at Rolling Stones Records was Earl McGrath, who had chosen that moment to resign, in a huff, from his job as head of Atlantic's publicity department. McGrath—a one-time (and not very successful) Hollywood scriptwriter who entered the music business almost by accident—was appointed to his new position against Mick Jagger's better judgment. "Mick was a little reluctant [to hire McGrath] because I don't think he likes social friends to get into a business relationship, and he likes Earl very much," says Ertegun. But Ertegun "talked to the boys and they somehow agreed that it would be okay," and for about one year it was. Then McGrath abruptly resigned again, in high dudgeon, saying, "I'm sick of working with drug addicts"— an ironic complaint since his prodigious intake of drugs was probably on a level with that of any of the Stones.

Perhaps the truth was that only Ertegun himself could successfully manage Atlantic's partnership with the Rolling Stones because only he had the stamina to keep up with them. But there were long-term implications to the need for Ertegun's exceptionally close involvement with the group— implications that, in the view of some of his colleagues, became increasingly apparent. "The Rolling Stones was a big deal for the Warner group because of our competition with CBS," says Jack Holzman. "Ahmet pulled it off but he paid a price for it. It was a very rich deal, but the price was all the time he had to spend nursing it, perhaps neglecting some other things."

Chapter 10
IN WITH THE NEW

In 1973, five years after moving to Florida, Jerry Wexler and his wife, Shirley, separated and he returned to New York. In the interim he had kept his hand in by occasionally producing records at a studio in Miami, and he had tried to keep in almost daily contact with Ertegun by telephone. If, however, he expected to be able to pick up the pieces at Atlantic, he was sadly mistaken.

Ertegun's description of the inevitable split between Wexler and himself is uncharacteristically brief; it is not a subject he likes to talk about. "He had difficulty slotting in," says Ertegun. "His main difficulty was with the staff at Atlantic: Most of them he had hired, but they had now taken over. When he came back a lot of the kids, who had just been kids running around, were now in high positions here. And it wasn't the same place he had left because over a period of five or six years things change. I think he became disenchanted—and he told me and Sheldon Vogel [then controller, now vice-president of Atlantic] that he thought he wanted to work out a way to retire. So they worked it out upstairs. He had lots of financial advantages to do that, and he decided to do that on his own. He was never asked to leave or anything like that. These rumors go around, but it was his decision."

Wexler's explanation for the final split is even more brief: "I just didn't fit into the company," he says. "Everything had changed. My apparatchiks had gone elsewhere."

There was, of course, much more to it than that.

Ever on the lookout for "authentic" music, and still resistant to the cacophonies of the "rockoids," Wexler signed the Average White Band, a British soul group, developed an interest in a new style of country music—one that blended traditional country-and-western ballads with rock. At Wexler's urging, Atlantic opened an office in Nashville, Tennessee, and Wexler signed to the label a country singer and writer who would eventually become so famous, and so popular in his native Texas, that the Texas Senate would rename the Fourth of July after him. Willie Nelson had been writing and recording songs for fifteen years with no great commercial success until he redefined country music by bringing together a band of "good old country boys" and young "hippies" from the world of rock. Wexler believed the resulting first album, *Phases and Stages,* would provide Nelson's breakthrough. When it did not, Wexler blamed Atlantic for failing to push the record and, according to Tom Dowd, "he just looked at Willie and said, 'You're in the wrong place.' So he got Willie off the label, because there wasn't the empathy for him there."

According to Dickie Kline, head of national promotion at Atlantic at the time, Wexler's disappointment was made worse by Atlantic's decision to close down its Nashville operation: "I believe that was a big hurt for Jerry, to give up what he really believed could happen, and I think that was one of the deciding factors to make him leave."

Another factor must surely have been Atlantic's reaction when Nelson's very next album, *Red Headed Stranger,* was released by Columbia Records (part of arch-rival CBS), and sold one million copies—and Wexler found himself blamed for letting Nelson go. As Tom Dowd explains: "The company felt 'We had a hit artist, and Jerry gave him away.' It wasn't Ahmet that felt that way, but some idiots there did."

If final proof was needed that Wexler and Atlantic were no longer on the same wavelength it came when the Jackson 5, the prodigiously successful black pop group, announced it was leaving Motown Records because of a dispute over artistic control. Wexler may not have anticipated just how all-conquering Michael Jackson would become as a solo artist, but he certainly believed in the Jacksons, and was determined Atlantic should sign them. His efforts came to naught because, he believed, Ertegun did not share his conviction.

These were bitter days for Jerry Wexler. Not only did he feel alienated in his own company; not only was his judgment no longer accepted; not only was he being second-guessed by "the kids running around"—some of those kids were now pretenders to the throne Wexler occupied. There could have been nothing more galling for him than the fact that the "kid" most widely slated to take over from Wexler as Ahmet Ertegun's alter ego was a man whom Jerry Wexler thoroughly detested.

David Geffen is a ferociously ambitious man who now runs his own eponymous record company, under the umbrella of Warner Communications, along with a successful film company. Presiding over his empire on Sunset Boulevard, Beverly Hills—in a building that is a curious mixture between a Swiss mountain lodge and a small French château, with a few Greek columns thrown in for good measure—Geffen's own office looks more like a comfortable California lounge than an executive suite. He too looks very informal, sitting on a cream sofa wearing faded Levis, a white T-shirt, and black suede shoes.

But Geffen—like a previous occupant of the building, Phil Spector—is anything but relaxed. Every question is a direct challenge to him, to be fiercely debated or angrily dismissed. Of his own history, he says abruptly: "Oh, you know, I can't tell this story except in four seconds because it so bores me."

Born in Brooklyn in 1943, his parents were Jewish immigrants from Russia and Poland. "I left school when I graduated at seventeen," Geffen says. "I went to college for a little bit but I wasn't a very good student. I decided it wasn't the best thing for me—I didn't like studying, and I still don't." His first job was in the stockroom of a Brooklyn dress shop. He had no thoughts of a career in the music business: "When Elvis Presley was happening, I loved Elvis Presley. When the Beatles happened, I loved the Beatles. But it never occurred to me for it to be a career. I was from Brooklyn and didn't know anything about show business. My mother was a corsetiere and my father was a pattern cutter. We just didn't know about these things."

He found his vocation some two years later when he went to work in the mailroom of the William Morris talent agency in New York. "I always thought I would find something I liked, and when I found it, I would be good at it. That's what I always hoped and believed. And when I got to the William Morris Agency, when I was twenty years old, I knew very quickly this was the right thing for me. I just knew it, and I knew I'd be good at it—and I was.

"It was like that song in *Chorus Line*—"I Can Do That." When I was delivering the mail around the halls of William Morris and listening to people talk, I thought, I can do that. I've always thought I can do anything I want to do."

Quickly rising from the mailroom of the agency, Geffen became a talent scout and then moved on from William Morris to the Ashley-Famous talent agency (which was purchased by the Kinney Corporation shortly before Kinney took over Warner Seven-Arts). From there he moved into artist management in his own right and was largely responsible for the formation of Crosby, Stills, and Nash—the group that emerged from the wreckage of Buffalo Springfield. That deal brought Geffen into the mainstream of the music business, it began his association with Ahmet Ertegun, and it provoked Geffen's first head-on collision with Jerry Wexler.

Assembling Crosby, Stills, and Nash was no easy trick. David Crosby, a former member of the Byrds, was under contract as a solo artist to Epic Records. Graham Nash was still a member of the British group the Hollies, and also under contract to Epic. And Stephen Stills was under contract to Atlantic. "So you can imagine, untangling it all was the most difficult thing, and the first person I called was Jerry Wexler," says Geffen. "I went to see Jerry Wexler to get a release for Stephen Stills—and he threw me out of his office."

Geffen speaks as if he still cannot quite believe it: "The truth of the matter is he threw me out of his office! He was really unpleasant, and I thought, My God, these people are a nightmare. We have to get away from Atlantic Records."

According to Geffen it was Ertegun, with his practiced diplomacy, who saved the situation: "The next day, I got a call from Ahmet Ertegun. He realized it was not a smart tactical move to throw me out of the office, so he called me up and he was extremely charming and extremely generous and flattering." Before long Ertegun was flying Geffen to California, and wining and dining him—"and I bought it, hook, line, and sinker, and was immediately in the Ahmet Ertegun fan club, which to some extent I have remained in my whole life. But particularly in those days, I thought Ahmet was the greatest thing since chocolate chip cookies, and I subsequently arranged that Crosby, Stills, and Nash would record for Atlantic Records. He handled me very well always, in those days."

This dangerously double-edged tone is often apparent when Geffen speaks of his relationship with Ertegun—a relationship that led to the setting up of Asylum Records in 1970. His antagonism toward Ertegun, though not as overt as it is toward Wexler, is still liable to crack his affable veneer. For example, Geffen's version of the events leading up to the formation of Asylum Records is more controversial than Ertegun's. "I got on with him very well, and we became great friends," says Ertegun. "And I saw in him a potential genius entertainment executive or entrepreneur; he was very bright, very fast. He was younger than me and he had a keen sense of where youth was going in America. He said he would love to start his own label—so I financed Asylum."

Geffen's version is longer, and laced with spite. He says, having successfully assembled Crosby, Stills, and Nash, and placed them with Atlantic, he asked Ertegun to sign another of the acts he managed, Jackson Browne—a then little known singer-songwriter based in California. "He wasn't interested," says Geffen contemptuously. "He passed. So then I went to every other record company in town: Clive Davis [of CBS], etcetera, etcetera—and they all passed. So then I went back to Ahmet and I said, 'Ahmet, look, I'm trying to do you a favor by giving you Jackson Browne.' And he said, 'Don't do me no favors.' And I said, 'Seriously, you'll make a lot of money.' And he said to me, 'You know what, David, I have a lot of money. Why don't you make a lot of money? Why don't you start a record company, and then you'll have a lot of money too.'

"He was being snide. So I thought, Fuck it. If I really believe in these artists I *should* start a record company. So I made a deal with Ahmet for Asylum Records . . ."

Under the terms of the deal, Atlantic financed Asylum Records for three years in return for a share of the profits. It proved to be a very astute move on Ertegun's part for the label was immensely successful in establishing the West Coast singer-songwriters Geffen had discovered. "I really expected it to be a tiny, tiny, nothing—basically a production deal," Geffen says. "But I'm very competitive and so once started I went for it, and within a very short amount of time I had twelve artists signed. And although in the first year I didn't release a single record, in the second year of the deal we released Linda Ronstadt, Jackson Browne, the Eagles, Joni Mitchell, etcetera, and everything started to happen."

By 1972, with only one year of the deal left to run, it was obvious to the Warner corporate executives that Asylum and Geffen were highly profitable commodities and should not be let go. As Geffen says: "It was very clear there was something valuable happening here, and it was also very clear they only had one more year left on the contract. So Steve Ross approached me about selling them the company, and I thought of the biggest amount of money I could possibly imagine in those days, and I sold them the company for seven million dollars altogether—five million in stock and two million in cash." Asylum became an Atlantic subsidiary which Geffen continued to run.

But Geffen—like Wexler five years earlier—immediately regretted his decision to sell to Warner, and he especially regretted being paid most of his money in Warner Communications stock. "In the following year Asylum went through the roof, and earned back one hundred percent of what the company cost on just a couple of records," explains Geffen. "But the stock, which I got at forty dollars a share, was down to eight dollars—so I was very, very upset, as you can well imagine. I wanted out of the deal, or more money, and I was very unhappy." (Warner Communications' stock has periodically been battered down, usually due to the poor performance of subsidiaries other than the movie and record divisions—which, overall, have done well. Those loss-making subsidiaries, most of which have since been sold, included the Atari computer and video games division, which lost Warner a spectacular $1 billion.)

The new boy genius of the music business clearly had to be placated at almost any cost. Warner Communications agreed to sweeten the original deal by guaranteeing that Geffen would not lose money on his Warner stock if the price failed to recover over a number of years. And, as a considerable bonus, Geffen was invited to take Asylum Records out from under the umbrella of Atlantic and merge it with Elektra Records (the independent label Warner had bought in 1970) to form a new label which Geffen would run. "Elektra was losing money and doing very poorly at the time, and they wanted me to take it over," says Geffen. He did so with a vengeance. "At the time, Elektra had something like forty-five or fifty artists. I dropped all but thirteen—and you never heard of any of the ones I dropped. It's not like I dropped an act and a week later they ended up being Motley Crue, or something like that, on another label. They were valueless. I kept all the ones I thought had value and that was a fraction of the people signed to the company. And altogether we had a very strong record company which was immediately very competitive with any record company in the world. And I built it into a very, very profitable, successful record company which, by the time I left, had the highest net profit of any record company in the world, and the largest amount of successes per release in any company in the history of the record business."

Jack Holzman, the founder of Elektra, who left the label to become a senior vice-president of Warner Communications (learning, he says, that "investment banking is the rock and roll of the 1980s"), says the merger of Elektra and Asylum was an obvious solution to two problems—how to revive Elektra's fortunes, and how to keep Geffen happy: "Geffen was very good with the artists he liked, and he knew how to keep them happy. So my suggestion to Steve Ross was that you give David Geffen a bigger sandbox to play in, and you take the Asylum label, bring it out from Atlantic, and merge it with Elektra."

It may have been an obvious solution but, as Holzman admits, it was not one designed to please Ahmet Ertegun: "Ahmet wasn't particularly happy about that. At the cocktail party for my departure, Ahmet's only comment about my leaving Elektra was he hated the idea of Asylum merging with Elektra because it meant he was going to lose the roster [of Asylum's artists]."

But as Geffen says, with no undue modesty, "On the other hand, it was hard [for Ertegun] not to rise to the occasion of the problems of the company, with Elektra Records doing as badly as it was doing."

If Ertegun was upset he remained apparently sanguine. Wexler, on the other hand, was increasingly enraged by Geffen and did not hide his hostility. There was at least one occasion when the two men almost came to blows.

"The classic fight was at my house," says Joe Smith, who then ran the Warner Brothers record label in Los Angeles

together with Mo Ostin. The occasion was an informal corporate meeting "to figure out how we can save money, or
something like that," and most of Warner's executives were
present, including Steve Ross.

Whatever the meeting was supposed to be about, the only
item on the agendas of Wexler and Geffen was Bob Dylan.
Dylan, who had been almost deified for ten years, had not yet
renewed his contract with Columbia Records and was being
hotly pursued by several labels, including Atlantic and Asylum. Eventually he would resign with Columbia but, shortly
before the meeting at Joe Smith's house, Geffen had
preempted the competition by doing a handshake deal with
Dylan which led to Asylum releasing the *Planet Waves*
album.

"Now it's around eleven-thirty," says Smith. "Geffen had
just signed Bob Dylan—and Wexler had been fighting for
Bob Dylan—and Wexler and Geffen did not like each other.
Wexler made some remark about 'You bought him, and you
paid so much money you're ridiculous.' And Geffen leapt to
the bait and started to scream and call him a has-been, a
washed-up old record man. And Wexler stood up screaming,
and says, 'You, you are an agent—you'd dive into a pile of pus
to come up with an act.'

"They were really talking hate. I thought Jerry was going
to have a heart attack or something like that. Everybody is
panicking, saying 'Sit down, we can't have this,' and Steve
Ross stands up and says, 'I'm going to leave now.' It was wild.
We get everything settled down but you are talking a very
heavy atmosphere in the room. Jack Holzman starts to talk
about something else but it's clear nobody's mind is on it."

Like most of Joe Smith's stories, this one has a funny ending. Smith's wife had prepared lunch—after much debate as
to whether she should serve poached salmon or cheese soufflé—and, in an attempt to make peace, Smith proposed to his
colleagues that they take a break from their meeting and go
to the dining room. "Okay, so she has set up the table terrific.
Now my wife is there, Miss Charm, and she's greeting every-

body, and all these men are coming in with these terrible looks on their faces. And we sit down and eat, and nobody is saying anything. So she says to me, 'Psst, come here.' I go over and say, 'What's the matter?' And she says, 'I told you we shouldn't have had the cheese soufflé.' "

Today Geffen, in a magnanimous mood, says, "I admire and respect Jerry." But he admits: "Jerry Wexler and I did not get along. He was kind of upset by my success and the attention I got, and the fact I signed Bob Dylan, whom he was sort of friendly with. He found it galling, and I'm the sort of person who doesn't take any shit from anybody anyway, so whenever shit was coming my way you can be sure that I was forthright about it. So Jerry had a real hard time with me."

The final straw for Wexler—and the greatest insult—came in June 1974, when Ertegun and Geffen decided to merge Atlantic and Elektra/Asylum to form what would have been one immensely powerful label. Under the terms of their plan, Ertegun and Geffen would become the joint heads of the new label, co-chairmen, and Wexler would be a mere vice-president. "Geffen wanted to be co-chairman, and I didn't mind the idea," says Ertegun. "Then I got this frantic phone call—I was in Germany at the time—from Jerry Greenberg and Sheldon Vogel, saying they were thoroughly opposed."

Jerry Greenberg, who had been hired by Wexler in 1967 as his assistant, had risen through the Atlantic hierarchy to become president of the company, filling the management vacuum created by Wexler's departure to Florida and Ertegun's frequent absences from New York. Greenberg was certainly not enamored of the proposed merger of Atlantic and Elektra/Asylum: "We all thought there were going to be too many problems and, from a corporate point of view, they would be better off having [separate] companies that were different. Geffen had his own style, his own way of running things, and his own taste in music . . . I had no problems working along with Geffen, because Geffen and I were real good friends. But all of a sudden we started figuring out, 'This guy has got to go and that guy has got to go.' It wasn't like putting two companies together and going 'boom, boom, boom.' It was putting two companies together and shrinking them."

Despite Greenberg's misgivings, however, it was Wexler and not he who mounted the most fierce opposition to the merger: "Jerry Wexler was the one who was really against it. Yes, Wexler really made a strong pitch that this was the wrong thing to do."

Faced with such solid resistance from his colleagues, Ertegun began having second thoughts about the merger. "So then I kind of postponed it, and David got very upset, and the whole thing fell apart," he says. "I think David was quite hurt. But I think everyone thought he would come on too strong, and be too disruptive."

For his part, Geffen does not accept this explanation. He says it mattered little that Wexler was against the merger: "Ahmet never cared about upsetting Jerry Wexler. Jerry was never a consideration." He also believes the objections of Jerry Greenberg and Sheldon Vogel were equally unimportant when it came to the final decision: "Ahmet is a big boy, and Ahmet does what he wants, and Ahmet is not that considerate of his employees. They don't have that big a vote. Ahmet's a little bit like the gorilla—he sits where he wants. By the way, it wasn't a rupture in our relationship. I didn't give a shit about it."

Geffen's explanation for the merger falling through is as cynical as one would expect: "Ahmet and I agreed on a merger but he got very upset because friends of his were calling him up to find out if it was a demotion for him . . . Ahmet was upset by the idea people would think that he was less than they thought he was, by virtue of this shared chairmanship."

As Ertegun says of Geffen, "David doesn't have a long attention span. He does something for a couple of years, loses interest, and then does something else. He's always looking for something bigger and better." After the merger fell through—and denied the chance to play in an even bigger sandbox—Geffen soon grew bored with the music business. He had once told Ertegun: "Everyone else is so stupid, let's take over everything—films, music, the lot." In pursuit of that belief, presumably, in 1975 he moved from Elektra/Asylum to the Warner film division, attacking his new position with customary élan. "The first job I had in the movie business was vice-chairman of the board of Warner Brothers Pictures," he says. "That was literally my first job, just like my first job in the record business was as chairman of the board of Asylum Records. I've always gone in and just done it because what I really believe is, there isn't that much to know." But after one year with the movie division he abruptly resigned ("David *always* gets restless," says Ertegun), and essentially retired: For the next four years he occupied himself by lecturing at the University of California in Los Angeles and at Yale, and collecting art. After a cancer scare (a false alarm, as it turned out), he emerged to do battle again in 1980, setting up Geffen Records in partnership with Warner Communications—a label which now counts among its successes Elton John and Peter Gabriel.

According to Mica Ertegun—who has all of her husband's astuteness about people, and more—Geffen, although charming, intelligent, and likeable in many ways, is not only ruthlessly ambitious but also a man incapable of loyalty to anybody.

Ertegun himself is always publicly loyal to Geffen. Privately, when asked if they are still friends, Ertegun replies: "He says we're best friends but we never really see each other. He sees me when I can be useful to him." Beyond that he will not go. He seems like a father, nursing some secret disappointment over an ungrateful son; a disappointment too painful to articulate.

But Tom Dowd, Atlantic's veteran producer, tells a story that offers some insight into how Ertegun really feels about

Geffen, and why. It concerns an incident that happened when Geffen, having left Elektra/Asylum, was living in Los Angeles with Cher after her marriage to Sonny Bono had broken down.

As Dowd tells it, he and Ertegun happened to be in Los Angeles at the same time and Ertegun, for once, had no definite plans for the evening. "Usually, when he is in California he has dinner plans, cocktail plans, lunch plans, Copacabana plans, and four meetings an hour," says Dowd.

Ertegun suggested to Dowd they go out to dinner with Bianca Jagger. Dowd arrived at the restaurant as arranged, and spent the next hour and a half drinking at the bar alone. He was not perturbed: Ertegun is notorious for many things, chronic unpunctuality being one of them. "Sure enough, at ten-thirty Ahmet arrived with Bianca Jagger and another lady—some countess. He's calling the waiters, ordering champagne, and I'm thinking, Oh God, I'm going to be a disgrace. We finish dinner at one o'clock—by which time they're sweeping the floor of the restaurant and putting the chairs on the tables. Mick Jagger's joined us by then, and Ahmet says, 'There's got to be a party somewhere—there must be a party somewhere.' So he gets a waiter to bring a phone to the table and he picks up the phone and dials a number: 'Hello, Bette [Midler], what are you doing? There's a party going on at Cher's—we'll pick you up on the way there.' Then he phones Cher—she's probably asleep as it's now getting on for two in the morning. 'Hello, Cher,' he says. 'I'm with Tom, and Mick, and Bianca, and Bette—we'll come over for a nightcap.' He doesn't crash a party, he manufactures one.

"So we pull up at Cher's house—Mick, and Bianca Jagger, Bette Midler, this countess, Ahmet, and me. Cher's looking beautiful in a gold lamé dress. She's living with David Geffen at this point, and we all go into the living room. Mick's sitting there at the piano, Cher is singing. Geffen is just sitting there in tennis shoes and shorts.

"And Ahmet says to me, 'Look at that creep. How can he

dress like that?' Then he says to Geffen, 'David, what a lovely outfit.' Then he asks Cher if we can have some champagne. She says, 'Of course, we always have some chilled.' But then David Geffen asks her, 'Where is the champagne?' Ahmet just looks at him and says, 'We never had that problem when Sonny was here.'

"That was Ahmet, pulling people's strings. Ahmet has a great deal of respect for Geffen but he doesn't like him as a human being. He has no allegiance to him—because David has no allegiance to anything except for dollar signs. And Ahmet will not renege on a human being, like David would."

Jerry Wexler left Atlantic Records in 1975, ending an extraordinary partnership that had lasted twenty-two years and had contributed incalculably to the development of the modern music industry. Wexler continued to produce musicals, soundtracks, and records for artists such as Bob Dylan and Dire Straits. The latter he signed to Warner Brothers Records for whom he became a consultant.

Today he divides his time between a book-filled house in East Hampton, Long Island, and a second home in Florida, with occasional forays to the mahogany and marble splendors of Manhattan's University Club (tempted there by its uncommonly fine wine and well-stocked library). Sitting in his East Hampton house, comfortable in faded jeans, an old cap, and a T-shirt commemorating the Montreux Jazz Festival, Wexler reflects on the past glories of his career with some sadness. "You're so close to someone when you produce records—so intimate, so tender. And then suddenly it's over. I'm left with a ballroom full of ghosts."

Ertegun—who can appear the most straightforward of men, hiding the myriad complexities of his character—explains Wexler's melancholy: "He is sad because he sees the music to which he gave his life is no longer important." It is wise, says Ertegun with a sigh, to retain some kind of perspective on the music that he and Wexler both love. "It is a mistake to invest the music we recorded with too much importance [and perhaps this is why the album covers that decorate the walls of Atlantic's reception area are placed indiscriminately, so that Dizzie Gillespie and Charlie Mingus are unceremoniously hung next to Genesis, Foreigner, and Pete Townsend]. It isn't classical music, and it cannot be interpreted in the same way. It's more like the old Fred Astaire movies: They're fun, but they're not great art. And they shouldn't be seen as great art."

Chapter 11
MADNESS AND MONEY

These were the salad days of the record industry, of fever-pitch competition to sign up rock stars whose value, in commercial terms, was spiraling ever upwards. By now power was concentrated in the hands of six major record companies which between them controlled between 80 and 90 percent of the market. (The six companies, in order of market share, were CBS, Warner, RCA, Capitol-EMI, MCA, and Polygram.) They conducted fierce bidding wars among themselves, wars that sometimes escalated to the point of madness. The worldwide sales of the Warner group of record companies alone were some $700 million, and money was available in such excessive quantities it was difficult to keep track of where it was going and which acts it was paying for.

Brian Lane, the streetwise cockney manager of the British groups Yes and Emerson, Lake, and Palmer (and later of Asia, the first supergroup of the eighties, formed from the remnants of those two bands), watched, with some bemusement, millions of dollars change hands in the most arbitrary manner. On occasion, he even received large payments from Atlantic for services which he had not rendered.

In the early fall of 1979, Lane received a telephone call from his very meticulous bookkeeper, who said, "It's good news about Pete. The bank says the money has arrived from Atlantic." Lane had no idea what his bookkeeper was talking about but asked how much money Atlantic had sent. "Four hundred thousand dollars," said the bookkeeper. Lane told him to put the money on deposit and then telephoned the bank in search of further explanation. The bank told him the advice note accompanying the payment read: "Advance re. Pete Townsend." Brian Lane had no connection with Townsend, the lead guitarist and main songwriter of the Who; nor, so far as he knew, did Atlantic—both the group and Townsend, as a solo artist, were under contract to MCA Records. Clearly the money had been sent to Lane in error. He decided to sit back and wait to see how long it was before anybody noticed.

October and November went by and Lane heard nothing from Atlantic. Just before Christmas he happened to meet another manager, in the Concorde Lounge at New York's Kennedy Airport, who was in a state of high excitement: He told Lane the Who had signed a new contract with Warner Brothers, and Townsend had signed a solo deal with Atco, Atlantic's subsidiary. Lane thought to himself, I know, and what's more I know where the advance is. But he said nothing.

January and February passed and still nobody mentioned the missing advance. By this stage Lane was thinking, What happens if nobody *ever* mentions it? In March of 1980 he went to New York to visit Atlantic and talk about money: not that advance, but a smaller one he was seeking for his group, Yes.

For all of Yes's phenomenal success during the 1970s, its members were short of money, and bickering among themselves. (For once the cause was not drugs: Most of the members of Yes were sober vegetarians.) The group was obviously coming apart at the seams, but it was working on a new album (which would be its last) and Lane asked Sheldon Vogel, Atlantic's controller, for $200,000 to keep his clients going. Much to Lane's annoyance, Vogel refused point-blank.

Deciding Ertegun might be a softer touch, Lane arranged to have lunch with him in Warner Communications' executive dining room. He was still waiting for the right moment to press his case for Yes when Vogel marched up to their table. "I want my four hundred thousand dollars back," he demanded. "What four hundred thousand?" said Lane—thus forcing Vogel in to a long and embarrassing explanation of how an advance that should have been sent to Warner's London office had instead reached Brian Lane's bank account. "It'll be pretty costly if you make a few more errors like that," said Lane, rubbing it in.

Lane then proposed that in order to keep the books straight, and to save embarrassment, "we call it quits": that Yes be given an advance of $400,000—twice what Lane had been asking for. "Ertegun was very confused, Sheldon was very angry, and I got my four hundred thousand," said Lane. He also got the interest which the money had been earning for almost six months.

This was not the first time Brian Lane had been the cause of flushed faces and ruffled tempers at Atlantic. Lane well understood that in the frenetic competition between record companies to sign new groups, the quality of the music, or the group's originality, played little part in the process. What counted far more were rumor, hype, winning streaks, and fantastic speculation as to how much a group might earn. In New York, at a time when Lane was enjoying a considerable winning streak, he fell into conversation with Dee Anthony, another successful manager (of, among others, Peter Frampton). "We were saying how if you'd had a hit record and were on a roll, you could walk into any record company with a reel of tape and they would deal with you," says Lane. They agreed it did not matter who the artists were, or how good they were. Indeed, they decided, *the group did not even have to exist;* all it would take to start a bidding war was rumor, and a little hype. To test their theory, Lane and Anthony concocted an imaginary group called Scorpio, pretending it was jointly managed by the two of them, and set out to see how much interest they could drum up.

The occasion was a dinner in honor of Ahmet Ertegun,

who had been named B'nai B'rith Man of the Year. The music business luminaries at the top table—the unwitting guinea pigs of this experiment—included David Geffen, Clive Davis, Joe Smith, Robert Stigwood, and Ertegun himself.

The first to be offered the bait was David Geffen. Coming up to Lane he said, "How are you doing? How's business?"

"It's great," said Lane. "I've got this incredible new band called Scorpio that I'm managing with Dee Anthony."

"Brian, I told you to keep your mouth shut," said Anthony in mock anger. "We are still getting the band together and now you've told David Geffen, everybody knows." Lane and Anthony argued loudly enough to ensure that everybody could hear them. By the time dinner was over, Scorpio was so well established that Joe Smith—the master of ceremonies for the evening, and one who specializes in insulting members of his audience—announced: "Not content with ripping off the bands they already have, Brian Lane and Dee Anthony are going to start ripping off this new band Scorpio."

No sooner had Smith finished his speech than Lane and Anthony received their first firm offer of a recording contract for Scorpio. Doug Morris and Dick Vanderbilt of Big Tree Records, a subsidiary of Atlantic, sent their lawyer to the two managers' table to offer $250,000 to sign the nonexistent group. "Are you out of your mind?" said Anthony, as if such a lowly sum was an unthinkable advance for a band of Scorpio's status. He did agree, however, to a meeting with Big Tree's management to negotiate a better price.

By this time Brian Lane was getting cold feet. He was worried the joke had gone too far, and that Ahmet Ertegun might not appreciate the humor. He decided to confess: "I went up and told him that Dee Anthony and I were just trying to show how naive and gullible the music industry is. I said I hoped it hadn't spoiled his evening." Unfortunately it was by then late at night, and Ertegun had drunk a great deal. Lane *thought* Ertegun heard his apology, but he could not be sure.

In the days that followed Dee Anthony persuaded Lane they should continue what they now called "Operation Scorpio" to see how far it might go. "It is a shame to waste all these appointments," said Anthony. By the end of the week they had received an offer of $500,000 for one album—and none of those who bid even asked who the members of Scorpio were. Having conclusively proved their point to themselves, Lane and Anthony declared Operation Scorpio a complete success, and forgot all about it.

But Scorpio had taken on a life of its own. A month later, and back in London, Lane received a telephone call from a furious Ertegun. "You're cheap and two-faced," said Ertegun. "We know what you've done. I've got Doug and Dick [of Big Tree] in the office here. That band Scorpio—" Lane protested he had told Ertegun at the dinner that the whole thing was a hoax but Ertegun had no recollection of what Lane had said then—and would not accept it now. "That's what you want me to believe," he said. "I know you've been wining and dining everyone else. Dick and Doug asked you first. That band's got to be on Atlantic."

Nothing would dissuade him, and Lane eventually agreed to travel to New York, at Atlantic's expense, to negotiate a deal. "The lawyers drew up the contracts, the check for [the first payment of] two hundred fifty thousand was handed over—and Atlantic still didn't know who Scorpio was."

Brian Lane still has a photocopy of the check, which he keeps as a memento of what a winning streak, a little hype, and fantastic speculation can achieve. He did not sign the contract, of course, and his refusal to do so finally convinced Atlantic's executives that Scorpio was a figment of their own imaginations. Fortunately for Lane, Ertegun appreciates a well-executed practical joke. He thought the episode "hysterical."

Ironically—and as another indicator of the surreal nature of Ahmet Ertegun's business—at almost the same time Atlantic was so desperate to sign a band which did not exist, the company was not entirely enthusiastic about signing a group whose records would outsell those of the Rolling Stones with ease (and to the chagrin of the World's Greatest Rock-and-Roll Band). Fortunately for Atlantic, Foreigner was signed by the label—and Ertegun immediately took an interest in them. The group's debut album sold three million copies (and went on to sell five million copies worldwide). Since then Foreigner's sales have exceeded twenty-five million records, and everybody at Atlantic has become a believer.

Foreigner symbolizes what Atlantic Records has become in the eighties—a vast, efficient, profit-generating corporation—just as Ruth Brown and Big Joe Turner once symbolized the small, funky label Ertegun and Jerry Wexler struggled to establish in the fifties. (When Ertegun recently organized a birthday party for Nancy Reagan's friend Jerry Zipkin, he asked LaVern Baker, another Atlantic star from the early days, to sing at the dinner. She and Foreigner's lead guitarist and songwriter, Mick Jones, took the opportunity to "jam" together. "That was kind of interesting," says Jones. "For Ahmet, it must have been the beginning and the now.")

Mick Jagger disparagingly describes Foreigner's music as "corporate rock, beer ads." He says he understands why Ertegun was attracted by groups such as Led Zeppelin—which, after all, "loved the blues"—but he has never been quite sure how Foreigner fitted into Ertegun's scheme of things. "It's just a commercial move, I suppose," he says. "The company needed the money. And it's been a huge money-maker for them." He does concede, however, that if Foreigner has a place on the roster of any self-respecting record company it is because Mick Jones "is not a complete bozo as far as music is concerned." (Ertegun says Jones is far from being a bozo. "Mick Jones is a great talent, both as a musician and as a producer. Even though, like Led Zeppelin, they did not get critical acclaim in the beginning, the fans loved them—and they didn't love them because the music was bad.")

Certainly Mick Jones is not a typical rock star. He does

wear the obligatory uniform of black leather but, as if in counterbalance, he has a slight paunch, and he is articulate and friendly. He has a close rapport with Ertegun and with other pioneers of the music business which stems from his fascination with the world from which Atlantic Records emerged. In a way he, too, has paid his dues in the industry. And the story of Jones's rocky path to superstardom offers fascinating insights into some of the darker corners of that world.

As a young boy growing up in Woking, England, Jones was inspired not by such stars as Elvis Presley but by Atlantic's R&B kings Solomon Burke and Ray Charles, and by Arthur Alexander (who made the first hit to come out of Rick Hall's Fame studios in Muscle Shoals). This was unusual in Woking. "I felt very special being aware of those people," says Jones. "There were only a handful of people in Woking who knew about them."

As a teenager Jones formed a band called the Hustlers which played the music of Solomon Burke and Roy Orbison in local youth clubs. The Hustlers also opened at the Wooden Bridge club in nearby Guildford for a then little known band called the Rolling Stones. Jones began his professional career as the twenty-fourth guitarist with Nero and the Gladiators (which had several minor hits in England). He moved to Paris to work with French rock singer Johnny Halliday, and then "had a little spell with the Beatles," who introduced him to the records of Marvin Gaye. In Paris he also met Otis Redding, another of his childhood heroes.

After this apprenticeship at the feet of several present and future rock legends, Jones returned to England and in late 1972 joined the newly re-formed rock band Spooky Tooth. The group did not last, and never made a hit record. When it "ground to a halt in New York" in 1974, Jones bumped into a fellow Englishman named Nigel Thomas who aspired to be another Ahmet Ertegun—though he was never remotely his equal in terms of talent or personal charm. Thomas, the one-time manager of English blues singer Joe Cocker (renowned for vomiting onstage), hoped to make himself into a music mogul through a label he was setting up called EAR. "He had these illusions of grandeur about forming this fabulous situation in America—and I got taken in by it," says Jones. He agreed to produce records for EAR and oversee the general running of the company. "I was really flattered and thought it was a chance for me to use some of my knowledge."

In fact, as things turned out, it was more of an opportunity to extend his knowledge of some of the more unsavory aspects, and characters, of the American record business. Fortunately for Jones, he had an expert tutor—a man far wiser to the tricksters and con men of the industry: the ubiquitous Hy Weiss. Thomas had somehow persuaded Weiss to act as a guide for Jones through the murky world of independent distribution.

"Hy became a great mentor to me," says Jones. "I thought I knew a lot about the music business, and suddenly I met this guy who could pull out the whole history of the music as we know it. He'd been around with Ahmet and Jerry Wexler, and everybody, and they'd all lived through all those things. He took me on a tour of independent distributors—all those old scoundrels. Hy really toughened me up. Our offices were in the Brill Building, in Freddie Bienstock's office [the wealthy music publisher who married Miriam Abramson], right next to Leiber and Stoller [the songwriters and producers] . . . I don't know how it all happened but it was meant to be because it really toughened me up a lot, and provided a challenge for me to survive in New York."

Among other adventures, the unlikely trio—the journeyman rocker, the Jewish hustler, and the flash English rogue— had the audacity to try and take over Stax Records, then in its death throes. "We went down into Memphis and we were going to take over Memphis," says Jones. "Al Bell had disappeared by then. They [the authorities] were still looking for him." But Steve Cropper was still in Memphis and the trio moved into the studios where he was working while they conducted their bold negotiations with Stax's major and unhappy creditor, the Union Planters Bank.

The negotiations ended in farce when Jones, Weiss, and Thomas went out to dinner with a representative of the bank. "I think we were convincing," says Jones. "I had a bit of credibility, because of the bands I had worked with—and I was a nice sensible English guy." Unhappily, when the bill for dinner arrived and Thomas attempted to pay it with his MasterCard, the request for credit approval was turned down. They were on the verge of a $50 million deal—and they could not even pay for the meal.

This episode only foreshadowed what was to come. Thomas could rarely pay his bills and Jones was to rely heavily on Weiss—and his sharp nose for business—when the crash finally came and he and Weiss had to extricate themselves from the wreckage. "I found myself, after a certain point, being at the wrong end of a lot of disappointed people; disappointed people that were owed money," says Jones. He and Weiss parted company with Nigel Thomas in 1975. Although this left them out of pocket "we valued our lives and our faces," Jones says enigmatically.

"Hy Weiss helped me get through it all . . . He is like my Jewish godfather. He has such great redeeming qualities about him: He's a scoundrel and a scallywag sometimes but he's lovable—and he's a very philosophical person. Meeting Hy prepared me for what was to come. It was a sort of transition."

What was to come, in 1976, was Bud Prager, a silver-haired music manager who works out of an office in the same shabby building in New York as Morris Levy. Prager was, as ever, broke and looking to make a deal. He had a rock group on his hands which he was convinced could be the next Cream or Led Zeppelin, but nobody wanted to know. "Foreigner was turned down by everybody," says Prager. "Two of the biggest-selling rock bands of all time with their first albums— Foreigner and Boston—were both turned down by all the record companies, which is a reflection of the signing abilities of the major labels."

After the EAR debacle, Jones had wisely given up any notion of becoming a mogul and had formed Foreigner with Ian McDonald, an English multi-instrumentalist (flute, saxophone, keyboards, reeds, guitar—and he sings, too) who had been one of the founders of King Crimson. Together they recruited four unknown musicians and produced a series of demonstration tapes which Prager thought were impressive. The record companies did not. It might have been thought that any group including McDonald would have had an edge with Atlantic because King Crimson had recorded for the label and produced an album that Pete Townsend, no less, endorsed as "an uncanny masterpiece"—but Atlantic turned Foreigner down along with all the rest. (The exception was CBS, for Prager had a score to settle with the company: "They had screwed me out of a lot of money so I figured I would screw them out of Foreigner. The band was never even offered to them.")

Prager did not give up, concentrating his attention on Atlantic. "Record companies are very cyclical, and Atlantic was in a big slump at the time. They had a tradition of bands like Cream and Bad Company, then there was nothing and the bottom had fallen out. They hadn't broken a new band for three years and I, the eternal optimist, felt that Foreigner would fill the void." Atlantic remained unconvinced by Prager's unflattering arguments, and Jerry Greenberg, the label's president, kept rejecting the demo tapes.

The Atlantic executive who was finally persuaded by Foreigner, and who persuaded Greenberg to change his mind and sign what became one of the most commercial rock bands in the world, is someone who might be expected to be more interested in the outpourings of psychedelic rock bands of the seventies, or an arcane branch of folk music. John Kalodner, now head of A&R at Geffen Records, wears long straggly hair well past his shoulders and denim from head to toe. Among his other eccentricities, he belongs to the Survivalists, the strange Californian tribe whose members undergo rigorous training in the Hollywood foothills to prepare themselves for survival in the everlasting winter of a nuclear holocaust. Yet Kalodner's proudest possession, carefully positioned under the rainbow blinds of his office, and next to his collection of freaky gonk toys, is one of Foreigner's platinum albums. (A platinum album, as defined by the Recording Industry Association of America in 1976, is one that has sold at least one million copies with a dollar volume of at least $2 million.)

When Kalodner heard Foreigner's demo tape of "Feels Like the First Time" he had a hunch the band could be successful, and he eventually persuaded Greenberg (an ebullient, curly-headed New Yorker) to attend a live audition of the group. Greenberg says he agreed to go mainly out of sympathy for Bud Prager: "Prager has had his ups and now he was down—but he could always have a winner," said Greenberg. After the audition, driving back to Atlantic's offices in a limousine, Greenberg told Kalodner he could sign Foreigner and make the band his personal project. It was not easy. Kalodner had to call twenty-six producers before he could find anyone willing to steer the band through the making of its first album.

The result, *Foreigner*, was released in March 1977 to be met by critical accusations of "formulaic commercialism"— and huge success. Three tracks from the album, including the song that had originally attracted Kalodner, stayed in the Top 20 singles chart for a year.

Even so, it was not until Foreigner was in the studio recording its second album, *Double Vision*, that the group was graced by a visit from Ahmet Ertegun—the one person whose approval Mick Jones desperately sought. Jones remembers being so nervous at Ertegun's presence that he was shaking and had to keep leaving the studio. At the end of the session Ertegun said, "Well, the ballad sounds interesting." Mick Jones thought: My God, we're doomed, we've failed. *Double Vision* sold *seven million* copies.

It was to be another seven or eight years before Jones felt he had finally gained Ertegun's approval (by which time all the original members of the band, save Jones, had departed). In 1986, when the new Foreigner (now a quartet) was in the final stages of producing its *Agent Provocateur* album, Jones persuaded Ertegun to revisit the studio to listen to the master tape. This time Ertegun appeared at least moderately interested in some of the material. But Jones had saved one track for last: "I Want to Know What Love Is," with its soaring gospel chorus. "About a minute into the song I looked at Ahmet and I could see tears rolling down his cheeks. He looked over at me, and held my arm, just grabbed me—and the tears started with me too. We just sat there, and for me it was the crowning moment of achievement: the person that I lauded and respected so much, that guy who has seen everything in life, I'd actually brought tears to his eye."

Ertegun is not always so indifferent to Atlantic's rock artists, and it was not only the Rolling Stones that merited his attention. Now in his sixties, he claims he is no longer on the cutting edge: "I used to know exactly what would sell but I'm not so sure now, because I don't spend all my time in clubs and bars looking for bands to sign. I have young kids to do all that now." But every so often, "I hear something that really moves me"—and in those cases the music mogul climbs out of his executive chair and rolls up his sleeves. Since 1976, when Ertegun attended a concert "in some midwestern town like Minneapolis," one of his greatest enthusiasms has been for Genesis, the progressive rock band from Britain, and, in particular, for its leader, Phil Collins.

On the face of it Collins is an unlikely subject for such devotion. He was not one of the original founders of the group (four students from Charterhouse, an exclusive British public school) but merely the replacement drummer. And when Peter Gabriel, one of the founders and the lead singer, left Genesis in 1974 to pursue a solo career, Collins seemed the last person likely to replace him. Indeed, Genesis wasted eighteen months auditioning more than four hundred possible replacements for Gabriel before deciding that Collins should get the job of lead vocalist, while continuing to be the drummer. Ertegun first saw Collins perform his dual act at the concert in the Midwest, and was instantly captivated: "He took over the stage like a master who owned it and danced around, playing drums and running down to the mike. They put on a great extravaganza of a show and that was when I really got into the group." Perhaps as a result (though Ertegun would disclaim it), Genesis as a group, and Collins as a solo artist, went on to become two of Atlantic's biggest money spinners of the eighties.

It was Jerry Greenberg who signed the band to Atlantic in 1973—the result, he says, of a lesson learned from Ertegun that Britain was a great source of untapped musical talent. Greenberg, following Ertegun's advice, would cross the Atlantic six or seven times a year, hunting out new acts. "I could see that in England Genesis was happening, but they weren't selling five records in America," he says.

Remembering how long it took to establish Genesis in America, and the amount of money Atlantic had to spend to keep them on the road, Greenberg still blinks and rub his eyes when he reads in newspapers today that Genesis on tour fills football stadiums. "I used to give them twenty-five thousand dollars when they lost money on their tours, when they played to two thousand people in Chicago," he says.

With a beguiling style of art rock combining flutes, oboes, a medieval flavor, and bookish references in the lyrics, they were not an easy act to sell to a mass audience. While Peter Gabriel fronted the band they performed what was essentially costume drama, with Gabriel wearing an outlandish range of headgear, from flowerpots to cardboard boxes. The theatrics reached their peak in *The Lamb Lies Down on Broadway*, a two-album set with attendant live show in which Gabriel played Rael, suffering various metamorphoses in a surreal Manhattan. "Genesis was the most intellectual

band of its time and their songs weren't just rhymes on moon
and June," says Ertegun. "They were very intelligent with
some fantastic arrangements that weren't easily understood
by the general public. They had a small, avid, but above-
average audience; they were a cult band."

After Gabriel left the group, and Collins finally secured his
job, Genesis abandoned costume drama in favor of spectacular laser-light shows. Ertegun loved the live performances
but did not really like the Genesis recordings, which he considered a tame version of the live act. "So he rolled up his
shirt-sleeves and went into the studio," says Collins. The occasion was the recording of the group's 1978 album, . . . *And
Then There Were Three* . . . , which included the track "Follow You, Follow Me." Ertegun took Genesis's recorded version of that song and remixed it. "We didn't use his version
but we knew what he was getting at," says Collins. "He saw
something more in there that wasn't coming out before."
The final version of "Follow You, Follow Me" gave Genesis
its first hit single in America, and . . . *And Then There Were
Three* . . . its first gold album (meaning, by the industry's new
definition of "gold," that it sold at least five hundred thousand copies, and earned at least $1 million).

In the process Ertegun and Collins became very close
friends. Ertegun is extravagantly admiring of Collins: "He is
personally one of the really, really good people I have ever
known; he has a depth of goodness. But it is a discreet goodness. He has no fake humility, but real humility. He has a way
of facing life and the world: He is a person who represents
goodness and beauty, and somehow it emerges in his music."

For his part, Collins was initially just star-struck: To him
Ertegun was a legend. But he soon began to appreciate Ertegun's shrewdness and never doubted it when Ertegun told
him, "Some people think I'm a fool—but I know what's going
on." Collins was immensely gratified when Ertegun decided
to take Genesis firmly under his wing.

The next step in Ertegun's master plan was to launch Collins as a solo singer. Collins had played Ertegun a demonstra-

tion tape of some songs with an R&B flavor which he had recorded in his garage in England. "I realized Phil could make a different sort of record than Genesis," says Ertegun. "I told him he should record these songs. There was something very magical about the original tape, so we used that. He produced it, and I helped a little bit at the end."

According to Collins, this is a very modest account of Ertegun's contribution to his solo career and to *Face Value,* his first solo album, which sold two million copies: "Ahmet was behind it from the very beginning, very firmly, even when I was an unknown quantity. I mean, who wants a solo album from a drummer?"

For example, when Ertegun listened to the tape of "In the Air," one of the tracks from the album, he said, "Where's the backbeat, man? The kids won't know where it is—you've got to put extra drums on it."

"The drums come later," said Collins.

"By that time the kids will have flipped over to another radio station," said Ertegun.

Collins went back to London and over-dubbed drums on top of the master tape—an unheard-of technique at the time. "He was quite right," says Collins.

But, though the story of Phil Collins has a happy (and for him and Atlantic a highly profitable) ending, it might have been very different. Beginning in 1980, the American record industry was hit particularly hard by the effects of worldwide recession, and Atlantic seemed to lose some confidence in its own judgment. Just as Collins was preparing to launch his solo career, the company made a series of blunders which almost deprived it of his services—and, in fact, did lead to the loss of other major artists.

Genesis's contract with Atlantic was up for renewal, and Collins, as a solo artist, had not yet signed with the label. As part of the negotiations the group, and Collins as an individual, wanted their own custom label (of the sort the Rolling Stones had been granted), to be called Duke. According to John Kalodner—Foreigner's mentor—Atlantic as a corporation was still only half-hearted about Genesis and Collins, regardless of what Ertegun personally thought. Genesis, with only one gold record, was not yet a priority for most executives at the company.

"Atlantic was hemming and hawing about making this deal [with Phil Collins], which I think had to do with the re-signing of Genesis, and the creation of Duke Records," says Kalodner, who was then at work on Collins's debut album, which Ertegun had encouraged the singer to begin recording.

Then, as the contract negotiations with Genesis and Collins continued, Kalodner himself was let go by the company. In high dudgeon "for throwing me out of there unceremoniously after seven years," he went to work for Geffen Records and told David Geffen he knew Collins was "available." To Kalodner's chagrin (and Atlantic's relief), Geffen, for once, did not recognize the opportunity, and neither did any other American record company: "Nobody tried [to sign Collins as a solo artist] because nobody thought Collins could do anything. Here is an old balding drummer . . . Not old, but here is like a little schlock drummer who was barely cutting it as the lead singer of Genesis—he was just starting to come into his own." But, Kalodner says, he did persuade Richard Branson, the owner of Virgin Records in London, to sign Collins: "That is why Collins is on Virgin in the U.K., because Branson immediately called Tony Smith [the manager of Genesis], and signed him. And the only gold record I ever got for Phil Collins is from Virgin. Phil Collins never sent me one, and Atlantic of course didn't. That was something that hurt my feelings."

The embittered Kalodner also claims the dubious distinction of being indirectly responsible for the departure from Atlantic of Peter Gabriel, who had remained with the label as a solo artist after leaving Genesis.

Kalodner had worked briefly with Gabriel in England on what should have been his third solo album, and "loved" the two very commercial and melodic tracks he heard. However,

when Gabriel finally delivered the completed album to Atlantic, those two tracks were missing. Kalodner was incensed
by what remained: eccentric, "left-field," esoteric music
which Kalodner—despite his cultivated "hippie" appearance—did not appreciate. His musical philosophy is a simple
one: "The purpose of a record company is to make music for
the mass audience . . . I was really mad at Peter Gabriel for
doing this, and not even considering that I had thought the
songs [heard in England] were good."

Kalodner advised Ertegun and Jerry Greenberg that the
album was too uncommercial to be released, and that Atlantic should consider dropping Gabriel from the label. Astonishingly, his bad advice seems to have been accepted on both
counts.

"The second this happened, I realized that I had made a
mistake," says Kalodner. (He had. The album was later released by Mercury Records and became a hit around the
world. One of the tracks, "Games Without Frontiers,"
reached number eleven in the American pop chart.) In order
to make reparation to Gabriel, Kalodner again tipped off
David Geffen, who had just offered Kalodner a job. Kalodner
being Kalodner, he also tipped off CBS. Geffen and CBS were
soon in a bidding war for Gabriel, which—fortunately for
Kalodner—Geffen won.

Ertegun disagrees with much of Kalodner's account of the
complex negotiations surrounding the various members of
Genesis, but admits he personally agreed to the release of
Gabriel from the label, a decision he now greatly regrets.
"Gabriel had made a social-significance album about 'peace
in the world' and so on and we thought it wasn't going to sell.
Peter Gabriel didn't particularly want to go, but his manager
was upset at our lack of enthusiasm for his new album." Gabriel's massive success for Geffen Records in 1986 with his
solo album *So* was a painful reminder to Atlantic of what it
had given away.

"That was one of our rougher periods," Ertegun now says.
"Peter Gabriel is a great artist, which teaches me that some-

times you have got to weather bad periods an artist is going through. When you have a really great artist, you should try to hold on for as long as possible."

But, when the Rolling Stones' contract with Atlantic came up for renewal in 1983, it was abundantly clear to both sides that a split was imminent. "I think they were both disenchanted with each other," says Prince Rupert Lowenstein. "I think the 'magical mystery tour' had ended and I don't think Atlantic was all that enchanted with the next contract, and I don't think the Rolling Stones were all that enchanted with Ahmet. Familiarity breeds contempt. The excitement had gone."

As far as Bill Wyman was concerned, what had made Atlantic so special had changed: Atlantic was no longer the embodiment of Ahmet Ertegun. "When we left I think he was just a figurehead. He was just traveling around the world socializing. He was sorry about the break with us—but I don't think it keeps him awake at nights. There's no rift or anything. We're still good mates."

In Lowenstein's view, Ertegun was doing a little more than socializing. In 1983—a year after Steve Ross had been declared the most highly paid executive in America—the price of Warner Communications stock collapsed because of the huge losses of its Atari computer subsidiary, and Warner became the target of a hostile takeover attempt by Australian newspaper magnate Rupert Murdoch. "That whole enormous mess that started then, I think made life very hard for Ahmet and all the people who were trying to run specific sections of the company," says Lowenstein. Added to that, the record industry as a whole was still in a severe slump, and though Atlantic itself had one of its best-ever years in 1981 (the nadir of the recession), and did well in 1982, vigilance and caution were the watchwords. There is no doubt these administrative problems preoccupied and distracted Ertegun, leaving the Stones feeling somewhat neglected.

For Mick Jagger, this was one of the inevitable problems of

dealing with large corporations—and Atlantic was now very much part of corporate America. "It's very hard dealing with these corporate entities. It's like being a painter, and having IBM release your paintings—two such disparate worlds," Jagger says.

There was some bad feeling at the time, perhaps in part because of Ertegun's direct involvement with bands such as Genesis. As Lowenstein says, "It depends on your mood at the time. It is like a personal relationship. You know that people are fond of other people as well; it is just if you feel slighted on one particular day, you mind." Nevertheless, he adds—extending the conceit—the Stones did not sit around moping over what was past: "The Rolling Stones, and any really major established act, is not quite a shy young girl who feels she has to have every other dance with a popular man." Besides, Mick Jagger wanted to leave: "I think we had become a bit stale on Atlantic. I think we'd lost a bit of steam on it. You can only have so long of a relationship."

Atlantic did make an offer to renew the contract but there were several other powerful suitors, including a very determined CBS, and Bill Wyman says when the new deals were laid out "Atlantic's offer came nowhere near the big one; no one came near CBS. And by that time all the companies were the same so it didn't really matter."

Ertegun, far from losing sleep over the potential loss of the Stones, says he actually advised Jagger to go elsewhere, and get as much money as he could—before he got too old. As Jagger's friend, he wanted the band to reap as big a financial reward as possible—but, as an astute businessman, he did not want Atlantic to be stuck with the bill.

He had no intention of competing in an auction for the Stones because he predicted the bidding would go astronomically high, far too high for any label to be able to recoup the cost through the group's record sales. As Lowenstein says about him: "Ahmet was not motivated by sentiment, he was motivated by cash for the company." But sentiment did dictate that Ertegun fly to London, as though he were engaged in serious negotiations, in order to push the bidding even higher.

The final price was indeed astronomical. CBS agreed to pay a total of $24 million—$6 million for each of the Stones' next four albums. For CBS to even recoup its advance, let alone make a profit, each album would have to sell three million copies. And on top of that, Ertegun says, "CBS must be spending a million on marketing and promotion for each album."

The Rolling Stones may have been the Greatest Rock-and-Roll Band in the World, but it did not routinely sell at least three million copies of its albums. Like it or not, "beer ads" music or not, that distinction belonged to Foreigner.

Chapter 12
THE GUYS WITH FUNNY NAMES

Until Morris Levy sold his record and music publishing business in 1988, he boasted of drawing a bigger salary than the president of any major record company, and, by some estimates, he was worth $75 million. You would never have known it from his offices. Levy presided over the shabby New York headquarters of Roulette Records like Mr. Bumble in Oliver Twist's Victorian workhouse. Dowdily painted in shades of brown and cream, the walls were peeling and showing signs of decay. The cubicles that served as offices were like cells in a beehive, each one occupied by a harassed worker, all within shouting distance of the Boss.

The door to Levy's office was always open and when his children were there they spilled in and out of the room. His four-year-old son, Zac, would tumble over the faded orange armchairs. Becket, aged seven, his precocious middle son—a small, pale, bespectacled boy—would pester the secretary for a toasted sandwich. "Have you asked Daddy?" she would inquire. "It's okay," bellowed Daddy, "he can have one." It was hard to reconcile this Morris Levy with his reputation—until, speaking on the telephone of some third party who had provoked his ire, Levy said, "Tell him to go and get cancer."

The certificates on the piano in Levy's office included one of his awards from B'nai B'rith: "For his contribution to human rights and inter-religious understanding . . . through devotion and leadership." The certificate might have added "generosity" for over the years Levy donated and raised millions of dollars for Jewish charities. The walls of his office were covered with photographs of some of the sources of his wealth: Count Basie and Dinah Washington, from the days when Levy's Birdland club offered the best jazz on Broadway; Tommy James and the Shondells, who recorded a dozen Top 30 hits for Roulette in the sixties; Frankie Lymon and the Teenagers, whose biggest hit, "Why Do Fools Fall in Love," was, supposedly, co-written by Levy—though, thirty years on, there are lawsuits still in progress that say otherwise. The walls were also decked with photographs of his families (Levy has five former wives, including the mother of Zac and Becket), and with the best of the fine-mettled racehorses Levy breeds at his 1700-acre farm in Dutchess County, upstate New York.

Sunnyview farm, now his main priority and estimated to be worth $15 million, is home to 250 racehorses, a sizable staff, and Father Louis Gigante—an aging Roman Catholic priest who finds sanctuary in one of Levy's outhouses.

Levy's home is a handsome white timber farmhouse that Levy has extended to such vast proportions it looks like a New England town hall. The centerpiece is the living room, modeled on one Levy saw in an English country mansion. There is a roaring log fire, a comfortable jumble of antiques and sturdy chairs, innumerable oil paintings of hunting scenes, and a large round oak dining table at which Levy presides over family meals.

As often as not the meals are cooked by Levy himself, because his housekeeper has not yet learned to prepare Italian food to his satisfaction (just as none of the farm workers knows as much as Levy about the breeding of fine horses and the care of young foals). He brings to the table a succession of dishes, urging his children and guests to "eat, eat." The conversation is about life and duty. "Family is very important," says Levy. "It's more important than anything else." On the wall, facing Levy's chair, is a tapestry which reads "Yea, though I walk through the Valley of Darkness I shall fear no evil, for I am the meanest son of a bitch in the Valley."

Certainly, most people considered Morris Levy to be inviolable. So it caused great ructions in the music industry when,
on September 23, 1986, Levy was arrested by FBI agents at
the Ritz-Carlton Hotel in Boston and charged with extortion.
The next morning, on NBC's *Today* show, Levy heard himself described to the nation as "the godfather" of rock and
roll, *the* connection between the Mob and the music business.

There is no doubt that Levy is very well connected in the
music business. Walter Yetnikoff, president of CBS Records,
is a close friend and a visitor to Sunnyview farm where he
shared the ownership of one of Levy's racehorses. When Yetnikoff held a small party to celebrate his fiftieth birthday,
Levy was among the select handful of guests. Sheldon Vogel,
president of Atlantic Records, is another close friend, and
Nesuhi Ertegun was a considerable admirer. "I always liked
Morris," said Nesuhi. "I have never seen him do anything
wrong. For me he was a good influence on whatever he was
involved in. I never even saw him get mad or angry."

There are those in the industry who feel they were exploited by Levy, but they are equaled or outnumbered by
those who have reason to be grateful to him. In 1978, Art
Kass, co-founder of Buddah Records and Sutra Records,
found himself $10 million in debt and unable to make an
overdue interest payment of $250,000. "I needed money immediately and I had one last phone call," says Kass. "There
was nobody else I could even ask for that sum of money. I
called Morris and he came straight down to the bank. Right
there and then he signed a note for two hundred and fifty
thousand dollars." Levy persuaded Kass's major creditors—
which included CBS—to delay bankruptcy proceedings and,
taking Buddah/Sutra under his wing, helped Kass repay or
write off all the company's debts. In return Levy became a
partner in Kass's publishing and record companies, and

therefore shared in the success when Buddah/Sutra signed
the Fat Boys rap group in 1983.

This is a formula Levy has repeated several times. "They
call this office the clinic," he said. "Labels get sick, they come
here for treatment and they get better. We cut their overheads, their mega payment plans, and nurse them. It is practical business applied to creative business."

Art Kass is enormously grateful to his benefactor. "Morris
always seemed to be around to help a person," he says. "He
would never go back on his word. He was a hard dealer, he
made good deals, but a written contract never meant anything to him—it was his word. One thing: Morris is straight,
straight up. Morris is somebody who gives a lot of favors so
when he asks for anything, people say yes."

Even those who are not fond of Levy are apt to sing his
praises. Seymour Stein, president of Sire Records, says, "A lot
of people don't like Morris Levy, a lot of people—and I have
good reason not to like him. But when I look back at all the
music that might not have reached people were it not for
Morris Levy, that makes him okay in my book." Stein, too,
has had occasion to ask Levy for a favor. When the Teamsters
union took over a pressing plant in New Jersey, Stein asked
Levy for help. Levy demanded a $50,000 donation to the
United Jewish Appeal ("Seymour Stein is cheap as the day is
long and he doesn't give to any charities," says Levy in justification) and the Teamsters were removed, in some unspecified fashion.

Perhaps as a result of all the favors, perhaps because he is
an irreplaceable character in record industry mythology,
Levy's contemporaries and young imitators alike were
shocked by his arrest and the allegations against him. Nobody
wanted to see Morris Levy end his career in prison, and to
most such an outcome was unthinkable. Seymour Stein, for
all his reservations about Levy, was quick to defend him: "I
don't know much about all these scandals that are going on,
but it seems to me that whatever Morris has done—if he's
done anything—there are much bigger fish to fry. I think

they're making an example of him, and I don't know why. They don't have to look farther than one of our own big corporations."

As for the allegations of gangsterism against Levy, they were largely dismissed by the industry. As Joe Smith, president of Capitol Records, says: "You never thought about the gangster thing with Moishe [as Levy is affectionately known] that much. It was always a joke, something to talk about. He was with the clubs, and, hey, he knew a lot of guys with funny names—the Three-Fingered Somebody, and Willy the Someone."

Unfortunately for Levy, not everyone found his friendships so amusing.

Somehow it comes as no surprise to learn that Father Gigante, the Roman Catholic priest who lives on Levy's farm, is the brother of Vincent "the Chin" Gigante, so called because of his prominent jaw.

"The Chin" Gigante first achieved notoriety in 1957 when Vito Genovese attempted to take over leadership of the five New York Mafia families, and Frank Costello, another leading underworld figure, stood in his way. On May 2, 1957, as Costello returned home, Gigante approached from behind and said, "This is for you, Frank." Costello was shot in the head. He survived but agreed to retire. Gigante was indicted for attempted murder but won acquittal when Costello failed to identify him as the assailant.

Today Vincent Gigante is, reputedly, the acting head of the Genovese crime family, supposedly the most powerful Mafia family in America. If the FBI is correct, Levy pays "tribute" to Gigante in devious ways—for example, by giving Gigante's mistress a third of the stock in Buddah/Sutra Records. In the words of an FBI affidavit: "Vincent Gigante has developed a stranglehold on Morris Levy's recording-industry enterprise, in effect turning Levy into a source of ready cash for the Genovese LCN [La Cosa Nostra] Family and its leaders."

Levy does not—indeed, could not—deny close association with Gigante and other Mafia figures he has known since childhood. He admits that Anthony "Fat Tony" Salerno is a "close friend." Salerno was head of the Genovese family until he went to prison in 1986. And a former head of the Genovese family, Thomas "Tommy Ryan" Eboli, was a partner of Levy's—until, in 1972, he was murdered on the street in Crown Heights, Brooklyn.

Of Eboli, Levy has this to say: "Tommy Eboli was a good businessman. He helped sell, he took care of the warehouses, he was very active, and he loved the job. I don't know what he did on the side."

Of his other dubious friends, Levy says knowing Mafia chieftains does not make him a mobster, any more than knowing Cardinal Spellman (whom he has met) makes him a Catholic: "The people I worked for when I was fifteen still like me and trust me. They will ask me to do them favors as a friend. Not illegal things, because they have their own people for that. They don't let me in on everything they do. They like me, but I am not one of them. I know a few things because I'm around and I keep my eyes and ears open."

It is manifestly true that Levy made no secret of his business relationships with underworld figures. His partnership with Tommy Eboli involved the distribution and sale of "cut-out" records—records deleted from the catalogues and offered for sale at large discounts. Since, as Levy says, "it was a remarkably easy way to make a buck," since most of the bucks are in cash, and given Eboli's status as a Mafia chieftain, the FBI put their partnership under microscopic examination. "The FBI used to check every record in the place, everything that went in and everything that went out," says Levy. "The FBI was always across the road. One day the FBI man fell asleep and we called him to wake him up. If there had been anything wrong they would have got us. But we kept it very clean."

Similarly Levy was never abashed about his relationship with Nathan McCalla, the black mobster he recruited to his payroll to discourage the extortion attempts of the Fairplay Committee. McCalla was given his own label within Levy's empire, Calla Records, and his own music publishing company, JAMF (which stood for Jive Ass Mother Fucker). In February 1975—two years after Levy was honored at a celebrated music industry dinner as "Man of the Year"—Levy and McCalla were indicted in Manhattan for assaulting a plainclothes police lieutenant, causing him to lose his left eye. Had the case gone to trial, Levy would have claimed he was defending McCalla against racial harassment. In circumstances never publicly explained, however, the charges were dropped.

Like Eboli, McCalla was murdered. In 1977 he was spirited away to the Bahamas after a rock concert in Maryland in which he was involved—and in which the Genovese family had, supposedly, invested—lost money because somebody sold counterfeit tickets. On his unwise return to America in 1980, McCalla was shot in the back of the head in a rented house in Fort Lauderdale, Florida.

Levy was never accused of either knowledge or involvement in the murders of his two Mob partners. Nor, despite the intense scrutiny of the FBI and the Internal Revenue Service (which routinely audited Roulette Records), was Levy accused of any criminal wrongdoing. For thirty years there simply was no evidence that Levy was guilty of anything more than "knowing a lot of guys with funny names."

That situation changed dramatically on a May night in 1985, in the parking lot of a New Jersey motel where a man named John LaMonte was punched once so hard that his face had to be reconstructed with wire. LaMonte, in fear of his life, offered to provide the FBI with evidence of the Mob's involvement in the record industry. For the next eighteen months, Morris Levy was the target of a full-scale federal investigation—and more than a few record company executives slept uneasily in their beds.

The comforting notion that the Mafia has never succeeded in infiltrating the record industry, that it operates only on the fringes, is belied by the recent career of Salvatore James Pisello.

Pisello, twice convicted of tax evasion, is reputed to be a high-ranking soldier of the Carlo Gambino crime family in New York and an alleged narcotics trafficker. Yet, in March 1984, when the National Association of Recording Merchandisers held its annual convention in Hollywood, Florida, Pisello was present, representing MCA Records, one of the six major record companies in America. Pisello's job at the convention was to sell some 4.7 million discount records held in MCA's inventory. He did so to John LaMonte, a convicted record counterfeiter and owner of Out of the Past Incorporated, a discount record distributor based in Darby, Pennsylvania. LaMonte agreed to pay $1.25 million for the records. The deal was underwritten by Morris Levy, who signed the purchase order.

This was not the first or the last deal Pisello would handle for MCA. The company lost money on all of them, while Pisello made at least $600,000. To many former and present employees of MCA, his presence at the company's headquarters in Los Angeles—where he had his own office—was inexplicable. He would terrify the record company's employees by boasting openly of his Mafia contacts. Nobody was sure how Pisello carved out his niche at MCA, but as Rick Frio, a former vice-president of MCA Records, says, "There had to be somebody on the inside that let it happen. It could only be two or three people at the top that could let it happen. You can't have somebody hanging around the office day in and day out without somebody at the top allowing it."

Pisello's relationship with MCA began in 1983. The origins are cloudy but he was somehow able to negotiate an exclusive record-pressing and distribution deal between MCA and Sugar Hill, an independent but ailing New Jersey record company that specialized in black artists, including Chuck Berry.

Sugar Hill was yet another company that had benefited from treatment in Morris Levy's "clinic." It was owned by Joe Robinson, one of the few black proprietors in the country, and his wife, Sylvia, once a singer, now a talented record producer. After the Robinsons' first attempt to form a record label had ended in bankruptcy, Levy gave them a production and distribution deal and Sugar Hill established offices in Roulette's headquarters at 1790 Broadway, under Levy's vigilant eye. Most things Levy touches turn to gold, and Sugar Hill was no exception. Sylvia Robinson produced "Rappers Delight" and "Funk You Up"—and suddenly Sugar Hill was at the forefront of a new dance fad. But, as is also customary with Levy, relationships turned sour and Levy asked to be bought out of Sugar Hill for $2 million, a generous return on his original investment in the company of $300.

Sugar Hill moved out of Levy's offices to a long white building in Englewood, New Jersey, with a brightly striped canopy over the door and a parking lot which was soon filled with limousines. Before long, however, the company was in serious financial trouble—in part because of the vagaries of the independent record distribution system, which made it virtually impossible for undercapitalized companies like Sugar Hill to survive. Joe Robinson found he could not pay his bills, including the $2 million he still owed to Levy. Enter Salvatore Pisello.

Robinson was in Los Angeles in 1983, attempting to negotiate a distribution deal with Capitol Records, when Pisello walked into his hotel. "I hadn't seen Sal for fifteen years," says Robinson. "He told me he was MCA's representative. He just walked into my hotel and said, 'Hey Joe, I can get you a deal with MCA.' I said, 'Okay, go and get it.' Two months later Pisello returned with a distribution offer from MCA. Robinson gratefully accepted the deal, and agreed to pay

Pisello 3 percent of future revenues as a finder's fee.

Even so, Sugar Hill's fortunes continued to decline. By mid-1985 the company owed $3.5 million it had received in loans and advances from MCA, and Robinson still could not pay the money he owed Levy. Reenter Sal Pisello.

Levy insists it was none of his doing that brought Pisello back into the picture. According to Levy, he, too, had not seen Pisello for years, since the days when the gangster ran a restaurant in Manhattan. He says he met Pisello again by sheer chance, at the Pritikin Clinic in California where Levy makes an annual pilgrimage to fight the flab. "Pisello told me that Sugar Hill owed me money and said, 'I'm going to get it for you.' I said, 'I don't need you to get my money for me.' "

In any event, Pisello then arranged for MCA to purchase from Sugar Hill the one asset the little company had left: the catalogue of master recordings of the defunct Chess label (together with those of its subsidiaries, Checker and Cadet) which Robinson had purchased in 1976. MCA paid $3 million for the catalogue—almost ten times what Robinson had paid for it. Whether that money was used to write off Sugar Hill's debt to MCA, or whether any of it was used to pay off Robinson's debt to Levy, remains unresolved. What is clear is that Sugar Hill got none of it. The company was forced into bankruptcy. (Today, Robinson says MCA "stole" $3 million from him, and tried to pin the blame on him for bringing in Sal Pisello.)

Though the Sugar Hill deal was financially adverse for everyone save Pisello (and, possibly, Levy), it did have the merit of being relatively straightforward. Not so the discount record deal that Pisello arranged between MCA and John LaMonte. Among the cast of middlemen—besides Levy—and other interested parties were Gaetano "the Big Guy" Vastola, a leading member of New Jersey's DeCavalcante crime family; Frederick Giovanello, a soldier in the Genovese family (who was arrested in 1986 for the murder of a New York policeman, though later acquitted); and Dominick "Baldy Dom" Canterino, allegedly the right-hand man to

Levy's friend (and, some would say, patron) Vincent "the Chin" Gigante. To Rick Frio, former vice-president of MCA, the involvement of even one legitimate middleman—let alone a virtual mafioso convention—was absurd. Record companies had long established a straightforward method to get their old records into the "bargain-buy" racks of record stores. "The way I would handle these deals was very simple," he says, shaking his head in bemusement. "I always knew who I was going to supply cut-outs to—there are only about ten major buyers in the country. It was always one-to-one. There was no purpose in having a middleman."

Certainly the middlemen did not help the deal. The 4.7 million cut-outs LaMonte agreed to purchase from MCA included releases by Neil Diamond, Elton John, the Who, Tom Petty, Steely Dan, and Diana Ross—artists whose work would not normally reach the cut-out market, but whose records were included to "sweeten" the deal. When the cut-outs arrived at LaMonte's warehouse, however, in July 1984—on board sixty trailer-trucks—all the "sweeteners" had been removed, leaving only the dross. LaMonte refused to pay MCA the $1.25 million he had promised, which Levy had guaranteed.

For the next ten months Levy and his dubious associates fretted over LaMonte's failure to pay up. Unfortunately for them, the FBI recorded many of their conversations because the bureau suspected "Big Guy" Vastola of involvement in drug trafficking, and had won court approval to tap his telephone.

"Moishe, Moishe," Vastola said to Levy, "you knew this guy was a cocksucker before you made the deal, didn't you?"

"That's right," said Levy.

"Why did you make the deal with him?"

"Because I thought he was a *controllable* cocksucker," said Levy.

Under great pressure from the Mafia, LaMonte did make some small payments to MCA, totaling $30,000. He also signed notes, payable to Levy, worth $600,000. But that was less than half of what Levy owed to MCA under the terms of his guarantee, and Vastola for one grew increasingly impatient.

"I don't like the way this thing is going with this kid [LaMonte]," Vastola told one of his cousins, yet another of the cast of unsavory characters. "I'm telling you now, I'm going to put him in a fucking hospital. I'm not even going to talk to him. I don't like this motherfucker, what he's doing? I mean, what are they making, an asshole out of me, or what?"

Levy's advice to Vastola, as recorded by the FBI, was "go out to that place, take over the kid's [LaMonte's] business."

"I'm ready to go over there and break his ass," replied Vastola.

True to his word, "Big Guy" Vastola confronted LaMonte in a parking lot in Hightstown, New Jersey, and crushed his face with a single blow. When, as a result, LaMonte was interviewed by the FBI, and agreed to tell all he knew, he was easily persuaded to cooperate with the government by wearing a "wire"—a hidden recorder—and allowing the bureau to place concealed video cameras in his office.

The FBI now extended electronic surveillance to Levy. His telephone was tapped and some of his meetings were secretly filmed by the bureau. In September 1985, Levy told Vastola, "I'm getting nervous, and I'm not the nervous type. MCA is getting hot, and they have a right to. I don't want them to sue because they can hurt me. If I have to send them the money, I will. I have to pacify them now." Later that month, in a meeting that was secretly videotaped by the FBI, Levy unwittingly implicated Dominick "Baldy Dom" Canterino (allegedly Vincent Gigante's lieutenant) in the scheme. At the meeting, which Canterino attended, Levy complained that he and Vastola "have paid Dom more money to make peace with MCA than we collected from LaMonte."

By now two grand juries, in Newark and New York City, were investigating the Mafia's infiltration of the record industry, and John LaMonte, a key witness, was under federal protection. Meanwhile, in Los Angeles, the Strike Force Against Organized Crime began an investigation into Pisello's relationship with MCA.

And in New York, and Newark, and Los Angeles, and half a dozen other cities, there was another, entirely separate investigation going on into the Mafia's supposed links with the music industry. This probe, by Brian Ross and Ira Silverman of NBC *Nightly News,* also concerned MCA—but every other major record company as well. Ross and Silverman were out to expose what everybody in the industry already suspected: that payola, the bribery of radio personnel, was once again flourishing in America, despite supposedly tough laws to discourage it. This time, Ross and Silverman believed, the Mob was intimately involved.

By 1985, American record companies were spending well over $80 million a year on "record promotion"—the business of getting their records played on the air. The good old days, when Hy Weiss could get airtime by giving a "jock" $50 to take his wife out to dinner, were long gone. For one thing, most record companies no longer handled promotion directly: Instead the companies subcontracted much or all of the job to "independent promoters" who dealt with the radio stations, allowing the record companies to keep their hands clean. For another, the trick to successful promotion was targetting very specific radio stations.

A critical factor in today's music industry is the charts, up to twelve pages of them, published each week by a Los Angeles–based trade publication, *Radio & Records.* These charts calculate the amount of airplay given to new record releases by some 250 contemporary hit radio (CHR) stations in America. The stations are divided into three groups, the most important being the "Parallel Ones" (or P-1s): sixty-two stations across the nation that regularly reach a million or more listeners. Each week these stations, and the less influential P-2s and P-3s, report to *Radio & Records* which new releases they have added to their playlists—thus forecasting potential hits. The resulting charts published by *Radio & Records* influence other radio stations to play the same records. The more often a record is played on the air the more likely it is to become a hit.

Influencing the stations that report to *Radio & Records* is what "independent promotion" is all about. Each station might replace no more than three or four records on its playlist each week and competition for those spots is intense. Promoters who can "deliver" the stations can therefore demand extravagant fees: in addition to a flat weekly payment, up to $15,000 for a highly sought after P-1 station. It has become a fact of life that in order to get sufficient airtime to stand much chance of breaking into the real charts, the ones that reflect actual sales, a record company has to reckon on spending between $40,000 and $150,000 on any and every new release.

The convenient fiction accepted within the industry is that the fat fees paid to independent promoters are not intended to facilitate bribes. They are, so the argument goes, merely a reflection of what is a highly competitive business, and a recognition of the expertise of the independent promoters and the extent of their contacts at the most influential radio stations. If promoters funnel some of the money to corrupt radio station programmers and disc jockeys—sometimes to pay for drugs or prostitutes—the record companies can, and do, protest their innocence.

Ahmet Ertegun rarely discusses the seamier side of the music business, but on the question of modern-day payola his view is forthright and succinct: "We let the whole thing get out of hand because we couldn't do what the independent promoters did."

In 1985 one of the kings of independent promotion was Joe Isgro. Again it comes as no surprise to learn that Isgro has a connection with Morris Levy: Levy gave Isgro one of his first jobs, as the Philadelphia promotion man for Roulette Records. Isgro is only one of many influential men in the industry who "worked for me when they were kids," says Levy with pride. "We used to call it going to school . . . At one time, three or four presidents of major record companies had all come out of Roulette." Levy did not consider Isgro to be a particularly promising pupil and gives him a report of "fair . . . not great." The secret of Isgro's success was "he created an empire of his own. He created his own little network of forty or fifty guys he could call on."

Isgro is an aggressive, stocky man with greased-back hair and a pencil-thin mustache. Dressed in black from head to toe, even to the black ring on his little finger, he can be intimidating to visitors to his lavish Los Angeles offices. They sit on low leather armchairs while he—across a vast smoked-glass table set on thick undulating legs like gilded sea serpents—sits on a much larger and higher chair, with his feet swung up on a corner of the table. From this superior position he is ready to pounce on any suggestion that his business is not entirely legitimate. He can also be persuasively eloquent in defense of his trade.

Independent promotion, according to Isgro, was entirely a creature of the record companies' making. Isgro was a member of Motown Records' promotion staff in 1979 when the economic recession began to bite. As an economy measure, most record companies cut back on promotion and marketing; overnight Motown reduced its promotion staff to just six men in the field.

Almost immediately the companies began to suffer. Isgro, who was among those let go, says, "They cut back in the areas that are most essential to getting hit records." So, Isgro and others decided to "become entrepreneurs." Isgro hired some of the people the record companies had laid off, paid their expenses, and became "an independent promotion consultant." At first the record companies were enthusiastic about the new system since they saved themselves the fixed cost of permanent promotion staff and only paid Isgro, and others like him, for specific services rendered.

Then, according to Isgro, the companies got too greedy for their own good. "There was a highly competitive situation," he says. "They began to think, We are paying Joe and Bob one thousand dollars, if we pay them two thousand we'll get an edge on Sam. This is what escalated the costs of independent promotion. It was not independent promoters who increased their rates; it was the fiercely competitive nature of record companies."

It was not long before record companies realized their creation had grown into a monster they could not control. As Hy Weiss says cryptically, "It's like someone who lives in a tent and brings in a baby elephant; eventually the elephant takes over the tent." The fees grew higher and higher as the power of the independent promoters became entrenched, and the record companies competed with each other for the promoters' special favors. Nobody, and no record release, was immune: To get the latest releases of even the likes of Michael Jackson and Prince on the air, and on the charts, the companies had to pay the promoters.

A senior official of the Recording Industry Association of America compares the grip of Isgro and his fellow promoters to gangs in Chinatown demanding protection money. "If you want to protect yourself, you pay. They had us by the balls and didn't want to let go. That is not the American way—that is a monopoly."

The key to the power of the promoters lay in the fact that instead of being "independent," as their name suggested, they operated as a cartel, known in the industry as "the Network." Members of the Network did run independent businesses in different parts of the country, but in order to get the spread of airplay which ensured chart positions in *Radio & Records*, and therefore increased sales, record companies would hire them *en bloc* as a loosely knit organization.

Joe Isgro insists he never heard the term "the Network" until he read it in the *Los Angeles Times*. He claims he and the other promoters ran independent, self-sufficient businesses serving particular geographical markets. He admits, however, the various promoters would "exchange information" with each other to make their individual efforts more effective.

The most disturbing aspect of this system was that the vast sums of money paid to the Network by the major record companies made it almost impossible for small independent labels to compete. This in turn led to a narrowing of the music that Americans could hear on their radios. John Marmaduke, past president of the National Association of Record Merchandisers, says, "I'm more concerned with the restrictiveness that results from all this. Because of the high cost of independent promotion, it makes it extremely difficult for a small record company to have a hit. As a result, oftentimes great music is not being heard and bad music is being played. If this was 1963 and Capitol Records was not playing ball, we might never have heard the Beatles—and that is a one-million-dollar mistake."

In late 1980, the two biggest record corporations in America, CBS and Warner, did attempt to rid themselves of the elephant in their tent. Warner decided to stop using independent promoters and CBS soon followed suit. Explaining the Warner position, Joe Smith, then chairman of Elektra Records, announced: "The costs of using indies have become unbearable. In the last several years, their rates have gone up four and five times . . . For some companies the expenditures represented the difference between profit and loss . . . It's something we're just going to have to do without."

That, as it turned out, was a considerable miscalculation. There is no better demonstration of the power and influence of "independent promoters" than the speed with which CBS and Warner beat their combined retreat.

According to Isgro, the other major labels stepped up their use of independent promotion, and costs continued to rise. "Competition became even more fierce," says Isgro. "The other companies saw that now the two monster companies were out, this was their chance to grab a share of the market-

place. Capitol, RCA, and Polygram all had banner years."
CBS and Warner, meanwhile, both suffered a steep decline
in airplay and a consequent slump in sales. (Sales of Warner
labels fell by $61 million in 1981, though it is arguable if all
this was attributable to the lack of independent promotion.
Some critics think 1981 marked a low in the general quality
of releases from the Warner labels, although Ertegun points
out that 1981 was the most successful year in Atlantic's history.) After not much more than a year, both Warner and
CBS abandoned their bold stands.

Isgro laughs ironically as he explains what happened next.
"CBS and Warner figured they couldn't just come back and
say, 'We're sorry, we've changed our minds.' Instead they
said, 'Listen, we were doing this before, we are going to do
that now'—and they just raised the ante again, and it became
even more competitive." He repeats his claim, even more
adamantly, that not once in his career as a promoter has he
increased his fees; the record companies were *always* the
ones to "raise the ante."

The circumstances under which independent promotion became a matter of public concern, thanks to NBC *Nightly
News*, are mysterious—and, Joe Isgro would say, downright
suspicious.

By mid-1985 some members of the Recording Industry Association of America (to which almost all record companies
belong) were urging the association's board of directors
(made up of leading record company executives) to investi-
gate independent promotion. For example, on July 15, 1985,
Jay Laskar, the president of Motown Records, wrote a letter
to the Association saying, in part: "We should be meeting
about the high cost of trying to get our records played on the
radio, which to a great extent, has nothing to do with the
records' quality but rather with who pays the most."

In October 1985, the board did meet, and initially voted to
retain private investigators and spend up to $100,000 to de-

termine, according to the association's minutes, "whether or not the conduct of independent promotion involves or results in criminal violations or other violations of federal regulations or law." There was, however, strong opposition to this plan of action, primarily from executives of CBS. They said CBS had already conducted its own investigation of independent promoters, and found nothing wrong. Perhaps more important, the CBS men raised the thorny point that since all the members of the association were competitors, any joint action—such as a group boycott of the promoters—might be a violation of antitrust laws.

To be on the safe side, the board of directors therefore decided to appoint a "legal committee" to establish the ground rules for any investigation. The committee's report, dated November 4, 1985, not only endorsed the use of twenty-four private investigators, it proposed that the investigators use electronic surveillance of some promoters, to collect solid evidence of any wrongdoing. (That extreme proposal would subsequently cement Joe Isgro's conviction that he was the victim of a conspiracy. "They mentioned video equipment. What was that for? It would not be admissible in a court," says Isgro, implying videotape could perhaps be leaked to television journalists.)

The association's board of directors discussed the legal committee's report at a meeting in New York City on November 7, 1985. The proposed investigation was not immediately approved, partly because of the board's lingering concern about the risk of antitrust violations.

By coincidence or not, at about this time Brian Ross and Ira Silverman—NBC TV's award-winning investigative team—began receiving telephone calls alerting them to the power, and supposed abuses, of some independent promoters. Ross and Silverman were already aware that various grand juries were probing the record industry. As longtime students of the Mafia they were also aware of, and bemused by, the connection between MCA Records and Salvatore Pisello. When, as Silverman puts it, "the dimes began to drop," the NBC team headed for California to commence one of their classic operations; in the art of secretly filming suspects, they have no equals.

From what they saw, and what they learned, Ross and Silverman gradually compiled a report on what they called "the new payola." It alleged that a small group of powerful promoters used whatever it took—money, cocaine, prostitutes, and threats of violence—to get records on the air. They also believed, but could not yet prove, that Joe Isgro and one other major promoter, Fred DiSipio (another of Morris Levy's "pupils," from Philadelphia), were directly and explicitly linked to the Gambino crime family in New York.

In late January 1986, Silverman and Ross discreetly followed Isgro from Los Angeles to Manhattan where he and Fred DiSipio checked into the Helmsley Palace hotel. The two promoters had gone to New York to attend the annual dinner of Ahmet Ertegun's Rock-and-Roll Hall of Fame—but, it seemed, they had other business as well.

Silverman had also checked into the Helmsley Palace and was in his room when he received an urgent call from Ross, who was keeping watch in the lobby. "You'll never guess who's just walked in," said Ross. Silverman rushed to the nearest elevator and went down to the ground floor. When the door of the elevator opened he found himself face-to-face with John Gotti, who just one month before had apparently succeeded in his bid to become head of the Carlo Gambino family. (The position became vacant on December 16, 1985, when Gambino boss Paul Castellano was gunned down on East 46th Street in Manhattan. Police attributed the killing to rivalry between the Manhattan and Brooklyn factions of the Gambino family. The authorities believed that Gotti ordered Castellano's murder but he was never charged with the crime, which remains officially unsolved.)

Gotti was not alone. NBC's cameras, hidden outside the hotel, filmed through the ground-floor windows three more top members of the Gambino family hierarchy: Joseph "Piney" Armone, second in importance only to Gotti; and two lieutenants, Joe N. Gallo and Frank de Chico. It appeared to Ross and Silverman that what they were observing was a Mob summit meeting, at which leading representatives of organized crime were in the hotel to confer with the two most powerful promoters in the record industry. When, one hour later, Isgro and DiSipio left the Helmsley Palace for their next gathering, NBC's cameras followed them to the Waldorf Hotel—where the two promoters mixed with the great and the good at the Rock-and-Roll Hall of Fame annual dinner.

"Two of the most powerful and feared men in the rock music business," said Ross in his commentary when NBC broadcast those extraordinary pictures on the *Nightly News* on February 24: "Joseph Isgro, who authorities say has described Mafia *capo* Armone as his partner . . . and Isgro's close associate Fred DiSipio."

In that and a subsequent report, broadcast the next night, Ross and Silverman went on to detail the association between Salvatore Pisello and MCA, and Morris Levy's connections to the Genovese family.

Watching the grainy images on television, a senior investigator for the New York Organized Crime Task Force attempted to understand the significance of it all. "It is like every other industry that they [the Mafia] control and monopolize," he said. "There is one main ingredient through which they control an industry. For example, they control the construction industry because they control sand and gravel supplies . . . There must always be one element, and in this case I think it is independent promotion. Somehow organized crime is getting its share of radio promotion. The question is do they control Isgro? And if so, how?"

The reaction of the record industry to NBC's sensational allegations was schizophrenic. On the one hand there were loud cries of "foul" from the Recording Industry Association of America. "We have no knowledge that any firm or individual with whom our companies do business is engaged in any illegal activity," the association said in a statement. If there was any evidence of payola the industry would take "immediate and decisive corrective action." But, "until such time, we find it unjustified and distressing that the recording industry is so indiscriminately maligned by insidious innuendo. Such broad and unspecific allegations unfairly taint the innocent."

Joe Isgro went on ABC TV's *Entertainment Tonight* to say, "I am not involved in any business aspect with any member of any organized crime in this country." Had he attended a Mob summit meeting in New York? "Unequivocally no."

And Ken Barnes, editor of *Radio & Records*, who had been interviewed by Ross and Silverman for their report, complained his quotes had been taken out of context to distort what he had said. *Radio & Records* published an editorial accusing NBC *Nightly News* of "low blows" and "a self-serving edit . . . Shame on you NBC, you're bigger than that now."

Yet, within seventy-two hours of NBC's broadcasts, almost all major record labels in America announced that they were suspending use of all or most independent promoters. Joe Isgro prepared to close up his offices on Sunset Boulevard. "I'm destroyed," he told *Rolling Stone*. "My whole business was ruined by insidious innuendo," he added, adopting the message of the recording industry's association. "In thirty-six hours I've been accused, tried, and found guilty for nothing. My business is destroyed."

Well, not quite.

Though Isgro threatened to sue NBC *Nightly News* for defamation he never followed through. Instead, with characteristic chutzpah, Isgro sued the Recording Industry Association of America, and MCA, RCA, Arista, Capitol, Warner Brothers, Atlantic, Elektra, Motown, Polygram, A&M, Chrysalis, and Geffen—in other words, every major label in America except CBS. His suit, filed in federal court in the Central District of California by the San Francisco law firm Cannata, Genovese (no relation) & Papale, claimed violations of the Sherman Antitrust Act, and demanded $25 million in damages.

The thrust of Isgro's complaint was that the record companies had conspired together to put the independent promoters out of business. He also alleged they had engineered the scandalous publicity as a cynical way to cut costs. "The companies could not stop the spiraling costs, costs which they were responsible for," said Isgro. "And they knew from 1981 [when Warner and CBS went out on a limb] that action had to be taken together."

Ahmet Ertegun dismissed Isgro's allegations as ludicrous: "The idea we all conspired to put Isgro out of business is silly. We couldn't all agree to do something together."

To which Isgro replied: "Ahmet Ertegun . . . had as much knowledge of promotion as the man in the moon. Ahmet Ertegun was flying round the world."

Within two years, nine of the twelve record companies sued by Isgro settled out of court, paying him unspecified amounts of damages. "Why have they settled? They are afraid I have the evidence," says Isgro with undisguised satisfaction. (The holdouts were MCA, Warner Brothers, and A&M Records.)

Meanwhile, neither Isgro nor any other major independent promoter was put out of business for long. Within weeks, if not days, some record companies simply amended the system by paying promotion money to artists' managers, leaving them to employ independent promoters. From the record companies' point of view this change in the rules of the game has two advantages. First, it keeps the promotion men at one farther remove. Second, the record companies can charge these promotion costs as an advance, to be paid back out of artists' royalties. "So they saved themselves fifty million a year," says Isgro.

Other labels simply waited until the fuss died down, and then found ways around the supposed boycott of "the Network." A senior official of the Recording Industry Association of America believes little has changed since the scandal erupted. "Truthfully, I think many companies are still dealing with them," he said. "I don't know, or want to know, how they are doing it, but where there is a will there is a way."

A federal grand jury in Los Angeles indicted two of Joe Isgro's promoters for violations of the payola statutes. Isgro said the two men were not his employees but merely subcontractors to whom he had given "desk space." He was not, he said, responsible for any transgressions of the law they may have committed. Isgro himself was not indicted.

What of his supposed links to organized crime and, in particular, to Joseph Armone, underboss of the Gambino family?

Isgro admitted he was an old friend of Joe Armone. "Whenever I am in New York I will meet him for a linguine dinner," said Isgro. "I have never denied—nor will I ever deny—my friendships, but I do most emphatically deny any illegal act or wrongdoing."

For now the linguine dinners are on hold. In January 1988, Armone was tried and convicted in Brooklyn on charges of racketeering, and sentenced to twenty-five years. The evidence against him included recordings of conversations, secretly made by the FBI, in which Armone boasted to Mafia associates of his "interests" in the music business. There was, he said, a lot of money to be made out of "radio promotion."

By the summer of 1986, Morris Levy was sick of it all: sick of the allegations against him; sick of the music business; sick of America. He said he wanted to sell his myriad record and publishing companies, his eighty-store chain of record shops, and even Sunnyview, his beloved farm—and move to Australia.

The first suggestion that his relocation plans would have to wait came in July 1986 when FBI agents questioned Howard Fisher, Levy's apparently harmless bookkeeper. As Levy puts it: "Law enforcement people captured the comptroller

of Roulette in a hotel room and held him and threatened him
for four hours."

Then it was Levy's turn. "They [the FBI] broke into my
office and said, 'Tell us what you know about these people'—
these people I have known for forty or fifty years. They said,
'They are going to kill you because you know too much.'

" 'Bullshit,' I said. They tried to persuade me I needed to
come into their Witness Protection Program for my own
safety. I told them I couldn't become one of their witnesses.
For a start, I don't like the other people they have as their
witnesses. And it would be a violation of all the principles by
which I live my life."

Levy was warned by the FBI he might be indicted, so his
arrest two months later came as no great surprise. He was
charged—along with Fisher, his bookkeeper, and "Baldy
Dom" Canterino—with conspiring to extort money from
John LaMonte. ("Big Guy" Vastola, who allegedly delivered
the crushing blow to LaMonte's face, was charged separately,
to be tried later.)

What shocked Levy was his conviction. In May 1988, after
a two-month trial in Camden, New Jersey, the jury took less
than five hours to find Levy, Fisher, and Canterino guilty
(though Fisher's conviction was later overturned by the
judge). "I am sick of telling people I'm innocent—and I don't
do it—but I swear to God this is faked," said Levy. "I just
tried to collect a debt that was owed to me."

Levy was sentenced to ten years' imprisonment. He appealed, and remained free on bond, but for the first time he
accepted the possibility of going to jail, of "serving my time."
Looking tired, and grizzled around the mouth, he said:
"They keep trying to get me. I'm an easy target because I'm a
maverick, and because I have connections . . . Even if I get off
this one, the government will keep trying to have a go at me."

He saw himself (with some justification) as the last of a
breed: one of the pioneers of the music business "when it was
a beautiful business"; a man whose time had passed; a
Horatio Alger figure replaced by "no-talent bums."

Chapter 13
LONG LIVE
THE KING

Ben E. King sits in the office of his old friend Ahmet Ertegun, reflecting on the ups and downs of his own musical career that spans thirty years—and on what has
become of Atlantic Records.

In the early sixties, as lead singer of the Drifters and Atlantic's best hope to replace Ray Charles, King made four solo
records in a row that crossed over from the soul charts to the
pop charts—no mean achievement at the time. After that his
career went into decline (though he remained popular in
Europe) until 1975 when he re-signed with Atlantic, and
scored an immediate hit with his album *Supernatural Thing*.
He remained with Atlantic for the next ten years until, finally
disillusioned, he drifted away from the label once more. By a
nice irony his departure coincided with the decision of the
Levi jeans company to use King's "Stand by Me" as the
theme for one of its television commercials. Twenty-six years
after Atlantic originally released it, "Stand by Me" rose to the
top of the charts once more.

"I think the saddest thing I've ever seen happen is the
black music section of Atlantic disappear almost completely," says King. "Somewhere along the way, somebody
stopped paying attention . . . Somewhere along the line
someone wasn't glancing over at that area, and black music
suffered on Atlantic. They lost a lot of great artists. Now they
are fighting to come back, but I don't think the new artists

that are out there today can compare to what they lost. Ahmet is just too busy to babysit like he did when I was here."

In part King blames the "ghettoization" of black music at Atlantic (and most other major record companies): the "Okay, black music, that's on the first floor, send it down there" syndrome. "It shouldn't be like that," says King. "Everybody should listen to the music, and if the music is good, put it out—whatever the hell it is."

While Atlantic is not alone in having a separate black music department, and neglecting it, the company's history makes that policy all the more poignant. Shelley Kerner, a frantically busy lawyer who represents many black artists from her cramped offices on Broadway, says, "The pain is a little more heartfelt with Atlantic because Atlantic's reputation was so much based on the black acts that it started and really worked." She points to what happened to one of her clients, Gwen McRae, who was signed by Atlantic in 1980 after receiving gold records and Grammy nominations as "the disco queen." Perhaps because McRae was introduced to the label by Ertegun, but assigned to the black music department, nobody at Atlantic could decide what direction her career should take. Ertegun was very enthusiastic at the beginning, Kerner says, and planned to produce personally a record pairing McRae with Ben E. King. But he soon "lost faith." Kerner's impression was that "Ertegun wasn't around very much . . . He was on the road a lot."

Today Kerner believes that Atlantic does not merely neglect black music but even discriminates against it. "According to their lawyers there is no truth in it, [but] I have a very strong suspicion that the kind of deals you can make with Atlantic for a black act are not the same as the kind of deals that you can get for a white act," she says. "We may be talking about a twenty-thousand-dollar difference between the budgets of unknown black and white acts. Although some of that can probably be justified on the basis that a white act may have a larger market, I think it's really a self-imposed limitation."

Ertegun acknowledges the "sad" fact that Atlantic has lost touch with its roots: "It's true, it is a fact we did decline from being one of the top two or three R&B labels. It's part of our tradition but somehow, for one reason or another, we've had a serious decline over the last twelve years or so."

Ertegun may be sad but he is also acutely realistic. In 1985, in anticipation of the fortieth anniversary of the company's founding, Atlantic issued a seven-album set containing the best of the rhythm and blues it had recorded since 1947. "It got great reviews, but it didn't sell much," says Ertegun—in total, about 15,000 copies. Shortly afterward Atlantic issued a new Genesis album, *Invisible Touch*. It got bad reviews but "it sold hundreds of thousands of copies." As Ertegun sees it, there is the rub: Like it or not, in today's fiercely competitive industry, which encourages the production of highly commercial popular music, there is little room for "minority tastes."

For a sentimental man Ertegun is surprisingly unemotional about what others would call the good old days. "In the fifties we were just a two-bit company, giving our artists a small percentage of two bits," he says. Since 1980, by contrast and to Ertegun's obvious satisfaction, Atlantic has doubled its volume of sales, and achieved unheard-of levels of profit.

"The problem is that Atlantic is Ahmet's company—but Ahmet is not there much, and so it is left to the accountant to run it," says Chris Blackwell, founder and owner of the British label Island Records. Island is distributed in the United States by Atlantic, and "the accountant" with whom Blackwell has to deal is Sheldon Vogel. "He hasn't got an interest in how to build something which is going to be exciting in the future," says Blackwell. "So there is no help. There is never anybody you can go to [at Atlantic] who has any sort of mind which is open to the entertainment business, which is really a gut-feeling business."

Blackwell admits that Vogel is simply doing his job. "He's not supposed to have vision—he's an accountant. Ahmet is the one with the vision. But if Ahmet is not around . . ." Unfortunately, Blackwell says, he can rely on Ertegun to be around less and less. "He's not interested, and why should he be? He's been in it for a long time. He's done everything. Ahmet is an ambassador now, more than anything." (Ertegun responds that, except for vacations, and when traveling on business, he is in his office every day. "Mr. Blackwell, on the other hand, can rarely be found in his New York office, spending much time on the Riviera, the Caribbean, or making movie deals in Hollywood.")

For most people who have to deal with Atlantic today, Sheldon Vogel is their nemesis, the man they love to hate. Bud Prager, the delightfully indiscreet manager of Foreigner, once told him, "If ever you run Atlantic Records, Sheldon, Atlantic is history."

"You do have a way with words, Bud," Vogel replied.

Vogel did decide, however, he should attempt to improve his relations with Atlantic's artists. Mick Jones, the lead singer of Foreigner, and an affable fellow, was awarded the dubious honor of being the first to participate in this experiment when Vogel invited him to lunch. "I figured they'd have a good time," says Prager. "Sheldon can be very funny and charming."

There were two very different views on how the lunch went. After it, Vogel told Ahmet Ertegun his meeting with Jones had been a great success. At that precise moment Jones, greatly piqued, was on the telephone to Prager. He complained that Vogel had spent lunch lecturing him on the necessity of including potential hit singles on every album (a formula Foreigner already employed with almost monotonous regularity). Jones was so offended by Vogel's insensitivity that he insisted Prager call Ertegun to find out how much it would cost for Foreigner to break its contract with

Atlantic. It took all Ertegun's skills to persuade Jones that, Sheldon Vogel notwithstanding, Atlantic was where Foreigner belonged.

"Everyone loves Ahmet and hates Sheldon," says Mick Jagger. Why? "Sheldon Vogel is so penny-pinching. They are fantastically penny-pinching at Atlantic." Jagger is astute enough to realize, however, that Vogel is a very convenient diversionary figure for Ertegun: He can blame Vogel for all the tough decisions that have to be made ("I'm sorry, Sheldon says you can't have twenty grand for the video") and remain everybody's friend and favorite uncle.

Nevertheless, since it is Vogel who takes the flak, and since Vogel has (to put it mildly) little empathy with artists, he is an unlikely candidate to succeed Ahmet Ertegun—either as the guiding light of Atlantic Records or as the most respected music mogul. Many people agree with producer Tom Dowd that Ertegun is in fact irreplaceable: that "when he goes, the charisma, the love, will change, and people will say, 'It's not like it was.' " But, though much of the industry has fallen into the hands of the accountants, though it is corporate men with no love or knowledge of music who increasingly call the shots, though the business of making records is now exactly that, there is still a handful of survivors who understand the legacy that Ertegun will leave.

According to Ertegun, the man most likely to succeed him as the head of Atlantic Records is Doug Morris, an affable one-time songwriter and singer who is now "one of the best record executives in the world today." Morris has been closely involved in the careers of Pete Townsend, Stevie Nicks, Debbie Gibson, and INXS, among others. He is also particularly skilled at record promotion. Succeeding Ahmet Ertegun as the dean of music, at least within the Warner group, is another matter. The most likely candidate for that role is Seymour Stein, the irreverent and hilarious head of Sire Records, which has been wholly owned by Warner since Stein sold the label in 1980. (Sire operates as a subsidiary of Warner Brothers Records under the control, more or less, of Mo Ostin.) Though not yet fifty, Stein seems to have been around forever. His fund of (thoroughly indiscreet) anecdotes goes back to the fifties when, as he tells it, Morty Craft attempted to bribe him to fix the charts in *Billboard*. Having learned his trade at King Records, at the feet of the great Syd Nathan, Stein is a survivor of those buccaneering days who has forgotten none of the lessons of his apprenticeship. Like Nathan, Stein is renowned for his meanness: "Seymour Stein, See Less Money" is the industry joke. He is also renowned, however, for his encyclopedic knowledge of modern music, and for the asset that makes him such a potent force: Seymour Stein has "great ears."

He started Sire Records, on a wing and a prayer, in 1966 after Red Bird's attempt to merge with Atlantic (or, in Ertegun's view, take over Atlantic) failed. He brought the British group Fleetwood Mac to America, and the Climax Blues Band, and Focus from Holland. In the seventies Stein became the first—and perhaps only—American record executive to understand the significance of punk and new wave, signing the Ramones, Richard Hell and the Voidoids, and Talking Heads. In the eighties, after Sire was bought by Warner Brothers Records, Stein was the first to recognize the potential of Madonna.

His description of how he signed one of the more unlikely superstars of pop music—delivered, as are all his anecdotes, at 100 miles an hour—is classic Seymour Stein: "I had met Mark Caymans [Madonna's manager] about a year, maybe a little more before. I liked him. I still like him. We're having a lawsuit right now which is wrong—he's really in the wrong, but I still like him. I like him so much that even though what he paid me was so dreadful I said to him, 'This isn't right for me, but you are, and I'd like you to keep in touch and keep sending me things.' And then, here I am in the hospital, vegetating [recovering from open-heart surgery]. My assistant at the time, Michael Rosenblatt, calls me up and says, 'Mark

Caymans has brought in this girl singer and she is fucking great.' And I said to him, 'Michael, you know I've been waiting for a year for Mark to bring in something. I want to do some business with him—send the tape right over.' And I heard the tape. It was 'Everybody,' a very rough demo of Mark producing 'Everybody,' and I loved it. I was also at that point suffering from cabin fever, or something, and I said, 'I want to sign her right now. Bring her to the hospital.' And I shaved; I must have had a ten-day growth. And I sent home for a new robe because the robe I had, I think it could have walked off by itself. And she came to see me. I'm sure she was shocked. She thought she was talking to a man that probably wouldn't be around. Knowing that sweetie-pie as I know her now . . . And I love her. We were with her just yesterday, and wasn't she fabulous? She was great. Anyway, I said to her, 'I want to sign you.' And I did the whole deal with her in the hospital."

Stein's methods are not universally admired in the industry. Elliot Rashman, manager of the British group Simply Red, acknowledges Stein's talent: "If you are Madonna, it must look wonderful. Nobody else would have touched her, but he saw something there . . . Stein has got the greatest ears in America." But, adds Rashman, he is totally ruthless: "The Seymour Stein philosophy is, you shop. You come over [to Britain] and sign twenty artists, and if one breaks that's fine. If you're on the artists' side, it's a horrendous game. All these groups think 'great'—and then they can never get him on the phone and there is never any more money. They have one single that comes out that nobody works on."

Simply Red is one group that Stein has not yet signed, though not for lack of trying. He claims to have discovered the band ("I don't want to sound like Jerry Wexler, but I made the first demo") but could not generate any enthusiasm among the executives at Warner Brothers. Instead Simply Red was snapped up by another Warner label, Elektra Records, which since 1985 has been run by Bob Krasnow—one of Stein's fellow apprentices at King Records. Elektra is the smallest of the Warner labels and within the corporation it has a reputation for being somewhat wayward. For example, Elektra's promotion department sent a pig's head, with a tape cassette stuffed in its mouth, to an intransigent radio station that would not play Elektra's records. What matters, however, is the bottom line. Before Krasnow, Elektra habitually lost money and there were rumors it would be sold. Since Krasnow, Elektra has enjoyed spectacular success. As he says, with characteristic candor, "Elektra is steaming. Now it's the consummate, all-world record company." That transformation has been due in part to Simply Red.

Krasnow regards Simply Red as "Otis Redding incarnate." For Nesuhi Ertegun (who was head of Warner Records' international division until his retirement in 1987), Simply Red represents "the best signing of a new band by the Warner group in the last ten years." The reason for Nesuhi Ertegun's enthusiasm is Mick Hucknall, the group's mop-headed, urchin-like singer, whose songs suggest to Ertegun an understanding of R&B music from Atlantic's earliest days. "He sends me telexes saying 'You should reissue these titles by Ray Charles,'" said Nesuhi Ertegun in amazement. "He knows the music that preceded him to an astonishing degree for a young guy."

Despite Ertegun's interest and support, Simply Red was not insulated from the internal politics of the Warner record division. After being signed by Krasnow in 1985, the group was shuffled around: from Elektra U.K., to Elektra U.S., then to Warner/Elektra/Asylum (WEA) U.K. Simply Red did not take to being shoved around, and the group has in Elliot Rashman a manager who is as tough and astute as they come. ("The horrible Elliot Rashman," Stein calls him. "Elliot Rashman is enough to make even me anti-Semitic, so you can imagine what he must do to some Wasp.")

Sitting in a yellow-ocher dressing room in London's Hammersmith Odeon where Simply Red is about to play to a packed house, Rashman describes how Krasnow flew to London to assure him the upheaval caused by Warner's internal politics would soon be over. Rashman was not in the least assuaged by Krasnow's attempt at reassurance and claimed that Simply Red would disband rather than tolerate any more turmoil. Says Rashman: "The only thing he didn't budget for was having somebody just as Jewish and hysterical as himself screaming, 'No, the band'll split up.' I sat there with my lawyer, because I wouldn't meet Bob without him, and Bob said, 'Do we really need your lawyer, can't we just talk about this?' " Krasnow took Rashman out onto the streets of north London to try to calm things down. As noisy juggernauts hurtled past them, Krasnow said, "As one Jew to another, I want you to trust me, everything is going to be all right." Rashman could not believe what he was hearing: "It all became a laugh and this thought kept running through my head: He's Walter Matthau, Neil Simon wrote this, I'm Jack Lemmon; I'm the putz and he's trying to sell me this thing."

Nevertheless Krasnow returned to New York believing he had succeeded in calming the waters. He had not reckoned, however, on the crafty determination and eye for the main chance of Seymour Stein.

Warner actively fosters competitiveness among its various labels. ("When competition is healthy it all works wonderfully," says Robert Morgado, who was chief of staff when Hugh Carey was governor of New York and who oversees the music division of Warner Communications. "When competitiveness becomes destructive my job is to make sure that doesn't continue. All our record companies compete in the same area—artists—so there have to be rules of the game. I leave it up to them until I hear that one of them isn't competing by certain elementary rules.") Aware that Simply Red was not entirely happy with Elektra, Stein did not hesitate to attempt to lure the group away. "We were making a breakthrough in Europe but Elektra were doing nothing in America," says Mick Hucknall. "Stein started telling us the people in Elektra weren't interested in us."

Stein's attempted piracy of Simply Red did not succeed.

Hucknall took all his promises with a large grain of salt, well aware of the terms of what he calls a standard Seymour Stein deal: "bad percentage, bad everything." Still, Stein should never be counted out. Hucknall says he is always prepared to listen to a pitch from Stein—"if he pays the legal bills, which he won't; he'll say he will, but he won't"—because, for all his faults, Stein has that unique advantage: his ears. "He obviously loves R&B and he has got ears for success, great ears," says Hucknall. "He has just got an edge to him that I like."

Seymour Stein is obsessed by music and the music industry, and particularly by the moguls who run it: their characters, their histories, and their relationships—about which he is constantly indiscreet. His sometimes bizarre assessments of them are filtered through the eccentric Seymour Stein view of the world. For example, his boss, Mo Ostin, would no doubt be perplexed to hear this assessment of himself by Stein: "If I look back at the last ten years with Warner Brothers, it is like thirteen weeks of my life when I was about ten or twelve years old. It is Saturday and I'm in the movie theater, and it is episode thirteen of *Don Winslow of the Navy*. The evil guy known as Scorpion has been killed off. His henchmen have names like M1, M22, and M331; you might as well call them Gitlin and David Berman [two executives at Warner Brothers]. Then it is like I peel off the mask of Scorpio and I'm shocked to find it is Mo Ostin. I mean it in the nicest possible way."

Stein's opinion of Ahmet Ertegun is rather more respectful. Had it been Atlantic rather than Warner Brothers that wanted to buy out Stein, he would have refused to sell Sire Records. "I felt Ahmet was too strong for me; it was my own insecurities, I suppose. We're not equally strong even now. If there was a patriarch of our business it would be Ahmet, nobody else. Maybe a little less now than ten years ago but, certainly, there is only one Ahmet. If I were to prove Mo Ostin wrong about something it would be a feather in my cap. If it was Ahmet, even if I knew I was right, I'd back down. I wouldn't want Ahmet to be perceived as wrong. If I were to prove Ahmet Ertegun wrong it would be like discrediting the president of the United States."

While any comparison between Ahmet Ertegun and one particular former president, Ronald Reagan, would be ludicrous (Ertegun is an unfashionably avid supporter of liberal and democratic causes), he does have something in common with the Teflon president: the ability to shrug off misfortune and criticism. Over the forty years of Atlantic's history, musical styles have come and gone, other record companies have waxed and waned, Ertegun's own partners have risen and then fallen, and Atlantic has become part of a vast corporate machine. Throughout it all, Ertegun has remained unscathed: inscrutable, charming, irreverent, successful, apparently admired by all.

He appears to exist in a special state of grace. At the all-day concert held in Madison Square Garden to celebrate the fortieth anniversary of Ahmet Ertegun's company, all of the powerful forces that are Atlantic Records—jazz, rhythm and blues, soul, and rock—were present, from Ruth Brown and LaVern Baker (both resplendent in sequins and satin) to Genesis, Bob Geldof, Foreigner, and Led Zeppelin. The musical eclecticism became dizzying, but there to hold it all together was Ertegun, this balding, plump man with his air of relaxed affability, moving from group to group—of glamorous celebrities, performers past and present, and the grandest of record executives—dispensing largesse and advice. Chameleon-like he adapts effortlessly to all social milieux, all sorts of people, all periods of time.

That the anniversary concert took place at all was a small miracle, largely attributable to Ertegun's finely honed diplomatic skills. Many of the groups of musicians called upon to perform had long since split up amidst sour acrimony, and it took endless telephone calls to reassemble them. Perhaps Ertegun's biggest coup in the fraught weeks before the concert was to persuade the three surviving members of Led Zeppelin to play together as the headline act—thus ending an eight-year rift among them.

But noticeable by their absence were the Rolling Stones. The eighteen years that had passed since Ertegun wooed them to Atlantic had done nothing to ease the complex courtship that is usually necessary to persuade the group to cooperate in any venture. In the end, the labyrinthine arrangements required to get the Greatest Rock-and-Roll Band in the World to Madison Square Garden proved too difficult for even Ahmet Ertegun.

And nothing could persuade Ertegun's former partner Jerry Wexler to go to the concert. "He was asked, but he didn't want to come," says Ertegun. "He said he was too ill . . ." He pauses to reflect on Wexler's refusal to attend, and then adds an unsatisfactory explanation: "It's seventeen years since Jerry left the company—or is it twenty years? Whatever, it's a long time. I think he feels that he's just left, but so much has happened since then, and the business is so big . . ." The truth is (as is the case with Ertegun's original partner, Herb Abramson), Ertegun and Wexler have little or nothing to say to each other anymore.

The same is not true of other associates and friends from Atlantic's earliest days. Perhaps one of the reasons for Ertegun's success is that he has stayed loyal, by and large, to his friends, and he has kept in touch with his musical roots. For example, on a recent rainy summer's night, Ertegun was not to be found along with the rest of the industry's high-powered executives at a party held in New York to celebrate the end of a tour by Prince. Instead he spent the evening down at Manhattan's South Street Seaport, listening to a concert to celebrate the music of Doc Pomus, the veteran Atlantic songwriter. Classic hits such as "Save the Last Dance for Me" and "This Magic Moment" were performed by a variety of artists, including Ben E. King. Ertegun sat next to Pomus, who has been confined to a wheelchair since suffering a severe fall in 1965. Unaffected by the fishy smells of the seaport, or the nastiness of the drizzling rain, Ertegun clapped with delight at the nostalgic parade of songs—being what he is: the ultimate fan.

Pomus and Ertegun have had their ups and downs. Pomus has his complaints about Atlantic Records, which is prone to all the tensions that might be expected of a major corporation. "Nobody is really friendly with anyone else there now," says Pomus. He remembers when "they were all music lovers, really soulful guys." In the early days of Atlantic, "the artists were all great singers, people whose music we all loved." Later on, the artists were "people who made a lot of money. Once they had a stable of great singers. Later on they had a stable of great money-makers."

Perhaps because of that, Pomus saw a profound change take place in Ertegun. "He became very inaccessible, tremendously preoccupied with business. During that time I hardly saw him." Pomus recalls that subsequently he met Ertegun by chance in a nightclub. Ertegun was none too sober, but appeared enormously enthusiastic about seeing his old friend after such a long time. He called his companions over to meet Pomus, saying, "This man really knows about music," and he insisted on having his photograph taken with the songwriter. After the long absence of any contact with Ertegun, Pomus was not impressed with this unexpected attention. He remarked to a friend, "I bet if I phone him tomorrow, he won't even take my call." The next day Pomus tested his theory—and proved himself right.

Nevertheless Pomus has once again joined the throng of Ertegun's admirers. "In recent years, something has happened to Ahmet. He resents the fact that he had become a stony-faced businessman. It was a very cold time in his life. When he had a pure attitude to music he was a creative person. After a while, he became so involved in the business side that he resented it.

"I have a whole different feeling about Ahmet now. In a certain way the whole Atlantic thing is coming around again.

All of a sudden, Ahmet is coming round . . . Ahmet has become the music man again. He has proved that he is the old Ahmet Ertegun."

Well, not quite. Nowadays Ertegun does not spend much time in the recording studio, and his name is more likely to appear in the pages of *Vanity Fair* and *New York,* linked with the likes of Betsy Bloomingdale and Kathleen Tynan, than it is in the music press. He certainly spends more time jet-setting to Paris or London, or lounging on his Turkish sailing boat, than he does visiting smoky dens in Harlem.

But his oldest friends remain convinced that Ertegun is first and foremost a music man, and that he is ultimately loyal to the right people. Tom Dowd, Atlantic's first engineer and producer, recalls a recent Rock-and-Roll Hall of Fame dinner, at which Ertegun's guests were New York society people. "As I walked by his table, Ahmet got up and introduced me to the people. He said, 'This is the producer, Tom Dowd. We're dear friends, and he's been with me since the beginning.'" Dowd was touched by the gesture, and believed it was genuine: "If it came down to it, push to shove, he'd say, 'They're not my friends, *you're* my friend.'"

That may be the greatest secret of Ertegun's success: his ability to make people believe he likes them, that they are his true friend, and he theirs. Cynical observers may sneer at his easy geniality, saying that it is hard-nosed business—not people or music—that comes first in Ahmet Ertegun's empire, and his life. Consider, however, the words of Hy Weiss, the bluntest and most outspoken of all the industry's insiders. He, like many other old-timers, remains constant in his appreciation of the Greatest Rock-and-Roll Mogul in the World.

"I happen to like Ahmet Ertegun," says Weiss in his gruff, down-to-earth voice. "No matter how the story goes, I happen to like him."

And then he provides what would be an undeniable epitaph for Ahmet Ertegun: "He's a class guy."

INDEX

italicized page numbers refer to photographs

ABC Records, 97, 98
Abramson, Herb, 37, 112, *151*, 288
  in army, 40
  departure from Atlantic, 44–51
  eclectic recordings, 34–35
  Ertegun, Nesuhi, and, 46–47
  founding of Atlantic, 33
  with National Records, 32–33
  talent searches, 33–34
Abramson, Miriam, *see* Bienstock,
  Miriam
AC/DC, *157*
Agent Provocateur (Foreigner), 243
Alexander, Arthur, 238
Allen, Henry, 182
American Bandstand (TV show),
  83, 84, 91
American Society of Composers,
  Authors, and Publishers
  (ASCAP), 56, 92
. . . And Then There Were Three . . .
  (Genesis), 245
Anthony, Dee, 234, 235, 236
Armone, Joseph "Piney," 271, 272,
  275
Ashley, Ted, 162, 163
Asylum Records, 221–24, 226–27
Ataturk, Kemal, 28
Atco Records, 48–49, 128
Atlantic Records:
  Abramson's departure, 44–51
  advance money incident, 232–34

anniversary concert, 287–88
black music, status in 1989,
  277–79
black producers, 179–81
British groups, pursuit of, 137–38,
  244
Brown and, 37–38, 142–43
business manager, first, 36–37
Charles and, 40, 97–98
corporate culture in 1950s, 38–39
eclectic recordings, 34–35
Elektra/Asylum, proposed
  merger with, 226–27
Elektra-Asylum merger, 223–24
Ertegun's successor, 281
Fairplay Committee and, 177–78
first success, 35
Foreigner signed by, 237, 241–43
founding of, 32–33
Genesis signed by, 244–45
institutionalization of, 164–65,
  169
Kinney Corporation takeover,
  161–65
Leiber and Stoller's departure,
  104–7
loss of artists:
  in 1950s, 97–99
  in 1980s, 246–49
Nashville office, 218
Nelson signed by, 218
payola investigation, 90

Atlantic Records (*continued*)
  protest campaigns aimed at, 39
  Red Bird, proposed merger with,
    111–15
  Rolling Stones and, 200–205,
    249–51
    see also Rolling Stones Records
  royalties, failure to pay, 184
  royalties of old records, payment
    of, 20–21
  sale to Warner, 144, 145–48, 159
  segregation of black and white
    music, 182
  Sonny and Cher signed by, 127
  Spector and, 100–103, 106, 123
  Stax Records:
    business arrangement with,
      129–35
    split with, 183–86
  subsidiaries, *see* Atco Records;
    Asylum Records; Duke
    Records; Rolling Stones
    Records
  Vogel's management of, 279–81
  white performers, shift to, 49,
    125, 127–28, 135–39, 141–43
Axton, Estelle, 128, 129

"Baby Don't Go" (Sonny and Cher),
    127
Baker, Ginger, 137
Baker, LaVern, *150*, 237, 287
Ballard, Hank, 60
Barnes, Ken, 273
Basie, Count, 20, 53, 88, 253
Baylor, Johnny, 176, 178, 187–88,
    189–91, 192–93, 194
the Beatles, 124, 200, 238
the Bee Gees, 138
Bell, Al, 132, 239
  Atlantic-Stax business
    arrangement, 131
  Atlantic-Stax split, 185, 186
  demise of Stax, 194–95
  Fairplay Committee and, 174,
    178, 188, 189–91, 192–93
  hired by Stax, 131

  partner in Stax, 187
  Wexler, assessment of, 133
Bell, William, 186–87
Bergman, Jo, 200, 201, 203
Bernstein, Carl, 17, 19
Berry, Chuck, 86, 202
Bienstock, Freddie, 50
Bienstock, Miriam Abramson, 38,
    52, 54, 104, 165, 168, 169
  Atlantic business manager, 36–37
  on Charles, 40, 97–98
  divorce from Abramson, 47–48,
    50
  on Leiber and Stoller, 116,
    119–20
  sale of Atlantic, 146–47
  on Spector, 101
Big Tree Records, 235
Birdland (nightclub), 52–53, 54
black activism in record business,
    see Fairplay Committee
black music, discrimination against,
    181–83, 277–79
black producers, 179–81
Blackwell, Bumps, 72, 125, 126
Blackwell, Chris, 279–80
Blane, Jerry, 69, 83, 90
Blind Faith, 162, 163
the Bluesbreakers, 137
Blue Thumb Records, 67
Bono, Sonny, 167, 168, 229
  sale of Atlantic, 147
  Sonny and Cher, 26, 127–28, 141
  at Specialty records, 125–26
  Spector and, 100, 126–27
Booker T. and the MGs, 132, 186
Boone, Pat, 73
Boston (rock group), 240
Branigan, Laura, *155*
Branson, Richard, 247
Brantley, Johnny, 84
Brill Building, 110
Broadcast Music Incorporated
    (BMI), 56
"Broken Arrow" (Buffalo
    Springfield), 136
Brown, James, 60, 62–63

Brown, Ruth, 26, 38–39, *150*, 287
  departure from Atlantic, 142–43
  signed by Atlantic, 37–38
Browne, Jackson, 222
Bruce, Jack, 137
Buddah/Sutra Records, 254–55, 256
Buffalo Springfield, 26, 135–36
Burke, Solomon, 124–25, *152*,
    164–65, 167, 168, 238
the Business (rock group), 24–25

Caesar and Cleo, *see* Sonny and
    Cher
Calla Records, 258
Calloway, Cab, 28
Canterino, Dominick "Baldy Dom,"
    261–62, 263, 276
Capitol Records, 97
Carter, Benny, 31
Cassotto, Walden Robert, *see* Darin,
    Bobby
Castellano, Paul, 271
"Cause I Love You" (Thomas), 129
Caymans, Mark, 282–83
CBS Records, 35–36, 198, 204, 210,
    241, 250, 251, 268–69
"Chains of Love" (Turner), 34
"Chapel of Love" (Dixie Cups), 111
Chappell music publishing
    company, 50
Charles, Ray, 26, *150*, 238
  departure from Atlantic, 97–98
  signed by Atlantic, 40
  the charts, 264–65
Cher, 229, 230
  Sonny and Cher, 26, 127–28, 141
Chesler, Lew, 148
Chess, Leonard, 70–71, 81
Chess, Marshall, 70, 206
  with Rolling Stones Records,
    207–8, 214–15
Chess, Phil, 70
Chess Records, 70, 145, 206–7
Children's Storefront, party for,
    17–20
Christy, Don, *see* Bono, Sonny
Clapton, Eric, 27, 137–38

Clark, Dick, 83, 91–92
Clay, Judy, 187
Climax Blues Band, 282
Cocker, Joe, 238–39
Cole, Nat King, 86
Collins, Phil, 17, *154*, *155*
  solo career, 245–47
  with Genesis, 243–44
Columbia Records, 140–41, 218
Cooke, Sam, 126
Copus, "Cowboy," 60
Cosnat distribution company, 67
Costello, Frank, 256
Covay, Don "Pretty Boy," 133, 134
Craft, Morty, 64–65, 282
Crayton, Pee Wee, 20
Cream (rock group), 27, 137–38
Cropper, Steve, 129–30, 131–32,
    133, 134–35, 174, 184, 187,
    188–89, 194–95, 239
Crosby, David, 220
Crosby, Stills, and Nash, 26–27, 136,
    220–21
Crosby, Stills, Nash, and Young, 136
Curtis, King, 171

Daisy Records, 107
Darin, Bobby, 26, 49, 97, 99, 103–4,
    151
Davis, Clive, 204–5, 210, 222, 235
Davis, Miles, 176
Decca Records, 199–200
De Chico, Frank, 272
Déjà Vu (Crosby, Stills, Nash, and
    Young), 136
disc jockeys' convention of 1958
    (Miami), 87–89
discount record deals, 259, 261–62
DiSipio, Fred, 271, 272
distribution companies, 66–68
the Dixie Cups, 111
Double Vision (Foreigner), 242
Dowd, Tom, 21, 34, 36–37, 39, 41,
    42, 48–49, 134, 135, 169, 218,
    228–30, 281, 290
Drake, Bill, 202
"Dream Lover" (Darin), 97

the Drifters, 39, 102
"Drinking Wine, Spo-Dee-O-Dee"
     (McGhee), 35, 36
Duke Records, 246, 247
Dunn, Donald "Duck," 131, 132
Dylan, Bob, 225, 226

the Eagles, 222
Eastman, Lee, 111
Eboli, Thomas "Tommy Ryan," 257
Eckstein, Billy, 33, 46–47
Ed Sullivan Show, 124
Elektra Records, 58, 223–24,
     226–27, 283–84
Ellington, Duke, 28, 98
Ertegun, Ahmet, *149, 151, 153,*
     155, 156, 157, 158
   Abramson's departure from
     Atlantic, 45–46, 50
   anniversary concert for Atlantic,
     287–88
   Asylum Records, 221–22
   bargaining, love for, 22–23
   black America, fascination with,
     29
   black music at Atlantic in 1989,
     279
   Buffalo Springfield and, 135, 136
   charitable activities, 17–21, 171
   childhood and youth, 28–31
   Clapton and, 137–38
   Collins and, 243–44, 245–46
   compositions by, 34
   Crosby, Stills, and Nash situation,
     221
   Darin and, 49
   diplomatic nature, 24–25, 26
   doing business, methods of,
     138–39
   drinking by, 202, 205
   Elektra/Asylum-Atlantic merger,
     proposed, 226–27
   Elektra-Asylum merger, 224
   Fairplay Committee and, 177,
     183
   Foreigner and, 237–38, 242–43,
     280–81

   founding of Atlantic, 32–33
   Freed and, 77, 79, 82–83
   Gabriel affair, 248–49
   Geffen, assessment of, 227–30
   Genesis and, 243–45
   girls in tow, 202
   Harlem, first visit to, 29–30
   home in Turkey, 22
   home in Manhattan, 17–18
   on independent promotion, 265,
     274
   Jagger, friendship with, 209–10
   Jagger's assessment of, 200–201
   jazz, early interest in, 28, 29–31
   jokes, love for, 23
   Kinney takeover of Atlantic,
     161–64
   Leiber and Stoller, dealing with,
     105, 106–7
   loyalty to friends, 288–90
   modern music, contribution to,
     26–27
   money, attitude toward, 37
   music he loves, perspective on,
     230–31
   "neglect" of Atlantic, 279–80
   optimism of, 144
   payola, involvement in, 81,
     82–83, 90
   Presley and, 99
   quitting Atlantic, consideration
     of, 161–63
   racial injustice, fight against,
     30–31
   Redbird-Atlantic merger,
     proposed, 111–15
   rockoids and, 167
   Rolling Stones:
     departure from Atlantic, 249,
       250–51
     "management" of, 210–16
     signed by Atlantic, 197, 198,
       200–205
   Rolling Stones Records, 209
   sale of Atlantic, 144, 145–47, 148,
     159
   Scorpio scam, 235, 236

secret of his success, 290
segregation in record business,
182–83
Some Girls controversy, 211–14
Sonny and Cher, signing of, 125,
127
Spector and, 103–4
stars' departure from Atlantic,
98–99
stature in record business, 21,
205–6
Stein's assessment of, 286–87
talent searches, 33–34
as "Teflon" executive, 287
vocals on recordings, 43
Wexler:
rift with, 112–13
working relationship, 41–43,
122, 123–24, 168
Wexler's retirement, 217, 230
wife, first, 122
wife, second, *see* Ertegun, Mica
Ertegun, Mica (wife), 17
background, 122–23
on Geffen, 228
interior design business, 25,
123
marriage, 123
Some Girls controversy, 211
Ertegun, Munir (father), 28–29, 31
Ertegun, Nesuhi (brother), 30–31,
52, 127, *149, 151,* 254, 284
Abramson and, 46–47
partner in Atlantic, 46
sale of Atlantic, 146
Esquire magazine, 30

Face Value (Collins), 246
Fairplay Committee:
Atlantic and, 177–78
background of, 175–77
blacks' attitude toward, 178–79
consequences of actions, 181–83
goals of, 173, 175
intimidation tactics, 171–75
Stax Records and, 187–94
Fame Studios, 139–41, 183

"Feels Like the First Time"
(Foreigner), 242
Fisher, Howard, 275, 276
the Five Crowns, 69
Flack, Roberta, 19–20
Fleetwood Mac, 282
Floyd, Eddie, 131, 132, 186
Focus (rock group), 282
"Follow You, Follow Me" (Genesis),
245
Foreigner (rock group), *154,*
237–38, 240–43, 280–81,
287
Foreigner (Foreigner), 242
"For What It's Worth" (Buffalo
Springfield), 135–36
Frampton, Peter, 234
Francesi, Sonny, 118, 119
Francis, Connie, 64
Frankie Lymon and the Teenagers,
57, 253
Franklin, Aretha, 26, 140–41, 170,
171, 180
Freed, Alan, 76–77
arrest in Boston, 86–87
audience, rapport with, 79–80
background, 77–78
black music, preference for, 79
Cleveland disc jockey, 78
criminal conviction, 93
downfall, 87, 93–94
egotism, 82, 83, 84
final days, 94–96
first job in radio, 78
hoodlums, involvement with,
84
live concerts, 80, 86–87
memorial service for, 96
New York, move to, 79
payola scandal, 82–83, 84–85, 91,
92, 93
TV show, 83–84, 85
WINS, contract with, 93
Freed, Lance, 78, 79, 80, 84–85, 86,
87, 92, 93, 95, 96
Frio, Rick, 259, 262
Fury Records, 172

Gabriel, Peter, 228, 243, 244, 247–49
Gales, Juggie, 170
Gallo, Joe N., 272
Gambino crime family, 259, 270–72
"Games Without Frontiers" (Gabriel), 248
Gaye, Marvin, 238
Gee Records, 57
"Gee Whiz (Look at His Eyes)" (Thomas), 130
Geffen, David, 219
 Asylum Records, 221–23
 background, 219–20
 Collins and, 247
 Crosby, Stills, and Nash situation, 220–21
 Electra/Asylum-Atlantic merger, proposed, 226–27
 Elektra-Asylum merger, 223–24
 Ertegun's assessment of, 227–30
 film work, 228
 Gabriel and, 248
 record company, founding of, 228
 Scorpio scam, 235
 Wexler and, 221, 224–26
Geffen Records, 228, 247
Geldof, Bob, 287
Genesis (rock group), *154*, 243–45, 246–47, 279, 287
Genovese, Vito, 256
Genovese crime family, 256–57, 258
George Goldner Enterprises, 111
Gigante, Father Louis, 253, 256
Gigante, Vincent "the Chin," 256, 262
Gillespie, Dizzy, 20
Giovanello, Frederick, 261
Goldner, George, 57, 95–96
 death, 120–21
 disk jockey conventions, 87–88
 disk jockeys, treatment of, 82
 Leiber and Stoller, work for, 108–11
 Levy and, 82, 108, 120–21
 Mafia and, 119–20

Red Bird, purchase of, 115–16, 119
Red Bird-Atlantic merger, proposed, 111–15
Gordy, Berry, Jr., 142
Gotti, John, 271
Green, Al, 32
Greenberg, Florence, 117
Greenberg, Jerry, 165–66, 226–27, 241, 242, 244, 248
"Green Onions" (Booker T. and the MGs), 132
Gulf & Western Company, 186, 187
Guralnick, Peter, 98

Hall, Rick, 139, 140, 141, 183
Halliday, Johnny, 238
Harlem Blues and Jazz Band, 19
Harris, Oren, 92
Hawkins, Ronnie, 68, 88
Hayes, Isaac, 185, 187, 191
Hayward, Brooke, 213, 214
Hibbler, Al, 98
"High School Dance" (Bono), 125
Hirshey, Gerri, 140
"Hold On, I'm Coming" (Sam and Dave), 185
Holzman, Jack, 203–4, 216, 224, 225
"Honey Love" (Drifters), 39
Hook, Jack, 84
Hot Buttered Soul (Hayes), 187
Hucknall, Mick, 284, 285–86
the Hustlers, 238
Hutchence, Michael, *157*
Hyman, Elliot, 148, 159

"I Am a Child" (Buffalo Springfield), 136
"If Loving You Is Wrong, I Don't Want to Be Right" (Ingram), 189
"I Got You Babe" (Sonny and Cher), 127–28
independent promotion:
 current status, 274–75
 growth of, 264–69
 industry abandonment of, 272–73
 investigations of, 269–72

promoters' lawsuit against
industry, 273–74
"I Never Loved a Man (the Way I
Love You)" (Franklin), 141
Ingram, Luther, 188, 189
Interstate and Foreign Commerce
Committee (House of
Representatives), 89–93
"In the Air" (Collins), 246
"In the Midnight Hour" (Pickett),
133
Invisible Touch (Genesis), 279
Isgro, Joe, 265–69, 270, 271, 272,
273–74, 275
Island Records, 279
"I Want to Know What Love Is"
(Foreigner), 243

Jackson, Al, 131
Jackson, Hal, 211, 213, 214
Jackson, Jesse, 171, 193, 212–13
Jackson, Mahalia, 140
Jackson, Michael, 219
Jackson 5, 218–19
Jagger, Bianca, 209, 229
Jagger, Mick, 17, 22, 71, 148, *153*,
229
Atlantic Records:
departure from, 249–50
signing with, 198, 200–205
blues, interest in, 206–7
business problems in 1969, 199
Chess and, 207–8
Ertegun:
assessment of, 200–201
friendship with, 209–210
Ertegun's "management" of
Rolling Stones, 210–11, 212
on Foreigner, 237
home in Manhattan, 198–99
McGrath and, 215–16
reputation, 197–98
Some Girls controversy, 211, 212,
213–14
on Vogel, 281
JAMF music publishing company,
258
the Jellybeans, 111

John, Elton, 228
Jones, Booker T.:
departure from Stax, 187, 189
Fairplay Committee and, 174,
178
recordings at Stax, 129, 131,
132
Wexler and, 134
Jones, Brian, 198
Jones, Mick, *154*
background, 237–39
business venture and Thomas and
Weiss, 239–40
Foreigner recordings for Atlantic,
242–43
formation of Foreigner, 241
Vogel and, 280–81

Kalodner, John, 241–42, 246–48
Kamasutra Productions, 117–19
Kass, Art, 254–55
Keen, Bob, 126
Keen Records, 126
Kellogg, Mercedes, 18
Kerner, Shelley, 278–79
King, Ben E., 39, 102, *155*, 167,
277–78, 288
King, Coretta Scott, 171
King Crimson (rock group), 241
King Records, 58, 59–60, 62, 63–64
Kinney Corporation, 159–65
Kissinger, Henry, 23–24
Kissinger, Nancy, 23
Klein, Allen, 199
Kline, Dickie, 60, 66, 170, 172–73,
175, 181, 218
Koko Records, 188
Krasnow, Bob, 58–59, 60, 64, 67,
283, 284, 285

LaBelle, Patti, 180
The Lamb Lies Down on Broadway
(Genesis), 244
LaMonte, John, 258, 259, 261–63
Lane, Brian, 138–39
advance money incident, 232–34
Scorpio scam, 234–36
Lansky, Meyer, 148

LaPier, Cherilyn Sarkasian, *see* Cher
Laskar, Jay, 269
"Last Night" (Mar-Keys), 132
LaVaughn, Reggie, 176
Lawrence, D. H., 30
"Leader of the Pack" (Shangri-Las), 111
Led Zeppelin, 27, 138, 167, 287–88
Leiber, Jerry, 32–33, 51
    departure from Atlantic, 104–7
    record businesses, 107–11
    Red Bird-Atlantic merger, proposed, 111–15
    sale of Red Bird, 115–16, 119
    Spector and, 101, 102
Levy, Becket, 252
Levy, Morris, 117, *151*, 172, 259
    arrest for assault, 258
    arrest for extortion, 254, 255–56, 275–76
    background, 54–55
    debt payment by, 68
    Fairplay Committee and, 177
    favors performed by, 254–55
    FBI investigation of, 263
    Freed and, 76, 78–79, 80, 83–84, 93–94
    Goldner and, 82, 108, 120–21
    home in Dutchess County, 253–54
    Isgro and, 265–66
    Mafia connections, 55–56, 254, 255–59, 262–63, 272
    music publishing, entry into, 56–57
    nightclubs owned by, 53, 54
    payola scandal, 81, 88, 89, 90–91, 92–93
    record companies, 57–58
    "retirement," 145
    Roulette offices, 252–53
    Sugar Hill and, 260, 261
Levy, Zac (Morris's son), 252
Levy, Zaccariah (Morris's brother), 53, 56
Lewis, Jerry Lee, 86
Lewis, Sir Edward, 201, 211

Lilly, Doris, 88–89
Little, Leroy, Sr., 173
"Little Red Rooster" (Rolling Stones), 197
Little Richard, 71–75, 126
Lowenstein, Prince Rupert, 200, 205, 209, 210, 211, 249, 250
Lymon, Frankie, 57, 85, 253

McCalla, Nathan, 177, 258
McCartney, Paul, 73
McDonald, Ian, 241
McGhee, Brownie, 35
McGhee, Stick, 35, 36
McGrath, Earl, 215–16
"Mack the Knife" (Darin), 97
McPhatter, Clyde, 39
McQueen, Steve, 210
McRae, Gwen, 278
Madonna, 282–83
Mafia involvement in record business, 116–17
    independent promotion, 271–72, 275
    Kamasutra Productions, 117–19
    Levy and, 55–56, 254, 255–59, 262–63, 272
    MCA Records, 259–64, 272
    Red Bird Records, 116, 119–20
    Seven Arts, 148
Mammarella, Tony, 91
Manners, Lady Theresa, 24
Marcos, Ferdinand, 65
Margaret, Princess, 22
the Mar-Keys, 132
Marmaduke, John, 268
Marquette, Peewee, 52–53
Masrati, Hy, 117
Mavaratti, Frankie, 177
Mayall, John, 137
MCA Records, 259–64, 272
"Memphis sound," 131–32
Mercury Records, 248
Miami Herald, 87, 88, 89
Midler, Bette, 229
Miller, Mitch, 65
Mitchell, Joni, 222
Moman, Chips, 128

"Money Honey" (Drifters), 39
"moralistic" responses to rock and
   roll, 39, 85–86
Morgado, Robert, 285
Morganfield, McKinley, *see* Waters,
   Muddy
Morris, Doug, 235, 281
Motedo, Jay, 189
Motown Records, 142, 195, 266
Murdoch, Rupert, 249

Nash, Graham, 220–21
Nathan, Nathaniel Nathan, 62
Nathan, Sydney, 59–60, 62–64,
   70–71, 282
National Association for the
   Advancement of Colored
   People, 181
National Association of Television
   and Radio Announcers
   (NATRA) convention of
   1968, 170–74, 179
National Records, 32–33
NBC *Nightly News*, 264, 269,
   270–73
Nelson, Willie, 218
Nero and the Gladiators, 238
the Network (promoters cartel),
   267–68
New Yorker magazine, 21, 22,
   205
New York Post, 88
Noonan, Tom, 61
Nureyev, Rudolf, 22

O'Gorman, Ned, 19
Old Town Records, 69
Ostin, Mo, 127, 225, 282, 286
Out of the Past Incorporated,
   259
Ovens, Don, 88–89

Page, "Hot Lips," 29
Page, Jimmy, 138, *153*
Paola, Elizabeth, 92
Parker, Colonel, 99
Parks, Mama Lu, 19
Payne, Cleo, 29

payola (bribes for disc jockeys),
   92–93
   disc jockeys' conventions, 87–89
   Fairplay Committee and, 175
   Freed and, 82–83, 84–85, 91, 92,
      93
   investigation into, 89–93
   in 1980s, *see* independent
      promotion
   types of bribes, 65–66, 81–82
Pele, *156*
Penniman, Richard, *see* Little
   Richard
Performance (film), 148
Phases and Stages (Nelson), 218
Philadelphia International Records,
   195
Philles Records, 126–27
Phillips, Dewey, 81
Pickett, Wilson, 24, 133, 134,
   136–37, 139–40
Pisello, Salvatore James, 259–61,
   264, 272
Planet Waves (Dylan), 225
Plant, Robert, *156*
platinum albums, 242
Polygram Records, 137
Pomus, Doc, 37, 38, 50–51, 68,
   288–90
Porter, David, 185
Prager, Bud, 240–41, 242, 280
Presley, Elvis, 99
producer's royalty, 104–5
promotion of records, *see*
   independent promotion

"Queen of the Hop" (Darin),
   97

Radio & Records (trade
   publication), 264–65,
   273
the Ramones, 99–100, 282
Rashman, Elliot, 283, 284–85
Rat On (Swamp Dogg), 179
Rayner, Chessy, 123
Recording Industry Association of
   America, 269–70, 272–73

Red Bird Records, 109, 110–11
  Atlantic, proposed merger with,
    111–15
  Mafia takeover, 116, 119–20
  sale to Goldner, 115–16, 119
Redding, Otis, 133, *152*, 185–86,
  238
Red Headed Stranger (Nelson), 218
Renta, Oscar de la, 18
Reprise Records, 127, 161
"Respect" (Franklin), 141
Richard Hell and the Voidoids, 282
Ripp, Artie, 87–88, 95, 96, 117–19
Robinson, Joe, 260–61
Robinson, Sugar Ray, 176
Robinson, Sylvia, 260
Rock-and-Roll Hall of Fame, 26
rock music, birth of, 135
Rock of Ages (book), 48
rockoids, 167
Roeg, Nicolas, 148
Rolling Stones, 27, *153*, 288
  business problems in 1969,
    199–200
  Chess studio, recording at, 207
  departure from Atlantic, 249–51
  Ertegun's "management" of,
    210–16
  history of, 197–98
  record companies interested in,
    203–5
  recordings for Atlantic, *see*
    Rolling Stones Records
  signed by Atlantic, 200–205
Rolling Stones Records:
  Chess hired for, 207–8, 214–15
  Ertegun's involvement, 209
  founding of, 205
  McGrath hired for, 215–16
  releases, 209, 211
Ronstadt, Linda, 222
Rosenblatt, Michael, 282–83
Ross, Brian, 264, 270–72
Ross, Carol Rosenthal, 160
Ross, Steve, *156*, 159–64, 222, 225
Roulette Records, 57, 84, 88, 90,
  177, 252

Rudin, Mickey, 161
Runyon Sales distribution company,
  66, 67
Rupe, Art, 73–74, 125–26

Sabit, Vahdi, 32, 113
Safice Records, 131
Salerno, Anthony "Fat Tony," 257
Sam and Dave, 132, 185
"Save the Last Dance for Me"
  (Drifters), 102
Savoy Lindyhoppers, 19
Scepter Records, 117
Scorpio scam, 234–36
Sea and the Shells, 180
segregation in record business,
  181–83
Sehorn, Marshall, 172, 173, 175,
  179, 183
Seven-Arts Company, *see* Warner
  Seven-Arts Company
Shaft (Hayes), 191
"Shake, Rattle and Roll" (Turner),
  43
the Shangra-Las, 111
Shields, Del, 173, 175
Sill, Lester, 101, 126
Silverman, Ira, 264, 270–72
Simply Red, 283, 284–86
Sinatra, Frank, 127, 161
Sire Records, 60, 281–82
Sledge, Percy, 140
Smith, Joe, 81, 82, 86–87, 88, 90, 91,
  148, 224–26, 235, 256, 268
Smith, Tony, 247
So (Gabriel), 248
"So Long" (Brown), 38
Some Girls (Rolling Stones), 211
  controversy surrounding, 211–14
Sonny and Cher, 26, 125, 127–28,
  141
"Soul Limbo" (Booker T. and the
  MGs), 186
the Soul Stirrers, 125
"Spanish Harlem" (King), 102
Specialty Records, 72, 73–74,
  125–26

Spector, Phil, 111
  background, 100
  Bono and, 100, 126–27
  car stereo of, 103
  Darin and, 103–4
  departure from Atlantic, 123
  eccentricities of, 99–100
  hired by Atlantic, 100–101
  "hooks" provided by, 102–3
  Leiber and Stoller replaced by,
    106
  personality, 101
  production assignments from
    Atlantic, 101–3, 106
  "wall of sound" productions, 100,
    126
"Splish Splash" (Darin), 49
Spooky Tooth, 238
"Stand by Me" (King), 102, 277
"Star Star" (Rolling Stones), 210
Stax Records:
  Atlantic Records:
    business arrangement with,
      129–35
    split with, 183–86
  "black mafia" takeover, 192–93
  catalogue, ownership of, 184–85
  demise of, 194–96
  Fairplay Committee and, 187–94
  Gulf & Western purchase of,
    186–87
  Jones-Thomas-Weiss takeover
    attempt, 239–40
  "Memphis sound," 131–32
  origins of, 128–29
  successful recordings, 132–33
  Weiss hired by, 191–92
Stein, Seymour, 70, 99, 284
  background, 60–61
  business philosophy, 283
  Ertegun, assessment of, 286–87
  Ertegun's successor, possible,
    281–82
  Leiber and Stoller, work for, 110,
    111
  Levy, assessment of, 255–56
  Madonna signed by, 282–83

  Nathan and, 61–64
  Simply Red, attempt to sign, 283,
    285–86
  Weiss and, 68–69
Steinberg, Phil, 117
Stewart, Jim, 187, 190
  Atlantic-Stax business
    arrangement, 130, 131,
    134–35
  Atlantic-Stax split, 183, 184, 185
  founding of Stax, 128, 129
Sticky Fingers (Rolling Stones), 209
Stigwood, Robert, 137, 138, 235
Stills, Stephen, 135, 221
Stoller, Mike, 32
  departure from Atlantic, 104–7
  record businesses, 107–11
  Red Bird-Atlantic merger,
    proposed, 111–15
  sale of Red Bird, 115–16, 119
  Spector and, 101, 102
"Such a Night" (Drifters), 39
Sugar Hill Records, 260–61
Sunlight Restaurant, 65
Supernatural Thing (King), 277
Swamp Dogg (Jerry Williams),
    178–81, 182, 193, 194
Sweet Soul Music (Guralnick), 98
Symphony Sid, 53–54

Talking Heads, 282
Taylor, Johnny, 187
Teamsters union, 255
Teddy Bears (rock group), 100
"There Goes My Baby" (Drifters),
    102
Thomas, Carla, 129, 130, 132, 187
Thomas, Nigel, 238–40
Thomas, Rufus, 129, 132
Thompson, Sonny, 63–64
Tiger Records, 107
Tommy James and the Shondells,
    177, 253
Townsend, Pete, 232–33, 241
Trow, George, 205–6
Turner, Big Joe, 20, 26, 33, 34,
    43

"Tutti Frutti" (Little Richard),
72–73, 74
Twintower Records, 65
Twittie, Conway, 64
Tynan, Kathleen, 17

Union Planters Bank, 194, 195, 240

Vanderbilt, Dick, 235
Vastola, Gaetano "the Big Guy,"
261, 262, 263, 276
Vee Jay Records, 145
Virgin Records, 247
Vogel, Sheldon, 181, 217, 226, 227,
233–34, 254, 279–81

WABC radio station, 93
Wakschal, Francine, 37, 38, 164
"wall of sound" productions, 100,
126
Ward, Clara, 140
Ward, Ed, 48
Warhol, Andy, 209
Warner, Jack, 148, 161
Warner Brothers Records, 148, 161,
268–69
Warner Communications, 223, 249,
285
Warner Seven-Arts Company:
Atlantic purchased by, 147–48,
159
Kinney takeover of, 159, 160–63
Mafia and, 148
Washington, Dinah, 53, 253
Waters, Muddy, 71, 207
Wayne, Ethel, 72
WEBB radio station, 124
Weiss, Hy, 130, 267
business venture with Jones and
Thomas, 239–40
distribution companies, 66–68
on Ertegun, 290
Freed and, 85, 96
Goldner and, 108–10, 120, 121
payola and, 65–66, 81
record company, 69–70
at Stax Records, 191–92
Stein and, 68–69

Wexler, Harry, 40
Wexler, Jerry, 52, 57–58, 98,
141–42, *151*
Abramson's departure from
Atlantic, 46, 47, 48, 50
on Boone, 73
Crosby, Stills, and Nash situation,
221
Elektra/Asylum-Atlantic merger,
proposed, 227
Ertegun:
rift with, 112–13
working relationship, 41–43,
122, 123–24, 168
on Ertegun brothers, 46
Fairplay Committee and, 171,
174–75, 177, 178
Fame Studios, 139, 140, 141,
183
Freed and, 82
Geffen and, 221, 224–26
hired by Atlantic, 40–41
Jackson 5 and, 218–19
Leiber and Stoller, dealing with,
104, 105, 106, 119
on Mafia involvement in record
business, 116–17
Miami, move to, 165–69
Nelson and, 218
in 1989, 230, 288
payola, involvement in, 81, 83, 90
pessimism of, 144–45
Red Bird-Atlantic merger,
proposed, 111–15
retirement, 217–18, 230
Rolling Stones, Atlantic's signing
of, 203
sale of Atlantic, 144, 145–47
Stax Records, 128, 129, 130–31,
132, 133, 134, 135, 183–85,
196
Swamp Dogg and, 180, 181
vocals on recordings, 43
white rock, attitude toward, 135,
167
work habits, 133, 165–66
Wexler, Shirley, 171, 217
"What'd I Say" (Charles), 97

"When a Man Loves a Woman"
(Sledge), 140
White, Ted, 141
the Who, 233
"Why Do Fools Fall in Love"
(Frankie Lymon and the
Teenagers), 253
WILD radio station, 91
Williams, Jerry, *see* Swamp Dogg
Williams, Larry, 126
WINS radio station, 76, 78, 79, 80,
87, 93
Winwood, Stevie, 162
Wood, Randy, 96
Woods, Noreen, 98, 145–46, 168,
212, 214

Woodward, Dino "Boom Boom,"
175–78, 187, 188, 189
Worcester, Earl of (Bunter), 24–25
WQAM radio station, 94
Wyman, Bill, *153*, 200, 201, 205,
207, 249, 250

the Yardbirds, 137, 138
Yes (rock group), 27, 138, 233–34
Yetnikoff, Walter, 254
Young, Lester, 31, 53
Young, Neil, 135, 136
"You Send Me" (Cooke), 126
Yo Yo Ma, 19

Zipkin, Jerry, 17, 237